3·9·76

BRITISH ECONOMIC THOUGHT AND INDIA
1600–1858

BRITISH ECONOMIC THOUGHT AND INDIA 1600–1858

by
WILLIAM J. BARBER

*A Study in the History of
Development Economics*

CLARENDON PRESS · OXFORD
1975

Oxford University Press, Ely House, London W. 1

GLASGOW NEW YORK TORONTO MELBOURNE WELLINGTON
CAPE TOWN IBADAN NAIROBI DAR ES SALAAM LUSAKA ADDIS ABABA
DELHI BOMBAY CALCUTTA MADRAS KARACHI LAHORE DACCA
KUALA LUMPUR SINGAPORE HONG KONG TOKYO

ISBN 0 19 828265 6

© *Oxford University Press 1975*

Printed in Great Britain by
Butler & Tanner Ltd,
Frome and London

Acknowledgements

THE obligations accumulated during the preparation of this study are far too numerous to be itemized in full. A special tribute is in order, however, to staff members of the British Museum and of the Indian Institute Library in the University of Oxford for their skill in blending custody of remarkable treasures with provision for efficient access to them. I am also especially indebted to the Oxford Institute of Commonwealth Studies and to its Director, Paul Streeten, for cordial hospitality during the preparation of the final draft.

I have been the beneficiary of the wisdom of numerous friends and colleagues who have read and commented on portions of the manuscript: among them, Lord Balogh, Jeffrey Butler, A. J. Gayer, E. O. Golob, Stanley Lebergott, L. O. Mink, and Sir Edgar Williams. None of the above should be held accountable for deficiencies which remain. Mrs. Gerry Cote and Mrs. Joan Halberg have been unfailingly helpful in converting my drafts into legible form.

I am grateful to the editors of *History of Political Economy* and the *Journal of Oriental Studies* for permission to restate portions of arguments which earlier appeared within the pages of their publications.

W.J.B.

Contents

Introduction

THIS study is an essay in the history of development economics—and an essay on some themes in the development of economics. Such a description of its subject-matter requires a few words of explanation and justification.

The assertion that development economics has a history—or at least one which antedates the Second World War—may be greeted with scepticism in some quarters. Nor would such a challenge be totally lacking in plausibility. After all, the current interest of the international community of economists in the problems of the less developed parts of the globe is of fairly recent origin. Certainly the past several decades have witnessed the production of economic studies of the Third World in unprecedented volume, a phenomenon which has coincided with several fundamental changes on the international scene.

During this period, most of the territories of the Third World have undergone a political transition from colonial to independent status. At the same time, the unparalleled growth in the populations of most of these countries has heightened concern about prospects for major improvement in their economic condition. Meanwhile, technological advance in the richer countries—combined with the considerable post-war success of industrial economies in forestalling major downturns in economic activity—has tended to widen the absolute income gap between the richer and the poorer countries and to direct attention to the importance of special measures to cushion some of the harsher consequences of international economic inequality.

The middle decades of the twentieth century, without question, have given fresh urgency and added new dimensions to the study of development economics. Indeed, if the formal origins of a specialism within a discipline were identified with the date at which it achieved regular curricular recognition within the world's major universities, one might readily conclude that development economics is indeed something new under the sun.

In fact, however, systematic attempts to come to grips with the problems of economic development did not begin in the mid-twentieth century. The study of these issues engaged the analytic energy of some of the ablest economic thinkers in earlier centuries. Much of that effort, to be sure, was focused on the conditions required for development in the analyst's home country. But one cluster of economic thinkers—those concerned with the activities of the English East India Company—involved themselves in an intellectual enterprise not totally dissimilar from the one which has preoccupied many later development economists. They sought to comprehend the economic reality of a remote and unfamiliar part of the world and to understand the implications of relationships between economies which were markedly divergent in their structures. From the beginning of the seventeenth century through the mid-nineteenth century, the East India Company was the most significant point of contact between Western thought and a part of today's Third World. Over this span of time, virtually all of the thinkers who would deserve a place in an economists' Hall of Fame were participants in the controversies surrounding the Company's activities and performance.

One of the central tasks of this study is to explore the properties of the conceptual systems used by our intellectual ancestors as they addressed the phenomenon of under-development. Those who grapple with the economics of the Third World —whether yesterday or today—can do so only within an organizing framework of ideas. Though these 'master models' are not always explicitly articulated, they are indispensable to the ordering of our perceptions of reality. Only with their aid can we impose intelligibility on the world we observe. But these systems, essential as they are to the sharpening of our vision, are necessarily selective. Each has its inherent limitations. With the detachment of time, it is much easier to observe them in our predecessors than it is in our contemporaries. Yet, by knowing our intellectual ancestors better, we may also learn something about ourselves.

An exploration of approaches to economic development formulated in the past has a further recommendation. It is a truism that the 'master models' constructed at any particular moment are influenced by intellectual currents and by the economic and political circumstances of their time. Their usefulness as guides to other times and conditions is thus restricted. New problems may be expected to cry out for new conceptual formulations. With respect to the physical sciences, it has been persuasively argued that periods of bewilderment—in which observed realities appear to run counter to the expectations of the reigning 'master model'—create the conditions required for such intellectual 'revolutions'. Whether or not fundamental change in the conceptual systems of economics proceeds so predictably is less clear. Consideration of the ebb and flow of debate over Britain's involvement with the East during the life span of the East India Company provides a useful vantage-point from which to inspect the response of economic thinkers to circumstances which have challenged the adequacy of conceptual systems.

Throughout the period under review, British contacts with India were prolific in generating analytical materials which had the capacity to interest the major thinkers who were to give shape to the discipline of economics. With changes in the role of the East India Company, the focal points of controversy shifted. Four key episodes—in each of which problems calling for a rethinking of basic presuppositions came to the surface—deserve inspection in some detail. With the beginnings in the seventeenth century, the dominant issue was one of comprehending a form of international commerce which failed to fit the conventional mould. By the middle decades of the eighteenth century, when sovereignty over sizeable territories in India had been asserted by the East India Company, the attention of political economists turned to the political and economic implications of alternative types of governing structures. In the first half of the nineteenth century, the central problem had again changed in emphasis; by then the paramount concern was with the formulation of economic policies appropriate to the circumstances of India. Finally, the dramatic events of 1857–58—when an uprising quite unforeseen touched off reactions which abruptly terminated the life of the East India Company—brought quite a different question to the surface. It was then necessary to ask: what had gone wrong?

In many obvious respects, the relationships between developed and less developed countries in the 1970s are a vast distance removed from those which prevailed during the lifetime of the East India Company. But the enterprise in which the energies of development economists have been engaged, both in those days and now, has some common ingredients. Though the particulars are quite different, the shape of the fundamental intellectual questions has a remarkable similarity. Then, as now, the work of a development economist begins with a choice of a conceptual framework—and that organizing framework, in turn, affects his perceptions of the relevant realities and his vision of unrealized potentialities. Now, as then, economic thinkers may be the victims of lapses in the analytic imagination by applying conceptual categories which are not fully adequate to the central issues at hand.

At the intellectual level, there is thus a kinship between students of development economics of the past and of the present. But those who come later enjoy one potential advantage. Through a study of 'master models' deployed by our forerunners—of the way they formulated questions and later reformulated them (or failed to do so)—we may approach a fuller understanding of the strengths and weaknesses of the conceptual systems of which we are at once the creatures and the creators.

PART 1

International Trade and Development: the Seventeenth-Century Controversies

In the early seventeenth century, an impression was current in the minds of some thoughtful Englishmen that they lived in an underdeveloped economy. There were some substantial reasons for this view. The economic structure of the country was still dominated by the keeping of sheep and by the crafts and commerce derived from this basic agricultural industry. For all practical purposes, England's economy displayed the essential characteristics of a 'mono-culture'.

In the later decades of the sixteenth century, the country's export base was not in the most robust condition. Religious wars on the Continent had disrupted important market channels. Potentially more serious was a puzzling change in the conditions of wool supply. The beginnings of land enclosures in Tudor times had led to new patterns of land usage. For reasons that contemporaries did not fully understand, fibres from sheep grazed on enclosed pastures were more difficult both to process and to sell. As the wool trade had begun to show symptoms of stagnation, it was not out of place to wonder whether traditional product lines could spur further expansion in the national economy.

Forceful stimulants to fresh thinking about national economic strategies came from other directions as well. Englishmen had the examples of several countries before them—notably, Holland, Portugal, and Spain—which, though their natural endowments were not necessarily far superior, appeared to be much richer. In each, the growth of wealth and power had been accompanied by innovative ventures which had transcended the resource limitations of the home country. At the same time, explorations of English seamen had awakened a sense of the world beyond Europe, and the privateering successes of Drake and Hawkins against the Spanish shipping had given Englishmen a taste of its fruits. By 1600 England was prepared to look outward for economic diversification.

Systematic contact between England and the part of the world which was to be moulded into the Indian Empire began in 1600 with the award of a royal charter to a company of London-based merchants affording them exclusive rights to the conduct of English trade in the area east of the Cape of Good Hope. Interest in the Asian commerce, to be sure, had a much deeper history. The exotic products of the East—pepper, spices, indigo, silks, and 'finely wrought' textiles—had long been known in English and in European markets. In an age which long antedated artificial refrigeration, there was already a well-established demand for some of these commodities. But reliable access to Asian sources of supply presented awkward problems. The overland routes through the Middle East to the Eastern shores of the Mediterranean were vulnerable to the whims of the Turkish Sultanate. For English merchants, the sea route around the African continent was subject to another set of risks. The Dutch and Portuguese traders who had preceded them did not welcome the entry of competitors. These hazards were well understood. Despite the disappearance of three vessels dispatched to the East in 1591 and the loss of another voyage commissioned a few years later, the interest of Englishmen in penetrating this remote sphere of commerce was not deterred.[1] On the contrary, Dutch successes in the late sixteenth century, combined with their exercise of monopoly power in raising pepper prices in Europe, strengthened the determination of English traders to gain an independent stake in this allegedly lucrative trade.

Though the charter members of the English East India Company lacked the advantage of prior direct contact with the East and were largely ignorant of conditions there, they were familiar with dealings in Asian merchandise. Most of the original subscribers were associated with the Levant Company (a trading group operating in Asian spices and textiles brought overland to the Mediterranean),[2] and they perceived their interests to be

[1] For background on this point, see G. D. Ramsey, *English Overseas Trade During the Centuries of Emergence* (London, 1957), esp. p. 67.

[2] In the early years of the East India Company, its governor—Thomas Smythe—also served the Levant Company in the same capacity. Of the 270 initial subscribers to the East India Company, it has been calculated that only seven could be regarded as 'gentry': the rest had a background as merchants. (See Theodore K. Rabb, 'Investment in English Overseas Enterprise', *Economic History Review*, 2nd Ser., vol. 19 (1966), p. 78.)

acutely threatened by the activities of Dutch traders who were circumnavigating the Cape. For Englishmen, the full organization of a long-distance sea commerce with the East was, however, a novel undertaking. When the first three vessels departed in 1601 with a cargo of money valued at £21,742 and of 'wares' valued at £6,860, a new chapter had been opened.

CHAPTER 1

Commercial Infancy and the Initial Formulation of an Official Model: 1600–1640

NOT surprisingly, the early voyages sponsored by the East India Company generated a host of unanticipated practical problems. But perhaps more interesting were the intellectual perplexities arising from this new mode and sphere of commerce. How, it was often asked by contemporaries, could the Company's practice of exporting precious metals be justified? Was not the nation's stock of wealth seriously compromised by such behaviour? How, in turn, could the national interest be advanced by an enterprise with such apparent indifference to the promotion of traditional English exports? Moreover, what justification could be offered for the exclusiveness of the privileges accorded to a small group of London-based merchants? Was this not official favouritism of the most objectionable form?

Questions of this sort were not long delayed. If the answers supplied were—at least in part—self-serving, the fact that they were articulated in writing and thus available for general discussion proved to be a remarkable stimulant to economic discourse. Throughout the seventeenth century, a substantial proportion of the more thoughtful contributions to economic literature was generated by England's involvement in the East India trade. This commerce was perplexingly different. Those who engaged in it seemed regularly to bend—if not to break altogether—the standard rules. The East India Company was in the vanguard of innovation in the seventeenth century: and, like most innovators, it was a magnet for critics.

I. THE QUESTION OF THE 'DRAIN'

Judged by the canons of the prevailing wisdom, gross heresy was perpetrated in the very provisions of the East India Company's charter. By royal decree, a private organization had been empowered to withdraw silver from the national stock of treasure for export to the East. The amounts were limited: according to the original stipulations, not more than £30,000 in value could be licensed for shipment abroad in any single year and only silver in coinage bearing the mark of another country was eligible for export. But these restrictions were soon relaxed. In 1616 the annual authorization to export silver was increased to £60,000 and, in 1617, to £100,000. When these concessions were shown to be inadequate to its needs, the Company—in 1629—acquired the right to export gold up to the limit of £120,000 and to send out up to a quarter of that sum in English coinage. Even though it could still be argued (at least until 1663 when restrictions were waived altogether) that the volume of the 'drain' was officially constrained, none could doubt that the East India Company had won concessions which departed significantly from well-established practice.

Attacks in England on the unorthodox behaviour of the East India Company grew in intensity during the first few decades of its life. Leading the assault were those who indicted the East India traders as 'enemies of Christendom' because they 'carried away the treasure of Europe to enrich the heathen'.[1] But if the Company's practices seemed to be at odds with inherited value systems, they also appeared to conflict with the immediate economic interests of England. It was alleged, for example, that withdrawals of precious metals to support the East India commerce were responsible for a shortage at the Royal Mint and for derangement in exchange rates. These charges were advanced with vehemence in the early 1620s—and they had some plausibility. In the twelve months beginning 1 April 1619, no silver was available for coinage at the mint.[2] Misselden supported such criticisms when he wrote that the East India commerce 'was the special remote cause of our want of money' and that 'the money which is traded out into those parts is continually issued out, and never returneth'.[3]

II. THE DOCTRINE OF THE BALANCE OF TRADE

The East India Company could ill afford to leave such charges unanswered. The survival of its charter was contingent on some

---

[1] Robert Kayll (also spelled Keale), *The Trade's Increase* (London, 1615), p. 32.

[2] Barry E. Supple, *Commercial Crisis and Change in England, 1600–1642* (Cambridge, 1959), p. 185.

[3] Edward Misselden, *Free Trade or, the Meanes to Make Trade Florish* (London, 1622), pp. 13, 20.

minimum level of public tolerance and understanding. Its privileges, after all, were subject to renewal at prescribed intervals—and they were always vulnerable to review.[4]

At this moment in its history, the East India Company was fortunate to have within its ranks a highly sophisticated economic thinker in the person of Thomas Mun. A trader of wide experience who held positions of high authority in the Company's councils, Mun was the major architect of a coherent brief on the Company's behalf.[5] His argument was communicated in three substantial tracts, two of which were published during his lifetime (one in 1621 and the other in 1628) and a third which appeared posthumously in 1664.[6] The latter document, though a more complete statement, was clearly an extension of the argument developed in 1628 and appears to have been written about thirty years before its publication.[7]

Mun saw his first task as one of convincing the sceptics that the East India trade genuinely augmented the wealth of the kingdom and that it was indeed the most profitable to the nation of any of the trades in which English merchants engaged. He was under no illusion that this assignment would be a simple one. On the contrary, he took it for granted that the influential public

[4] In 1624, for example, James I hinted that he was prepared to become an 'adventurer' in the Company, a proposition which was not warmly received by the membership despite a calculated threat that the Company's charter might be revoked. Nor did a proposal of 1628 that one-fifth of the Company's stock be 'made over' to Charles I 'in return for his favour and protection' win support within the Company. The Crown responded to this rebuff by issuing a patent to a rival organization, authorizing it to trade in those parts of the East where the East India Company had not already established itself. This enterprise—direct involvement of the Crown notwithstanding—failed disastrously. See William Foster, *John Company* (London, 1926), esp. pp. 121–8.

[5] Thomas Mun (1571–1641) spent the early years of his adult life as a trader in Italy. He became a director of the East India Company in 1615 and was elected to the position of Deputy Governor in 1624, though he declined to serve. For further background, see Raymond de Roover, 'Thomas Mun in Italy', *Bulletin of the Institute of Historical Research*, vol. 30 (1957). In addition to his work as a merchant, Mun served as a member of various official committees examining monetary questions in the 1620s. For comment on his contributions in that capacity, see Barry E. Supple, op. cit., esp. pp. 211–16.

[6] These documents were entitled: *A Discourse of Trade from England unto the East Indies* (London, 1621); *The Petition and Remonstrance of the Governor and Company of Merchants of London, Trading to the East Indies* (London, 1628); and *England's Treasure by Forraign Trade* (London, 1664). Subsequent references to these tracts will be by their dates of publication.

[7] On this point see J. D. Gould, 'The Date of *England's Treasure by Forraign Trade*', *Journal of Economic History*, vol. 15 (1955).

would not readily comprehend the wisdom of 'export of treasure' to the East because:

This position is so contrarie to the common opinion, that it will require strong Arguments, to maintaine and proove it before it will bee accepted, especially of the multitude, who bitterly exclaime when they see any Monies carried out of the Realme; affirming thereupon that we have absolutely lost so much Treasure, being an Acte against the long continued Lawes of this Kingdome . . .[8]

Yet he was confident that a general audience, if properly instructed, could grasp the central issues. He explained his decision to compose the first of his tracts by noting that 'clamorous complaints' against the trade had 'growne so loude and generall, that (my selfe being one of the Society) it hath much troubled my private meditations, to conceive the means and true grounds of this confusion. But at the last I resolved my selfe, that the greatest numbers of these exclaimers, are led away in ignorance; not having as yet, discerned the mysteries of such waighty affaires . . .'[9]

Mun did not quarrel with a central premiss of orthodox doctrine of his time: i.e. that a major goal of national economic policy should be the acquisition of precious metals. Moreover, he saw—as did his contemporaries—that only through trade could countries like England, which lacked significant gold and silver deposits at home, augment their supply of precious metals. The point at issue was how this objective could best be reached. One group of critics of the Company's practices maintained that no international transactions should be encouraged unless they promised to generate an immediate enlargement of the national stock of treasure. Mun insisted, on the other hand, that such guidelines were far too constricting and, if enforced, would oblige the nation to forego uniquely profitable avenues of commerce. The relevant test, he argued, was neither the outcome resulting from individual transactions nor that from bilateral dealings between England and any other single country. Judgements should instead be based on the results flowing from a multilateral chain of transactions, such as those developed by the East India traders.

[8] Mun (1628), p. 27. The same passage, with minor stylistic emendations, is repro-duced in Mun (1664), p. 14.
[9] Mun (1621), p. 6 (as reprinted in *Early English Tracts on Commerce*, ed. J. R. McCulloch (Cambridge, 1970)).

To support this conclusion, Mun invited his readers to consider the details of the intricate linkages between England and the East. The first step in initiating the trade was obviously one of providing from England those articles which could be used overseas to procure the commodities for which there was a known demand in Europe. What had England to offer to buyers in Asia? It was soon clear that tropical climates did not provide promising conditions for the sale of England's staple export—wool. Nor was there thought to be a substantial market in the East for English metal products. Successful conduct of the commerce was thus heavily dependent on the export of money. Mun reassured the critics that the merchant would 'rather carry out wares by which there is ever some gains expected, than to export money which is still but the same without any encrease'.[10] But he also wished his countrymen to understand that 'there are many Countries which may yeeld us very large and profitable traffique for our money, that otherwise afford us no trade at all because they have no use of our wares, as namely the East Indies for one . . .'[11] Mun did not emphasize the point—though he did acknowledge it—that merchants who transferred silver from Europe to Asia stood to reap substantial gains through arbitrage.[12] There can be no doubt that the shipment of silver to the East was good business.[13]

The early consignments of the Company to the East fell into the pattern Mun had sketched. From the first voyage in 1601 up to July 1620, 79 ships were dispatched. Measured by value, their outgoing cargoes were heavily dominated by silver. In the aggregate of export values for these two decades (amounting to about £840,000), silver accounted for £548,000. The remainder was distributed over such items as broadcloth, lead, and tin. While suppliers of domestic exports took little comfort from these results, Mun assured them that this was 'a good Addition,

---

[10] Mun (1664), p. 18.

[11] Mun (1628), p. 35.

[12] As he observed in 1621, '. . . who knoweth not, that gold in the East-Indies hath no ratable price with Silver? Neither hath the silver coyne of England any equall value with the Spanish Rialls according to their severall prices here . . .' (Mun (1621), p. 17.)

[13] For a valuable discussion of the silver premium in Asia, see K. N. Chaudhuri, 'The East India Company and the Export of Treasure in the Early Seventeenth Century', *Economic History Review*, 2nd ser., vol. 16 (1963–4), pp. 23–28.

and vent of our wares, into such remote places; where heretofore they have had no utterance at all'.[14]

The ultimate objective of transactions in the East was the procurement of Asian goods for sale in European markets. But, as latecomers to this sphere of commerce, English traders faced some formidable obstacles. The Dutch had already asserted themselves in the areas of most promising supply, particularly in Java (the main source of pepper) and in the islands of the Moluccas group (where cloves, maces, and nutmegs were obtained). Following a period of experimentation during the early voyages, English merchants sought to gain a foothold in the Dutch sphere of influence by proceeding circuitously. The fine textiles of India were much in demand in the Indonesian islands. To obtain them the English East India Company established its first permanent 'factory' (the term used to denote a trading station) at Surat on the north-west coast of India. Silver brought from Europe was there exchanged for textiles which, in turn, were bartered for pepper and spices in the Indonesian islands.[15]

Mun did not elaborate the mechanics of this 'country trade' within Asia. For an English audience, it was more important to clarify the nature of the Company's operations in Europe and to demonstrate that their over-all impact enhanced the wealth of the kingdom. This phase of the discussion hinged on a distinction between those imports which would be retained in England and those which would later be re-exported to third markets. The bulk of the retained imports Mun regarded as 'essentials': i.e. such items as pepper, spices, and drugs which would, he maintained, be acquired by English consumers by one means or another. But much depended on the nationality of the supplier. England's interest would be best served when an English

---

[14] Mun (1621), p. 18.
[15] For a fuller discussion of this network, see K. N. Chaudhuri, *The English East India Company: a Study of an Early Joint Stock Company* (London, 1965). It should be noted that the attempts to penetrate the Dutch sphere had heavy costs. Mun reported, for example, that 12 of the 79 ships dispatched in the first two decades of the Company's existence had been captured by the Dutch. A temporary *modus vivendi* was achieved in 1618 when a treaty was negotiated to afford access of English traders to one-half of the pepper trade of Java and to one-third of the trade of the Spice Islands of the Moluccas. This truce was short-lived. In 1623, the Dutch arrested English traders on the spice island of Amboyna and ten of them were killed. This episode was to live on in legend as the 'massacre of Amboyna'.

company—rather than a foreign one—served the home market. As Mun stated this proposition in 1628: 'Suppose wee therefore that Pepper were constantly worth two shillings the pound here in England, if we should then fetch the same from Holland the merchant may pay there to the Stranger twentie pence the pound out of this Kingdomes Stocke, and gaine well by the bargaine, but if he fetch this Pepper from the East Indies, he cannot give there above five pence the pound at the moste to obtaine the like gaine when all charges are considered; which doth sufficiently shew the great advantage we have to buy our Wares in those remote Countries . . .'[16] Not only did direct procurement by Englishmen check the outflow of precious metals to foreigners; it also served the long-term interest of English consumers. Prices in England of cloves, maces and nutmegs, it was noted, had roughly doubled after the 'Hollanders', following the loss of Amboyna, had 'engrossed' trade in these commodities.

Retained imports, important though they might be, occupied only a minor place in Mun's argument. Much more significant was the re-export trade. Mun contended that the bulk of the cargoes brought from the East would ultimately find their way into third markets. Some would do so directly: for example, a major share of the English East India Company's stocks of pepper would be marketed in Europe.[17] In other cases, Asian imports would be processed in England to add to their value before shipment to third markets; e.g. raw silk acquired in the East was woven into a finished product in England and utltimately sold to the luxury market on the Continent. Traffic in East India goods thus permitted England to run a substantial trade surplus in its commerce with third markets. This meant, in turn, that the nation acquired far more treasure than it had surrendered when embarking on the East India commerce. These gains, however, would not have been possible had the Company been obliged to live within the standard rules prohibiting the export of precious metals.

In his pamphlet of 1621, Mun sought to clinch this argument

[16] Mun (1628), p. 8.

[17] For the year 1627, Mun reported that 'wee brought in Pepper from the Indies to the value of two hundred and eight thousand pounds sterling, whereof one hundred and fourescore thousand pounds was within few weekes after shipped, or sould to be transported into forraigne Countries . . .' Mun (1628), p. 3.

with some estimates of the relevant magnitudes. An export of £100,000 in money to the East Indies would, he calculated, procure goods there which would be valued in Europe at £500,000. Of that total, he estimated that less than a quarter (specifically £120,000) would be consumed in England. Cargoes valued at £380,000 were destined for re-export. If earnings could be enhanced to this extent while, simultaneously, foreign suppliers were displaced from English markets, the final impact on the nation's wealth (as the orthodox defined it) could only be resoundingly positive. As he summed up the general case in 1628:

> ... when we have prepared our exportations of wares, and sent out as much of every thing as wee can spare or vent abroad; it is not therefore said, that when wee should add our money thereunto to fetch in the more *money immediately*, but rather first to inlarge our trade therewith by inabling us to bring in more forraigne wares, which being sent out againe into the places of their consume, they will in due time much increase our *Treasure*: For, although in this manner wee doe yearely multiply our importations ... *yet our consumption of these forraigne wares is no* more than it was *before*; so that all the sayd increase of commodities brought in by the meanes of our ready mony sent out as afore written, doth in the end become an exportation unto us of a farre greater value then our sayd monies were ...[18]

It was, in his view, not a question of whether or not England could afford to part with the treasure which initiated commerce with the East. The reality, as he saw it, was that the country could not afford to do otherwise. The East India trade was uniquely well suited to the accumulation of precious metals through the favourable balance on over-all trade which it generated.

While Mun's primary intention was to build an economic case in defence of the East India trade, he was not insensitive to the political arguments which could be invoked on the Company's behalf. The Company, he insisted, further served the national interest because its activities tended to weaken the position of European rivals. Treasure acquired through the re-export traffic drained the wealth and strength of foreigners. At the same time, the East India Company contributed importantly to national preparedness by developing a reserve naval capacity and by sharpening the skills of shipwrights and seamen. These external benefits, though not readily susceptible to precise calculation, were national blessings acquired without cost to the state.

[18] Mun (1628), pp. 28–9.

III. THE BROADER ANALYTIC VISION

Mun's treatment of the matter of the alleged 'drain' was designed, in the first instance, as a justification—within the framework of orthodox categories of interpretation—of a pattern of international trade and finance which appeared to many to be highly irregular. He made no attempt to conceal that he was an interested party in the debates raging over the East India commerce. But an important dimension of his case would be missed if it were to be dismissed as no more than an act of special pleading.[19] Though few of his presuppositions were set out explicitly, Mun was responsible for the formulation of a conceptual framework which was to influence the shape of economic debate throughout the seventeenth century.

Mun's initial rejoinder to the charges levelled against the activities of the East India Company was his demonstration that the triangular network of commerce produced a net increment to the national supply of treasure. But he was not interested in the accumulation of precious metals for their own sake. Much more important were the implications of a favourable balance of trade for the expansion of the English economy. Mun did not have in mind a mechanism which might readily occur to a modern student: i.e. that a merchandise trade surplus would tend to generate a foreign trade multiplier which would have stimulating effects on the home economy analogous to those associated with an increment in home investment. The favourable balance with which he was concerned had little to do with an expansion of domestic exports, but relied primarily on the re-export of goods procured in the East. The East India commerce, as he saw it, offered to England a unique opportunity to break out of the status of a relatively stagnant monoculture.

But how could the dynamic stimuli required for fundamental economic change be generated from foreign trade by a country in which the potential for export in domestic product lines appeared

[19] It has, for example, been argued by Lynn Muchmore that Mun's strategy should be regarded as an attempt to shift 'the terms of reference from the short run to the long run in order to de-emphasize the role of the money supply as the determinant of economic conditions.' ('A Note on Thomas Mun's *England's Treasure by Forraign Trade*', *Economic History Review*, 2nd ser., vol. 23 (1970), p. 501.) It is thus suggested that Mun's emphasis on the balance of trade should be regarded primarily as a diversionary tactic to confound those critics who had charged the East India Company with the responsibility for the monetary crises of the 1620s.

to be limited? Mun's answer was that the nation should 'trade with its money'. By regarding precious metals as themselves articles of commerce, the range of trade goods would immediately be enlarged and diversified. Such a strategy, if properly conducted, would—as Mun had attempted to demonstrate when disposing of allegations of a 'drain' to the East—produce still more money. But precious metals were also to be thought of as providing the potential for new investment. Twentieth-century economists—accustomed to a concept of investment organized around the needs of an industrial rather than those of a commercial era—may easily misread Mun's message. In his day, the type of investment which mattered most was not the formation of fixed capital. Far more interesting was investment in the working capital required for the expansion of overseas commerce. For this purpose (and most especially in the East India trade) money and working capital came to the same thing. Those who have charged seventeenth-century thinkers with 'confusing' money with capital have not fully appreciated this point.[20] It has been well understood, however, by the economic historians.[21]

Acquisitions of precious metals through a well-managed trade created, however, only the potential for worthwhile investment. In Mun's view, the national interest would be best served and growth in the national economy most usefully stimulated when these increments in treasure were re-invested as working capital to enlarge the long-distance commerce. But precisely because money and commercial capital had common properties, this objective could easily be frustrated. There was always the risk that newly acquired precious metals would be used as money and thus 'leak' into the domestic expenditure stream. This outcome

[20] See, for example, Jacob Viner, *Studies in the Theory of International Trade* (New York, 1937), p. 32.

[21] F. R. W. K. Hinton, for example, has observed: 'In the seventeenth century, a man accumulated money in order to invest it and in investing circulated it. It was really, therefore, capital and currency at the same time.' ('The Mercantile System in the Time of Thomas Mun', *Economic History Review*, 2nd ser., vol. 7 (1954–5), p. 282.) Charles Wilson has also emphasized that English seventeenth-century argument was 'rooted in the views of individual merchants about the requirements of their business. Trading capital *in money* was regarded as an indispensable link in the exchange of goods.' The necessity of this link was clearest in the two most 'difficult' trades: the East India commerce and the 'Eastland' trade with the Baltic for the acquisition of naval stores. See 'Treasure and Trade Balances: the Mercantilist Problem', reprinted in Charles Wilson, *Economic History and the Historian: Collected Essays* (London, 1969), pp. 54–5.

was undesirable on two counts. In the first place, the availabilities for commercial investment abroad would, to that extent, be reduced. In addition, the enlargement of the internal money supply might be expected to drive up prices. As Mun put the latter point, 'all men do consent that plenty of mony in a Kingdom doth make the native commodities dearer, which as it is to the profit of some private men in their revenues, so it is directly against the Publique in the quantity of the trade . . .'[22] The elements of a crude quantity theory of money—with fears that an expanding money supply would produce price adjustments tending to erode the balance of trade—are thus latent in his doctrine.

Unfavourable price effects could, of course, be averted if increments in treasure flowed into idle hoards or, as was then common practice, into the households of the wealthy in the form of plate. But this outcome, though less unsatisfactory, was also to be discouraged. Part of the potential for growth through commercial re-investment would simply have been wasted.

Within this perspective, the ideal situation was one in which the bulk of the treasure earned through foreign trade was ploughed back into the enlargement of overseas commerce by being shipped abroad. This use of money as capital would avert unfortunate price adjustments at home. Part of Mun's strategy might thus be regarded as the seventeenth-century counterpart of the late nineteenth-century practice of 'sterilizing the gold flow'. But the argument went beyond that. It was also an investment-oriented approach to a particular form of development. Mun could link the two notions when urging that a country which 'had gained some store of money by trade' should not 'lose it again by not trading with that money'.[23]

How was this objective to be accomplished? In Mun's judgement, the outcome to be sought was most likely to be achieved when the bulk of the gains in treasure accrued as profits to merchants engaged in foreign trade. In this view of the world, overseas merchants were expected to carry society's main burdens of saving and investment; in much the same way, the classical economists of the late eighteenth and early nineteenth centuries looked to industrial capitalists as the natural accumulators. Mun

[22] Mun (1664), p. 17.
[23] Mun (1664), p. 18.

did not offer elaborate statistical breakdowns purporting to document this point, though Gregory King was to do so toward the close of the seventeenth century.[24] Mun seems to have regarded this matter as too self-evident to require supporting evidence.[25]

IV. RE-INVESTMENT, RE-EXPORT LED GROWTH, AND THE DOMESTIC ECONOMY

One of the remarkable attributes of the 'model' developed by Mun was the central role assigned to activities which largely bypassed direct contact with the domestic English economy. While expansion in foreign trade was crucial, the suppliers of traditional English exports were not likely to be significant gainers. With care to avoid overstatement, Mun did, however, remind his readers that the East India Company's sales of English woollens and tin and lead products—though not overwhelming in volume—still offered a 'vent' which would not otherwise have been available.

Stimuli radiating from the long-distance trades were likely to have a more significant impact on income and employment elsewhere in the home economy. There were some obvious direct linkages with certain support industries—e.g. shipbuilding—and with the services sector of the economy. Mun estimated in 1628 that some 2,500 seamen were employed in the commerce with the East Indies and that 500 were engaged in its re-export traffic. Another 1,000 were then estimated to be employed in shipbuilding and in maintenance services.[26] From this point of view, the very remoteness of the East India trade gave it a unique recommendation. The longer the distances traversed and the

[24] See Gregory King, *Natural and Politicall Observations and Conclusions upon the State and Condition of England* (1696), p. 31 (as published in *Two Tracts by Gregory King* (Baltimore, Md., 1936)). King's calculations reported that the 'merchants and traders by sea' had the highest average propensity to save of any group in the community.

[25] It is of passing interest to note that Keynes once maintained that the roots of British overseas investment could be traced to Drake's looting of Spanish treasure, part of which went into the launching of the Levant Company. In his interpretation: 'Out of the profits of the Levant Company, the East India Company was founded; and the profits of this great enterprise were the foundation of England's subsequent foreign investment.' ('Economic Possibilities for Our Grandchildren', *Essays in Persuasion* (London, 1951), p. 362.)

[26] Mun (1628), pp. 2–4.

lengthier the time periods required to negotiate them, the larger would be the proportion of domestic content in the final value of the product. In this sense, the East India commerce was the most profitable trade in which the country engaged. As Mun put this matter: 'Also we ought to esteem and cherish those trades which we have in remote or far Countreys, for besides the encrease of Shipping and Mariners thereby, the wares also sent thither and receiv'd from thence are far more profitable unto the kingdom than by our trades neer at hand . . .'[27]

The East India Company was also the generator of employment opportunities in its capacity as an importer of intermediate goods. The dye-stuffs it procured in India helped to stimulate job opportunities in the textile trades. Perhaps more important was the linkage between the raw silks imported by the East India Company and employment for England's weavers.

At least in the early years, itemization of the increments in employment in England which could be attributed to the East India commerce did not yield a dramatically impressive set of numbers. Nevertheless, these gains were net additions to income and employment for Englishmen, won by pre-empting market space formerly occupied by suppliers of different nationality. England's participation in the East India commerce on the terms Mun had designed had no displacement impact on established producer interests in England. Retained imports were largely to be confined to the 'necessaries' and to intermediate goods. Consumer luxuries which might compete with home production were intended primarily for re-export.

But there was another side-effect of growth in this sphere of commerce which brought significant benefits to England. Part of

---

[27] Mun (1664), p. 10. Estimates of the magnitude of 'value added' in the East India commerce can be derived from a document prepared by the East India Company about 1620; Mun's estimates for this period, when they differ, are shown in parentheses.

Quantities imported	Price per unit in the Indies	Prices per unit in England
2,500,000 lbs. of pepper	2*d.*	20*d.*
150,000 lbs. of cloves	9*d.*	6*s.*
150,000 lbs. of nutmegs	3*d.* (Mun, 4*d.*)	6*s.*6*d.* (Mun, 2*s* 6*d.*)
50,000 lbs. maces	8*d.*	6*s.*
200,000 lbs. indigo	13*d.* (Mun, 14*d.*)	5*s.*
107,140 lbs. of raw silk	7*s.*	20*s.*
50,000 pieces calicoes	7*s.* (Mun, 6*s.*)	20*s.*

These data are reported by Bal Krishna, *Commercial Relations between India and England, 1601–1757* (London, 1924), p. 61.

the gain would accrue to the state in the form of increased receipts from customs duties. With the King's coffers thus swollen, his capacity to augment national wealth and strength was increased. Mun counselled the wise prince to suppress temptations either to spend these gains on conspicuous consumption or to immobilize his treasure in idle hoards. The national interest would be best served by 'investing' them in shipbuilding and in the development of fortifications.[28] Both national power and employment would thus be augmented.

V. IMPLICATIONS FOR THE APPROACH TO ECONOMIC POLICY

Mun's primary contribution was the formulation of an 'official model' of economic growth in which the long-distance trades in general (and the East India trade in particular) could be seen to be crucial components. A strategy for economic policy also emerged clearly from this analysis. In modern terms, this dimension of the argument may best be understood as analogous to the 'infant industry' argument for protection. The infant in this case, however, was not a manufacturing enterprise. It was instead a novel form of commercial undertaking.

Mun was certainly on sound ground in insisting that English commerce in the East was in its infancy. Other countries had already established themselves with success in that sphere of trade. The latecomer could thus mount a reasonably convincing case for special shelter, and, in large measure, the terms of the original charter provided it. The award to the East India Company of the privilege to export precious metals was a concession to the problems of a commercial infant and to the unusual circumstances facing it in the East. But no less important was the award of monopoly rights to shield the Company from the competition of other Englishmen. At least one set of risks to which venture capital was exposed had thereby been minimized. Moreover, the implicit support of the state to the East India Company buttressed the leverage of its agents when dealing with Asians and, to some extent, with commercial rivals from Europe.

The analogy of the 'infant industry' is also apt when one considers the major characteristics of the East India Company's operations. Just as the 'infant industry' argument for protection is usually mounted most successfully when markets have already

[28] Mun (1664), pp. 59–60.

been identified by foreign suppliers, so also did Mun maintain that protection for an infant commercial enterprise would open space for English suppliers at the expense of foreign ones. All that was needed to enable English merchants to win control of their home market was a minimum amount of official encouragement and shelter. In short, the case rested on the merits of a special form of import substitution.

While part of Mun's argument was thus built on the advantages of displacing foreign suppliers in the import trade, another part rested on the prospects of export enlargement (particularly through re-exports) via participation in the East India commerce. In both instances, trading links with the East would become complementary to—and not competitive with—the production pattern of the home economy. Those commodities which dominated the lists of retained imports (e.g. peppers and spices) presented no problem. There were no satisfactory domestic substitutes; supplies brought into England by the East India Company meant disturbance only for foreigners. Nor did raw materials imported from the East create any difficulty in England. On the contrary, they strengthened the production pattern of the home economy and improved England's export capabilities. The importation of final consumer goods—particularly those which were not 'necessities'—was an altogether different matter. Mun counselled restraint in this category of imports. Should, for example, Indian textiles be imported in volume to satisfy the demands of English consumers (rather than for re-export), two unhealthy consequences might follow. In the first place, the national capacity to generate 'investable' treasure would be diminished. Secondly, a heavy weight to final consumer goods of this type in the import bill might be at the expense of home producers of competing goods.

In substantial measure, responsibility for determining the volume and the composition of retained imports fell on the merchants themselves. Mun saw that there might be situations in which private profit-maximization in the short-term and the longer-term public interest would diverge. Situations might arise in which 'the gaine of the Marchant, which he doth sometimes justly and worthily effect' meant that 'the Common Wealth be a looser'.[29] By the same token, the merchant might lose, though

[29] Mun (1628), p. 14.

the nation gained.[30] If such a conflict should occur, the interests of the community should take precedence. In 1628, he observed: '. . . when the merchant by his laudable endeavours may both bring in and carry out Wares to his advantage, to buying them and selling them to good profit, which is the end of his labours: Yet neverthelesse, the Common-wealth shall decline and growe poore by a disorder in the people, when through pride and other excesses they doe consume more forraigne Ware in value, then the Wealth of the Kingdome can satisfy and pay by the exploitation of our owne Commodities, which is the very qualitie of an unthrift, who spends beyond his meanes.'[31]

VI. IMPLICIT PRESUPPOSITIONS IN MUN'S ANALYSIS

At the time Mun wrote, the presuppositions required for his 'model' to be translated into practice were reasonably well in accord with reality. The re-export commerce, upon which so much of its success depended, appeared to be capable of indefinite expansion. The profits of trade could thus be re-invested to enlarge the volume of commerce without requiring any fundamental changes in its pattern. But these conditions might not hold in perpetuity. Expansion of commerce along the lines Mun envisioned depended both on a highly elastic supply of the standard trade commodities in the East and on a highly elastic demand for these commodities in third markets. Should these conditions no longer obtain, a rethinking of the original premises would obviously be called for. Obstacles to the growth of trade within its established channels at any point in the chain of transactions would cloud the prospects for growth—at least along the lines Mun had charted. But it was also conceivable that growth in the volume of trade would itself produce different forms of contact between the East India commerce and England's home economy. In this respect, Mun's categories of analysis might be stripped of their relevance through the very fulfilment of his vision.

But another limitation was inherent in Mun's view of the world.

---

[30] Mun was at pains to emphasize the latter point to his colleagues in 1628. In face of the Company's heavy losses in the 1620s, morale among the traders was low. At one point, members of the Company voted to disband and it was only after strong intervention by the Governor that this decision was reconsidered and reversed. See K. N. Chaudhuri, op. cit., p. 19.

[31] Mun (1628), p. 16.

Why, one might well ask, should gains in precious metal won in overseas commerce be continuously ploughed back into the expansion of trade? Was not the country's welfare more a function of expanded consumption, than of expanded investment beyond its shores?[32] In this regard, Mun's analysis was subject to weaknesses similar to those which can be found in certain twentieth-century models of development. Some of the planning strategies devised, for example, for the Soviet Union and for India have asserted—as did Mun—a necessary priority for a particular type of capital formation if the maximum rate of growth is to be achieved. Whereas Mun identified investment in long-distance commerce as the key, twentieth-century variations on this theme have usually insisted on the crucial importance of investment in the producer goods sector of the economy.[33]

Arguments of this general structure, whether formulated in the seventeenth or in the twentieth century, have a number of common properties. Defence of the choice of priorities rests, for example, on broadly similar propositions: i.e. import displacement and foreign exchange conservation, minimization of 'backwash effects' on home manufacturers of consumer goods (particularly in the traditional crafts), and considerations of national independence and military strength. By the same token, investment-specific development strategies tend not to focus central analytic attention on the consumption aspirations of the community. This objective does not drop from sight completely, but is typically treated as a matter which can be dealt with satisfactorily only after the investment base in the economy's strategic sector has been solidly laid. Though Mun did not compromise his advocacy of thriftiness, he was prepared to encourage some

[32] This type of question has been raised by Lynn Muchmore, 'A Note on Thomas Mun's *England's Treasure by Forraign Trade*', *Economic History Review*, 2nd ser., vol. 23 (1970), and by George Wilson, 'Thomas Mun and Specie Flows', *Journal of Economic History*, vol. 18 (1958).

[33] In the 1920s, for example, an obscure Soviet economist named Fel'dman maintained that the route to growth for a poor economy was to be found by assigning priority to the capital goods sector of the economy. Not only would the capital stock be increased thereby, but the real saving of the community would necessarily increase because a rising proportion of the economy's outputs literally could not be consumed. A similar scheme of priorities has been urged on the Indian Planning Commission, notably by Professor P. C. Mahalanobis, Head of the Indian Statistical Institute. In the context of independent India, concentration of industrial investment in the producer goods sector has another recommendation: competition between machine-made consumer goods and the outputs of the traditional crafts can be minimized.

improvement in consumption and for quite practical reasons: '. . . all kind of Bounty and Pomp is not to be avoided, for if we should become so frugal, that we would use few or no Forraign wares, how shall we then vent our own commodities? what will become of our Ships, Mariners, Munitions, our poor Artificers, and many others? doe we hope that other Countreys will afford us money for All our wares, without buying or bartering for Some of theirs? this would prove a vain expectation; it is more safe and sure to run a middle course by spending moderately, which will purchase treasure plentifully.'[34]

Mun's conceptual framework, though not without its limitations, can nonetheless be absolved from most of the charges which twentieth century commentators have levelled against the general tradition of 'mercantilist' thought. Among one school of critics, it has been fashionable to dismiss the literature of the mercantilist era as misguided, irrational, or both. Why, they have asked, should any sensible person (or nation) hoard dead metals which yield no return and forgo thereby opportunities to raise consumption by purchasing imports? Moreover, would not the increment in the domestic money supply arising from a favourable balance of trade lead to subsequent increases in domestic prices? And would not this outcome, in turn—by making exports less competitive and imports more attractive—tend to erode the initial favourable balance of trade?

If the term 'mercantilism' is understood in its generic sense— i.e. as a body of economic literature about merchants and largely written by them—Mun's contributions can readily be subsumed under this rubric. His work cannot easily be faulted, however, on grounds of incoherence or internal inconsistency. A model of considerable ingenuity informed his writings. Though it was not set out in formal fashion, it was highly consistent within the context of its own assumptions. Even the point which neoclassical economists have held to be the fatal flaw in mercantilist thinking—i.e. an alleged failure to perceive the implications of price adjustment and specie flow mechanisms associated with an influx of precious metals—was incorporated within Mun's scheme of analysis.[35]

[34] Mun (1664), p. 60.

[35] J. D. Gould has commented perceptively on Mun's treatment of these matters; see 'The Trade Crisis of the Early 1620s and English Economic Thought', *Journal of Economic History*, vol. 15 (1955).

It may be noted in passing that little support for a more sympathetic twentieth-century interpretation of mercantilist economics can be found in Mun's writings. In his 'Notes on Mercantilism', Keynes credited this tradition with establishing a sophisticated connection between the money supply and levels of interest rates. In this interpretation, a high degree of rationality could be attributed to a strategy designed to increase the national supply of treasure because it would tend to lower interest rates and, in turn, to stimulate domestic investment and employment. Mun was little concerned with the mechanism of interest rates in organized capital markets. The investment he had in mind was accumulated from the profits of overseas trade; moreover, it was to be primarily allocated as working capital for overseas commerce, rather than to the formation of fixed capital at home.

It is not difficult to understand why seventeenth-century economic thought has often seemed to twentieth-century men to be a mass of shapeless dough. The literature of that age was bewildering in its volume and in its diversity. But if attention is concentrated on the yeast provided by the East India commerce,[36] a rather different impression emerges. This strand of development thinking had its own inner logic and its own intellectual dynamics.

As seventeenth-century men understood Mun, he offered a conceptual framework which enabled them to comprehend the unique characteristics of the East India commerce. Admittedly, this framework served the purposes of the East India Company. But it also did more. Contained within it were the essential ingredients of a model of a commercial revolution.

[36] The importance of the East India commerce as a prime mover of debates in the seventeenth century has been widely recognized. Lipson, for example, has noted that the economic issues raised by the East India trade 'played the leading role in the development of economic thought prior to Adam Smith's *Wealth of Nations*' (*The Economic History of England*, (6th edn., London, 1956) vol. 2, p. 270). Schumpeter, writing from a quite different perspective, has observed: 'because of its prominence, the East India Company attracted the lion's share of public attention and hostility. This accounts for a large part of the literature in question'. As will be noted later, there is substantial reason to differ with his subsequent judgement: 'so far as I can see, however, there is nothing in it to interest us except the arguments and counter arguments about the Company's exportation of monetary metal and about the competition which—though harassed by legislation and administration— it offered to English woollens by the importation of Indian wares. However, these arguments and counter arguments enter into the general discussion concerning the balance of trade.' (J. A. Schumpeter, *History of Economic Analysis* (London, 1954), p. 348.)

In large measure, Mun's model shaped the agenda of discussion throughout the remainder of the seventeenth century. Charges that the Company's export of treasure dissipated the wealth of the Kingdom—though they did not disappear entirely —commanded little attention. The issues which later came to dominate debate were largely controlled by Mun's categories and turned, in particular, on whether or not the conditions required for the realization of Mun's vision were being satisfied.

CHAPTER 2

Problems of Commercial Maturity: 1660–1700

I F the middle decades of the seventeenth century, the fortunes of the English East India Company mirrored the turbulence of the society of which it was a part. Indeed at the height of the English Civil War, the very survival of the Company was in doubt. Under the rule of the Protector, the state felt no obligation to honour charters issued by the Crown, but was instead under pressure to uproot such residual manifestations of privilege. The East India Company was in an exposed position for yet another reason. At least by repute, it had backed the loser. Even though the Company's support for the King had been less than enthusiastic, its credentials were suspect.[1] If Cromwell had scores to settle, he also had debts to pay. His constituencies in the outlying ports had long smarted at the exclusive privileges of a London-based company of merchants in the lucrative East India trade. In 1653 Parliament terminated the charter of the East India Company and opened the commerce to all comers.

The immediate impact of this change in the rules was a scramble for the prizes of the Eastern trade. Though the principle of free entry had been honoured, a stable equilibrium did not follow. It was widely acknowledged that the trading conditions which ensued were chaotic. Supply prices in the East were bid to unprecedented levels in the competition of English merchants for cargoes. Many of the new entrants, unacquainted with the peculiarities of commerce in Asia, soon found their expectations disappointed. Ease of entry was accompanied by

[1] In 1640, for example, Charles I—frustrated in his attempt to obtain a loan in the City—called upon the East India Company to advance him its total stock of pepper (valued at more than £63,000) for which he agreed to make payment at a later date. The King's fiscal problems were temporarily alleviated when the Crown marketed this inventory, even though the proceeds were less than the sum he had contracted to pay the Company. The Crown, however, defaulted on this involuntary 'loan'. (See E. Lipson, *The Economic History of England* (6th edn., London, 1956), vol. 3, p. 315.) In addition, the Company had undertaken in the mid-1630s to deliver all of its supplies of saltpetre to the King.

ease of exit. When members of the old East India Company threatened to abandon their network of outposts in Asia and to forfeit the concessions won from local rulers, Cromwell's government capitulated and restored its monopoly privileges.

The resurrected East India Company of 1657—if not then in the most flourishing health—was at least no longer an infant. In its new embodiment, it was to embark on a novel organizational experiment. A precedent for the conduct of the East India commerce on the basis of a joint stock principle had been set in the earliest voyages. But, in the years before 1657, the interests of shareholders had been limited to specific voyages and had been liquidated in distributions following the disposal of inward cargoes. Strictly speaking, the share capital raised in 1657 was subscribed for a seven-year period. Before the terminal date had been reached, however, the proprietors voted to keep the subscriptions in place. Thus the foundations of a 'permanent' joint stock—with its implications for corporate immortality—had been laid. In its time, this method of commercial and financial organization was a departure from standard practice sufficiently radical to provoke public anxiety.

Commercial maturity brought with it a new set of problems. Though Mun's conceptual categories tended to shape the agenda of debate, their adequacy to the circumstances of the later decades of the seventeenth century was increasingly open to question. These phases of controversy were coincident with changes in the economic climate which were to germinate some remarkable analytic innovations.

I. GROWTH AND PRODUCT DIVERSIFICATION

In the 1660s and 1670s, the volume of commerce conducted by the East India Company expanded dramatically. Its magnitude —as measured by the value of bullion and goods the Company exported from England—was slightly in excess of £1,400,000 in the decade of the 1660s. In the decade of the 1670s, this figure had more than doubled, approaching £3,500,000. By contrast, exports by the Company in the most active trading decade in the first half of the seventeenth century (1630–9) fell short of £900,000 in value.[2]

---

[2] See Bal Krishna, *Commercial Relations between India and England 1601–1757* (London, 1924).

Growth in the volume of trade brought a number of new practical problems to the surface. As the Company's directors discovered, most of the familiar staples in the import lists—commodities such as pepper, spices, indigo—faced relatively inelastic conditions of demand, both with respect to price and with respect to income. Significant expansion in earnings thus depended heavily on adjustments in the commodity composition of the import traffic. In this phase of its history, the East India Company's behaviour was not unlike that of a twentieth-century 'conglomerate'.

In Restoration England, a shift in this import pattern in more profitable directions was enormously facilitated by a change in consumer tastes. Indian-made textiles, which—in modest quantity—had been a part of the trade from its earliest days, became articles of high fashion in the 1670s. The new enthusiasm for muslins and calicoes was by no means discouraged by the East India Company. Its officials in London directed agents in the field to enlarge their procurements.[3] In the 1670s, the Company commissioned several experienced weavers and dyers from England to visit parts of India to instruct local craftsmen in designs most likely to win wide acceptance in English and European markets.

But these were not the only signs of change. Experiments were also launched to introduce a totally unfamiliar product—tea—into the European consumption pattern. The promotion strategy used was one which an advertising agency three centuries later would have understood well. In the 1680s, a presentation of the finest teas was made to the Royal household and with maximum publicity.[4] Though many decades were to pass before tea was to become a mainstay of the commerce, demand for this product of the East rose without interruption thereafter.

Growth in trade volume was thus accompanied by significant

[3] Bal Krishna has reported the upsurge in the orders for Indian textiles sent from the London headquarters to the Company's factors in the East as follows: for the years 1673–8, requisitions were sent for 3,903,500 pieces; for the years 1680–3, orders more than doubled, amounting to 8,564,000 pieces (op. cit., p. 140).

[4] In 1685, the Directors instructed their agents at Ft. St. George (later Madras):

In regard Thea is grown to be a commodity here and wee have occasion to make presents therein to our great friends at Court, we would have you send us yearly 5 or 6 canisters of the very best and freshest Thea. That which will colour the water in which it is infused most of a greenish complexion is generally best accepted.

(Letter Book VII, p. 425, as cited by Bal Krishna, op. cit., p. 151.)

diversification in the import bill. When Mun wrote in 1621, he could report that retained imports in England from the East India commerce were as follows: pepper, £33,333; other spices, £38,000; and indigo, £37,000.[5] By 1677, retained imports of calicoes (valued at £160,000) headed the list, followed by raw and manufactured silks (valued at £30,000). The early mainstays of the trade had shrunk in significance, absolutely as well as relatively. Pepper imports were valued at only £6,000 and 'indigo and other drugs' at £15,000.[6]

By the 1670s and 1680s, it was abundantly clear that the East India trade was no longer primarily a supplier of 'necessaries' (as Mun had used that term) to the English market. It had now become an important source of less essential manufactured products. Nor was the East India Company the only channel through which these goods entered England. Though the Company was the only legal trader in East India goods, their availability in England was nevertheless swollen by the operations of 'interlopers'.[7] The Company deployed its resources to suppress encroachments on its chartered privileges, but its efforts fell short of complete success. Nor could it always rely on English courts for support. Chief Justice Pollexfen in 1680 set aside one of its complaints against an 'interloper' on the grounds that the Company's charter was of doubtful validity because it had been awarded by the Crown rather than by Parliament.[8]

[5] Mun (1621), p. 55.

[6] *A Treatise Concerning the East-India Trade being a most Profitable Trade to the Kingdom and Best Secured and Improved by a Company and a Joint Stock* (London, 1680), p. 9. This tract has incorrectly been attributed to the pen of Sir Josiah Child. William Letwin has suggested that the author was more likely one Robert Ferguson who was commissioned to undertake this task by Papillon, then a senior member of the East India Company. Ferguson was paid a gratuity for his efforts. The first edition of this tract appeared in 1677. See William Letwin, *The Origins of Scientific Economics: English Economic Thought, 1660–1776* (London, 1963), p. 33.

[7] According to Bal Krishna's estimates, the private trade amounted to more than a quarter of the official trade in 1675, and to about half of the official trade during the years 1678–97 (op. cit., p. 125). These estimates of the private trade include allowance for the 'indulged' trade conducted by the company's directors and employees as well as for the commerce of totally unauthorized privateers.

[8] Pollexfen observed in passing that the Company was 'an invisible body subsisting only in *intelligentsia legis*, a body politic without soul or conscience'. (As quoted by P. J. Thomas, *Mercantilism and the East India Trade* (London, 1926), p. 17.) For its part, the Company reminded the state that it had a stake in the suppression of the 'interloping' traffic, pointing out that such unauthorized traders 'will save (as they call it) a great deal of the Custom on fine goods of small Bulk, whereas the Company upon Honour and Duty to His Majesty, do always pay the full customes to a penny, and

In light of these changes in the character and composition of trade, it might have been expected that the official model would be appropriately modified. A few shifts in emphasis were indeed detectable in the tracts commissioned by the Company in the 1670s and early 1680s. The fact that calico had become the most important single commodity in the import lists was duly noted. It was now argued, however, that this item should be regarded as a 'most useful and necessary commodity' rather than as a luxury. Moreover, textiles supplied through the East India trade, it was maintained, had favourable effects on the balance of trade because they displaced 'a like quantity of French, Dutch and Flanders Linnen, which would cost at least three times the price of it'.[9] Within this perspective, English consumption of Indian-made textiles was thus treated as an extension of the earlier pattern of import substitution in which the burdens of adjustment were borne by Continental rivals. No conflict with producer interests at home was recognized in this argument. On the contrary, it was to maintained that 'without question it would be much the Interest of this Kingdom to promote and encourage the Manufacture of Linnen in Ireland.' If this could be accomplished, 'the Callico now consumed here, might be transported to other Markets abroad, and to bring us a farther Addition of Stock to the Nation '.[10]

In the early 1680s, a sign of change could also be seen in the increasing prominence assigned to two subsidiary points in the Company's briefs. Greater attention was given to the employment opportunities in England which were linked to the East India traffic. In 1681, for example, it was noted that more than 40,000 families won their livelihood from processing raw silk brought from the East and that this number might easily be trebled within a few years. The East India Company, it was claimed, had recently 'found out a way of bringing Raw Silk of all sorts into this Kingdom, cheaper than it can be afforded in Turkey, France, Spain, Italy, or any other place where it is made'.[11] A heavier weight was also attached to the Company's

---

produce their true and original Invoices to the Kings officers at any time'. (*The East-India Company's Answer* (London, 1681), p. 14.)

[9] *A Treatise Concerning the East-India Trade being a most Profitable Trade to the Kingdom*, p. 10.   [10] Ibid., pp. 10–11.

[11] *A Treatise Wherein is Demonstrated that the East-India Trade is the most National of all Foreign Trades* (London, 1861), p. 8. This tract has also been incorrectly attributed to Child; see Letwin, op. cit., p. 33.

contributions to national security. India, the pamphleteers of this period reminded their readers, was the source of saltpetre—'that absolute necessity'—without which 'we should be like the Israelites under the Bondage of the Philistines, without means of defending our selves; If we had no India-trade, possibly in time of Peace we might purchase it, though it would cost us double what it now doth. But in case of War, where could we have sufficient? . . . What use will our Ships and Guns be of, if we want Powder?'[12] Moreover, national strength on the seas (which the Company helped to provide) was uniquely suited to the preservation of the liberties of Englishmen: 'A Naval power never affrights us; Seamen never did nor ever will destroy the Liberty of their own Country: they naturally hate Slavery, because they see so much of the misery of it in other Countreys. All tyrannies in the World are supported by Land-Armies: No absolute Princes have great Navies, or great Trades . . .'[13]

The basic framework of discussion, despite marginal adaptations, remained the one constructed by Thomas Mun. Spokesmen for the Company in the early 1680s continued to insist that, though trade volume had increased markedly, its basic structure was unchanged and that it remained a 'most profitable' trade for the kingdom.[14] It was further argued that the re-export trade in Indian goods continued to be the predominant interest of the Company and that its transactions necessarily augmented the wealth of the kingdom. Data cited for the year 1675, for example, maintained that the Company had procured goods with a value in Europe of 'at least £860,000' and that £630,000 of these 'returned' were 'transported to foreign markets'.[15] In 1681 it was argued 'above four-fifth parts of the Commodities Imported by this Trade, are again Exported into foreign parts . . . by the

[12] *Treatise Concerning the East-India Trade being a most Profitable Trade to the Kingdom* (1680), pp. 9–10.

[13] *A Treatise Wherein is Demonstrated that the East-India Trade is the most National of all Foreign Trades* (1681), p. 28.

[14] One of the tracts commissioned by the Company set out the criteria of a disadvantageous trade as one that 'takes off little from us in Commodities, and furnisheth us with little or no Good for our Foreign vent in other places, but with abundance of either unnecessary and superfluous things to feed our vain humours and fantasies, or with such, though useful, as hinder the consumption of our manufactures. . . .' (*A Treatise Concerning the East-India Trade being a most Profitable Trade to the Kingdom*, p. 2.) In the view of the author of this tract, the trade with France fitted these characteristics. The East India trade definitely did not.

[15] Ibid., pp. 7, 9.

Returns of which, more then treble the Bullion is Imported, that was first Exported to India . . .'[16] Lines such as these might easily have come from the pen of Thomas Mun.

II. EXPANSION IN THE EAST INDIA TRADE AND GROWTH IN THE ENGLISH ECONOMY: COMPATIBLE OR INCOMPATIBLE OBJECTIVES?

By the 1690s, events had been begun to press for a more fundamental change in doctrine. There were no longer any doubts about the divergence of the new reality from Mun's image of the structure of the East India commerce in relation to the English economic scene. Petitions circulated in Parliament calling for prohibitions against further importations of finished Indian textiles on the grounds that they seriously damaged the position of the woollen interests at home. Rates of duty on Indian textiles had already been sharply increased, but this remedy was held to be insufficient. The weaving trades sought relief—not only through protection from foreign competition, but also through legislation requiring the Company to stimulate sales of English goods in Asian markets. On the latter point, success was readily won. In the renewal of the charter in 1693, the East India Company was instructed to carry out at least £100,000 worth of English products annually.

For several decades, trends in the commodity composition of the Company's import trade had pointed in the direction of a possible clash of interests. Two unrelated sets of events in the late 1680s—both of which were derivative from England's commercial rivalry with Continental countries—hastened a collision. The first stemmed from a change in trade relationships following an edict by the French government in 1686 banning the entry of Indian textiles supplied by English merchants. By this time, France was sensitive to the interests of its own East India Company, founded in 1668. As access to one of the important markets for re-exported Indian textiles was closed, the English domestic market took on greater relative importance.[17] Dutch initiatives

[16] *A Treatise Wherein is Demonstrated that the East-India Trade is the most National of all Foreign Trades*, p. 6.

[17] Ironically, an earlier round in the trade war between England and France had eased one of the East India Company's marketing problems. In 1678 Parliament—retaliating against Colbert's exclusion of English cloth from France—legislated to prohibit further importation of French silks and linens. The finer textile products of India thus found new market space available to them in England's domestic economy.

in the East further complicated matters. In 1682 the English Company's procurement base for pepper at Bantam (on the island of Java) was seized by Dutch arms. Though pepper had long since been displaced from a position of prominence in the import lists, the loss of these cargoes implied that concentration on the newer product lines would be intensified. Meanwhile, the Company attempted to re-establish itself in the Indonesian archipelago by building up a more secure base for the procurement of pepper on the island of Bencoolen.

These forces, in combination, imposed considerable strain on the official model. After all, Mun's image of the long-distance commerce as the leading sector in economic expansion rested on the presupposition that England's imports of East Indian products were complementary to, rather than competitive with, home production. In particular, it was assumed that imports retained in England from the East India commerce would be dominated by necessities, while luxury consumer goods would generally be avoided. Most non-essentials in the list of trade goods were to be re-directed to third markets. This scheme of things was no longer in close touch with the reality. In the last decade of the seventeenth century, the impact of imports from India on English producers, particularly of textiles, was making itself felt.

That a change in the structure of the trade had occurred was soon to be acknowledged even by commentators sympathetic to the position of the Company. Davenant, writing in 1696, observed that about half of the landed value of East India goods was now consumed in England. Though he emphasized that the re-export trade was still substantial and that the goods shipped abroad could be sold for about four times what they would command in England, a striking shift in the proportion of the trade absorbed by English buyers was still noteworthy.[18]

Critics of the Company were not slow to seize on this point. The author of a hostile tract reminded his readers in 1697 that advocates of the East India commerce had formerly assured the public that their dealings in Indian manufactures could not injure the nation 'because [they] were not spent in England, but transported to foreign markets, and thereby occasioned the importation of more bullion than ever was exported'. But as this

[18] Davenant, *An Essay on the East India Trade* (London, 1696), pp. 15–16.

spokesman for the weavers added, 'the Truth (which was formerly denyed) being now owned . . . [was] that one half of the said Goods are consumed at Home, and that those Manufactured Goods do hinder the Consumption of what are Fabrickt by our own People.'[19]

The form in which part of the case of the weavers' interests was presented bears arresting witness to how well Mun's teaching had been absorbed. The argument rested on the premiss that England's advantage from the East India commerce derived from the re-export of Indian goods and from gains in money which could be acquired thereby. If the East India merchants had forgotten this lesson, the petitioners for the weavers insisted that they should be obliged to relearn it. Banning Indian textiles from England would compel them to pursue marketing efforts abroad with greater vigour. As this position was stated in 1697: 'This is a profitable Trade to England in its Exportation . . . I own this may be a profitable trade by due Regulation, and therefore I am for this Bill; . . . but the Design of this Bill, is to oblige the India Merchant to set up Factories to sell goods in Holland, Hamborough, Germany, Portugal, Spain, as well as Manufactures in India, to make them, and by this means they will truly bring in Bullion into England, as well as carry it to India . . .'[20] Mun's 'model' had thus been appropriated to attack the East India trade as it had now evolved. His analytic guns had been captured by the Company's enemies and were pointed in the reverse direction.

The stamp of Mun's thought can also be seen in another dimension of the arguments presented by this school of critics in the 1690s. Little space was allocated to the charge that the East India trade 'drained' the national supply of precious metals. Though reference might still be made to the loss of bullion to the East, this practice was no longer a matter of major contention. Mun's view that precious metals should be regarded as potential resources for investment had won broad acceptance. It was now asked, however, why this potential should flow into investments which produced their major employment-generating effects abroad. The East India traders were charged with preferring 'the

[19] *England and East India Inconsistent in Their Manufactures, being an Answer to a Treatise Intituled an Essay on the East-India Trade* (London, 1697), p. 3.
[20] *Reasons Humbly Offered for the Passing a Bill for the Hindering the Home Consumption of East-India Silks, Bengals, etc.* (London, 1697), pp. 15–16.

Welfare of the Moguls Subjects, the advancing of his Lands, and the imploying of his People' to the welfare and employment prospects of their own countrymen.[21] These criticisms of the East India Company also found expression in the jingles of the time.[22] The outcome would be far happier, it was maintained, if capital mobilized through trade were to be directed into capital formation at home. This doctrine was set out as follows in 1697: 'I would to God all the Merchants in England that carry out our Silver to promote and set up Forreign Manufacturies, were so sullen as to do so no more, but would Employ their Stocks in setting up new Species of Manufactures in England, in Towns and Places where the Poor have no Employment . . .'[23] A modern reader might well be expected to note a striking similarity between this view and the attitude of some representatives of organized labour in the United States toward American foreign investment in the 1970s.

Arguments derived from Mun's vision of the structure of the East India commerce were supplemented by allegations which have since become a standard part of protectionist polemics. The cheapness of labour in India, it was maintained, directly jeopardized the livelihood of English textile workers. With employment already slack, it was intolerable to permit a trade which put at risk the jobs of some 250,000 workers.[24] Moreover, the prosperity of the nation was closely linked to the fate of the trade in wool and woollen fabrics. Not only was this sector the mainstay of domestic exports; its linkage with agriculture was so direct that any recession in the woollen textiles trade would immediately

---

[21] *England and East-India Inconsistent in Their Manufactures* (1697), p. 28.

[22]
> Whilst they promote what Indians make,
> The Employment they from the English take,
> Then how shall Tenants pay Their Rents,
> When Trade and Coins (are) to India sent?
> How shall folks live, and Taxes pay,
> When Poor want work, and go away?
> Such cargoes as these ships bring over,
> In England were never seen before.

England's Almanac, 1700 (as quoted by Shafaat Ahmad Khan, *The East India Trade in the XVIIth Century* (London, 1923), p. 215.

[23] *Reasons Humbly Offered for the Passing a Bill for the Hindering the Home Consumption of East-India Silks, Bengals, etc.*, (1697), pp. 17–18.

[24] Ibid., p. 3.

spread distress throughout the country. Land values would be depressed and landowners would correspondingly suffer.[25]

To reinforce the employment and prosperity arguments for protection, spokesmen for the weavers introduced a national security argument of their own. A thriving and settled class of weavers, backed in turn by a self-reliant yeomanry, gave the nation its best insurance against invasion. As this case was stated: 'These poor People, when employed, highly conduce to the Happiness and Safety of England . . . since England hath been a Place of Manufactury, no Neighbour hath dared to Insult our Coast, or Invade us without our consent; for these poor People are not only themselves ready to oppose, but by their Imploy-ment, give Incouragement to Navigation, and to breeding of Seamen to navigate our Coasting-Vessels and to supply their necessities with Coals, Corn, Malt, Cheese, Butter, etc. by which means the King always hath Seamen ready to furnish his Men of War, that are the Bulworks of the Nation, and our Merchants are supplyed with Seamen for longer Voyages.'[26] There is a striking symmetry between this rhetoric and that which Gandhi used more than two centuries later when he appealed for the rejuvenation of the household spinning crafts of India and saw their revival as essential to 'rebuilding our villages'.

III. COMMERCIAL MONOPOLY: A RESTRAINT ON GROWTH?

Attacks on the special privileges enjoyed by the East India Company had long been familiar, but they were mounted with renewed vigour and with different modes of argument in the late seventeenth century. These critics, as had the weavers, developed part of their case within the framework Mun had constructed. It was now accepted that commerce with the East Indies was of

[25] 'If it be said, that this Trade hath a good foundation, because Materials are plenty, and Labour cheap in India; it being argued that these Manufactured Goods are spent both Abroad and at Home, in the room of our own. This instead of being an Argument for recommending this Trade, will appear the most dangerous part of it: For unless our Wooll fall into nothing, and the Wages of those that work it up to 2d. per Day, and Raw Silk and Silk Weavers Labour proportionable, the India goods will occasion a stop to the Consumption of them; because those from India must otherwise be Cheapest and all People will go to the Cheapest Markets, which will affect the Rents of Land, and bring our Working People to Poverty and force them either to fly to Foreign parts, or to be maintained by the Parishes . . .' (*England and East-India Inconsistent in Their Manufactures*, pp. 17–18.)

[26] *Reasons Humbly Offered for Passing a Bill for the Hindering the Home Consumption of East-India Silks, Bengals, etc.*, (1697), pp. 5 and 6.

national importance—and that its importance derived from the stimulus it provided to England's economic growth. But, if the desirability of this objective was established, then it would appear to follow that the volume of the trade should be expanded at the maximum possible rate. Whereas lobbyists for the weavers' interests charged the Company with violating the rules of the game by changing the character of a growing import trade, a second group of critics maintained that the Company's management had broken faith with the tradition of Mun by failing to promote the growth of trade with its full energy. According to these allegations, the monopoly form of organization had necessarily restricted the rate of commercial expansion.

These new charges stemmed largely from members of the Turkey Company, a group of London-based merchants whose trade had fallen on evil days. As had members of the Levant Company at the beginning of the century, they sought access to the special opportunities which the East India commerce appeared to present. Two main factors were responsible for their distresses at the time: increasingly severe restrictions imposed on their activities in the Middle East by the Turkish Sultanate and the encroachments on their established markets in raw silks and luxury textiles by the East India Company which followed from the new emphasis it had given to these commodities. The Turkey merchants sought a wider scope for their energies. But the exclusive privileges of a chartered monopoly barred them from direct trade with the East.

The central propositions of the Turkey Company were set out as follows in 1681: 'Compare the largeness and extent of the Companies Priviledges from the Cape of Good Hope to the Streights of Magellan, which is near two third Parts of the Trading World, with the smallness of their Stock, and by such Comparison it must needs appear that their stock is far too little, for the trade of so many vast and rich Countries. And 'tis evident in Fact, that no Trade at all is driven to many of them . . . and yet while they Trade not thither themselves, they violently keep out others who would Trade, for their Stock being so small, they only manage such Trades which yields very great and excessive Profit, and neglect others, which probably might Answer, though not so immense a Profit, yet a very good Advantage, and more proportionable, to the time and hazard, than any

Trade in Europe . . .'[27] Freer entry would thus attract additional resources to enlarge the trade. The national economy would correspondingly be enriched because 'the more Merchants, and other people, would be set on work, the more Ships and Marriners employed, the Trade more Extensive and National, the Commodities of those parts made Cheaper, and more got to the Kingdom in general, besides to his Majesty in particular, by his Customs'.[28]

From the perspective of the members of the Turkey Company, the corporate organization of the East India Company necessarily restricted the availability of capital for commerce. This judgement can be understood only against the background of the 'regulated company' form of commercial organization. Most of England's overseas trading groups (apart from the Royal Africa Company which was chartered as a joint-stock undertaking in the mid-seventeenth century) were organized along these lines. Under such arrangements, merchants who had served a stipulated period of apprenticeship could be admitted, upon payment of a fee, as 'free men' to membership in a trading company. This pattern derived from the medieval guild mode of organization. Admission to membership in a regulated company, though it established that a merchant had acquired certain skills, did not imply any pooling of capital. Each participating merchant traded on his own resources and the profits or losses arising from his ventures were solely his own affair. When measured against these standards, the East India Company was a curious specimen indeed. Few of its shareholders—the petitioners of the Turkey Company estimated that the number would not exceed more than one-fifth of the total—would be qualified as bona fide merchants.[29]

In view of the novelty of the concept of a permanent joint stock in those days, it was not remarkable that its features were imperfectly understood. Those whose views had been moulded within a 'regulated company' could readily conclude that a permanent joint stock necessarily imposed constraints on expansion—or at least on expansion along socially healthy lines. Whereas the Turkey Company regularly admitted new 'free men', the East India Company had not enlarged its share capital

[27] *The Allegations of the Turky Company and Others against the East-India Company* (London, 1681), p. 5. According to Letwin (op. cit., p. 30), this document was prepared by Sir John Buckworth and Sir Dudley North.

[28] Ibid., p. 5.   [29] Ibid., p. 4.

since the award of the charter in 1657. The critics acknowledged that the Company had, on occasion, transcended the limits of internal financing by borrowing at interest. Such proceedings, however, were held to be highly irregular and, moreover, the interest rates obtained by the Company seemed to be suspiciously low. As the petitioners of 1681 viewed the problem: 'But in case any misfortune happens to what danger will all the Lenders of so great a part of the Treasure of the Nation be exposed, when the flourishing Estates of particular men cannot be made liable to these Debts, contracted under the Common Seal, which give Life and Being to them, and from whence they arose; So that the East-India Company against the Rules of Justice and Reason, securely enjoy the benefit of the Trade, and yet have little share in the hazard and loss thereof.'[30]

But another theme ran through the critique of monopoly in this phase of the debate—and it is one which has long since become familiar in discussions of such issues. The Company was now charged with promoting an unfortunate distribution of income and wielding socially dangerous power. The Turkey Company opened this round of discussion with the charge that it was 'the certain effect of a Monopoly to enrich some few and empoverish many'.[31] Particularly when a trading organization with chartered privileges was organized on the basis of a joint stock, it appeared to follow necessarily that effective control would be exercised by a relatively small body of men. In 1681 it was alleged 'that the whole Management thereof is fall'n into the hands of 10 or 12 men, and in all likelihood in a few years may come into the hands of 3 or 4 . . .'[32] The structure was also vulnerable to another charge: that leading figures in the Company could swell their personal fortunes by conducting a trade on their own account while using the Company's commercial facilities. This privilege (known as the 'indulged trade') was available to members of the Company, in proportion to their share holdings and—on a more limited basis—to ship-captains and seamen in the Company's employ. The result, it was alleged, was that participants in the 'indulged trade' preferred 'their separate, and private Trade, before the Publique joint-Stock . . . And hence it comes to pass, that many of the choicest and richest Goods, are sent home, on the private accompt of Particular Men,

[30] Ibid., p. 3.　　　　[31] Ibid., p. 2.　　　　[32] Ibid., p. 4.

which are seldom or never sent home on Account of the Joint-Stock. The Particular and distinct Interest, being always preferred before the General and Publique.'[33] In this view of the Company's affairs, the whole system was seen to be saturated with corruption.

In the early 1680s, spokesmen for the Company had little difficulty in blunting the edge of these complaints. The company, they noted, was not restrictive in its membership. In 1681, one of its pamphleteers endorsed the view 'that all Monopolies, of what Nature or Kind soever, are Destructive to Trade'. He hastened to add, however, that 'if there be any thing in the East-India Company's Charter, or any Charter of Incorporated Merchants; that hinders any of His Majesties subjects of England, Scotland, or Ireland, from coming into that Trade, upon as good Terms as others of His Majesties Subjects did, or yet may, it would tend to the general good of the Kingdom, that such Barrs or Hinderances were removed.'[34] In short, the East India Company was not a closed monopoly; anyone with the required resources could buy in. It was further pointed out that entry into the East India commerce was much freer than into the Turkey trade. The Company imposed no apprenticeship conditions or licensing fees. Moreover, the critics had misunderstood the nature of the Company's management structure. Centralized decision-making reflected a concentration of skill. In the management of large affairs, professional direction—so long as it was subject to checks imposed by the shareholders at large—was in the best interests of efficiency.[35] The Company's official spokesmen acknowledged, however, that the 'indulged trade' was not altogether fortunate. The practice was broadly justified with arguments similar to those invoked to support stock-option plans for executive officers in some twentieth-century corporations. Spokesmen for the Company did not claim that the system was faultless, but

[33] *The Allegations of the Turky Company and Others against the East-India Company* (*London*, 1681), p. 5.

[34] *A Treatise Wherein is Demonstrated that the East-India Trade is the most National of all Foreign Trades*, p. 2.

[35] It was argued in 1681 that 'The more any Adventurer hath in the Stock, the more he is engaged to study and promote the good of it, by all possible means within his power. An Adventurer that hath the smallest Interest, may be as just and true to the stock, as he that hath the greatest: but I can never believe that a small interest will awaken a man so often in the night, nor keep him so long from sleeping, in the meditation of any business; that the very great and principal concern may do.' (Ibid., p. 21.)

observed that it would not be 'the work of a Year, nor of an Age, or two, to build up an East-India trade to perfection . . .'[36]

In yet another respect, an analogy with corporate behaviour in the twentieth century can be found in discussions within the circles of the senior membership of the East India Company in the 1680s. The ranks were sharply divided over the issue of increasing the number of shares. Enlargement of the share capital at this stage would, of course, have gone part of the way towards silencing those critics who had alleged that the joint-stock form of commercial organization restricted a beneficial growth in trade. In fact, the Company's access to the short-term loan market— and on extremely favourable terms—had been more than suffi- cient for its financial needs. Factional lines within the Company were sharply drawn between the position of Sir Josiah Child, who had succeeded to the governorship in 1681, and that of Papillon, a highly experienced merchant who had earlier been one of Child's closest associates. Child's opposition to enlargement of the equity capital carried the day. His case rested on the recogni- tion that an increase in the share issue would tend to dilute control. Papillon, who favoured a widening of the stock, was soon thereafter removed from a position of authority in the Company.

By the 1690s, those who protested against an unhealthy con- centration of power within the Company had greater substance for their charges. As Governor, Child carried far more weight than had any of his predecessors. But he still needed powerful allies—and he was inclined to seek them at Court. Though some degree of collaboration between Company and Crown had always been inherent in the structure of a chartered enterprise, Child brought collusion between them to a level far beyond anything witnessed earlier.[37]

While Child's policies generated heated divisions within the Company's Court of Proprietors, they provoked even sharper controversies outside it. The barrage of attacks launched in the 1690s set records for their vehemence. The economic implications

---

[36] *The East India Company's Answer*, p. 8.

[37] In the 1680s, for example, Child persuaded the Company to vote a present of 10,000 guineas to the King. This generosity was not unrelated to the Company's re- quest for support in the capture and punishment of 'interlopers'. The King, shortly thereafter, signed such a proclamation. (See Letwin, op. cit., pp. 34–5.) Khan has estimated that loans and gifts (restyled under Child as 'voluntary contributions') to Charles II totalled more than £324,000 between 1660 and 1684 (op. cit., p. 150).

of chartered monopoly, though occasionally introduced into the argument, were no longer the primary issues. Instead the major focus was political—a shift in emphasis which reflected the new direction Child had given to the Company following the loss of Bantam to the Dutch. By the late 1680s, fortifications in the East had come to be regarded as the essential instruments by which 'our servants, shipping, and estate could be secured'.[38] Outlays for military establishments were greatly enlarged and the foundations for the transformation of the Company into a territorial power in the East had thus been laid. In its new posture, the Company soon found itself in armed conflict with local rulers—and increasingly vunerable to assaults on its privileges at home. Its enemies in England charged the Company (with ample justification) with military adventurism which had stained the national honour and placed the legitimate trade in jeopardy.

Even those who were most outspoken in their denunciations of the Company's conduct did not, in this phase of debate, challenge the claim that the East India commerce was of vital importance to the nation. On the contrary, it was precisely because of its importance that steps to ensure that it was well and honourably managed were so essential. Even Child's severest critics credited the East India Company with contributing 'in value and profit one full sixth part of the trade of the whole Kingdom'.[39] The central difficulty arose from the fact that his strategies—which were seen as 'Hostilities and Depredations unreasonably exercised towards the Subjects of the Great Mogul and other Potentates in India and Parts adjacent'—had 'already deprived the Nation of trade in Bengale, Surat, and other Places and put the rest and whole of that invaluable Trade of East-India upon the utmost hazard of being inevitably, utterly, and irrecoverably lost to the Nation'.[40] Moreover, Child was depicted as a tyrant who had trampled on the liberties both of his countrymen and of innocent people abroad. Not only had his military interventions blotted the national honour abroad, but his methods at home had tended to subvert the integrity of English

[38] Child, Dispatch of April 1688 (as quoted by Khan, op. cit., p. 205).

[39] See, for example, the pamphlet entitled *Some Remarks upon the Present State of the East-India Company's Affairs: with Reasons for the speedy Establishing a New Company* (London, 1690).

[40] *An Essay towards a Scheme or Model for Erecting a National East-India Joynt-Stock or Company* (London, 1691), pp. 3–4.

government. With considerable justice, it was asserted that the profits of the Company had been diverted to purchase political support.[41] Charges of bribery and corruption were rampant.[42] To paraphrase the idiom of a later age, the East India Company was now perceived as the lynch-pin in a sinister 'military–mercantile complex'.

In the confused politics of the years following the Glorious Revolution of 1688, critics of the Company had an unusually receptive audience. Equilibrium in the relations between Crown and Parliament had yet to be reached. While Child might have the support of the Crown, the aggrieved could turn to Parliament. They did—and with some measure of success. An unintended delay in a tax payment in 1693 provided an opening for challenging the faithfulness of the Company to the stipulations of its charter and the debates which followed produced an Act of Parliament of 1698 which changed the rules. The exclusive right to trade with India was now to be conferred on those who subscribed to a state loan of £2,000,000. Though subscriptions were open both to individuals and to members of corporations, the annual amount of trade in each case would not be allowed to exceed the sums subscribed. A new company was formed and it dominated the subscription list.[43] This situation generated com-

---

[41] Somers has noted that an expenditure of £170,000 for 'secret service money' was noted in the books of the Company during the period of confusion over the status of the Company's charter in 1693. This outlay was believed to have been used 'in bribing courtiers and members of Parliament'. See Somers, *A Collection of Scarce and Valuable Tracts*, vol. 10 (1813), p. 618.

[42] As a pamphleteer in 1691 put the matter, 'That the Arbitrary Management of this Company by the Governor and Committees, hath all along conduced to, and greatly advanced the introducing Popery, Slavery, and Tyranny into this Nation, during the Reigns of the two last Kings, (more especially since the year 1681) by too great Severities in unhappy unexampled ways exercised towards and upon the Free-born Subjects of England, their Persons, Goods, Estates, and Liberties, as has been made evident at the Bar of the honourable House of Commons.' (*An Essay towards a Scheme or Model for Erecting a National East-India Joynt-Stock or Company*, p. 3.)

[43] The £2,000,000 loan was distributed as follows: the old Company, £315,000; the new Company, £1,662,000; independent traders, £23,000. An official of the old Company protested that its members had not been given an adequate opportunity to raise the full subscription which, it was asserted, the Company was fully capable of doing. Moreover, a gross injustice would be perpetrated unless the members of the old Company were compensated for the more than £1,000,000 they had invested in fixed assets in the East. The legislation of 1698, it was further noted, would bring ruin to 'some Hundreds of Families (many of which are Widows and Orphans) who have no other Subsistence, but their Interest in this Stock'. (*The Case of the Governor and Company of Merchants of London Trading to the East Indies* (London, 1698), p. 10.)

petition of a sort, though not necessarily in a form which any of the parties involved regarded as optimal.

IV. MODIFICATIONS IN THE OFFICIAL MODEL

With the appropriation of some of the basic insights of Mun's 'model' by the opposition, defenders of the East India Company were required to introduce rather different modes of argument to buttress their position in the 1690s. Somewhat unsystematically —but nevertheless quite deliberately—the positions toward which the briefs for the Company moved in the mid-1690s gave major emphasis to the benefits to consumers which would be available from an unrestricted import trade in which buyers could purchase in the cheapest markets.

At this stage in the debate, it was acknowledged that the importation of East Indian textiles might, in some degree, interfere with English textile manufactures. But it was further asserted that the principal issue at stake was 'Which way the Nation in General is more Cheaply supply'd'.[44] The nation stood to gain when the people of England were 'willing, and pleased to Wear Indian Silks, and Stuffs, of which the Prime Cost in India, is not above a Fourth part of what their own Commodities would stand them in here; and if they are thereby thus enabled to Export so much of their own Product, whatever is so sav'd, is clear Gain to the Kingdom in general'.[45] This argument amounted to saying that the substitution of Indian textiles for domestic woollens should be welcomed, not feared. The availability of wool for export would be enhanced as the claims of domestic consumers were reduced. Such an outcome was indeed a part of the natural order of things. In terms which approached a statement of the doctrine of comparative advantage, it was now maintained that 'the various Products of different Soiles, and Countries, is an Indication, that Providence intended they should be helpful to each other, and mutually supply the Necessities of one another.'[46]

This line of argument was pushed a step further in a tract which pleaded the case of the East India Company in 1696. As this author diagnosed the problem: '. . . if the Case be, as is owned by all, that we want people for our Work; and not Work

[44] *An Essay on the East-India Trade* (1696), p. 32.
[45] Ibid., p. 30.   [46] Ibid., p. 34.

for our People, then the bringing in of foreign Manufactures at half the Price we can make them here at Home, whilst at the same time we can find Imployment for our People, we by that Means save so much Money. This I take to be very clear. And the only Question is then, What other Imployment we have for our people? . . . we want Seamen, we want Hands in the West-Indies, we want Husbandmen, we want many more Hands in the Woollen Manufacture that it might be wrought Cheaper, and carried on to such a degree that it is capable to be improved; and the Linnen Manufacture which . . . may do well here in time will employ more hands; not to mention the Fishery and other things.'[47] The author of this statement did not claim that full employment obtained at that moment—a situation he explained as being attributable in large part to the dislocations of war. But part of the distress of the working population—and of the weavers in particular—was explained by the high costs of production in English manufacturing.[48] Remedies should not be sought in prohibitions against imports but through productivity improvement at home. Vigorous competition was indeed held to be therapeutic for the depressed sectors of the economy. According to this pamphleteer, 'our Manufactures are never so well Wrought as in a time of dull Trade, when we pay less for Workmanship, and yet the Poor live as well then as in time of greatest Plenty, if they have but a full stroke of Work.'[49] Within this framework, the textiles imported from India could be depicted as healthy stimulants to efficiency which, over the longer run, would benefit the nation by disciplining English woollen producers to become more competitive in export markets. This counsel, to be sure, did not win applause among the weavers.

Even so, a marked change in the course of debate on the East India commerce had occurred. As first devised, the categories of analysis had been moulded in a context in which it was necessary to justify a freedom to export—in particular, a freedom to export precious metals. But the rules set out by Mun were no longer applicable. In new circumstances, the case built by

[47] *Some Reflections on a Pamphlet Intituled England and East-India Inconsistent in Their Manufactures* (authorship attributed by Viner to Gardner) (London, 1696), pp. 9–10.

[48] It should be noted in passing that the population supported by poor relief in the mid-1690s was estimated at 1,200,000.

[49] Ibid., p. 16.

spokesmen for the East India Company appealed increasingly for a freedom to import—and particularly freedom to import finished consumer goods, even at the risk of displacing some local producers. The statement of the argument in the 1690s was by no means analytically complete. Yet a major step toward a new approach had been taken.

But the new formulation of the problem also provided the basis for a novel justification for the monopoly basis of organization of the East India trade. The Company's pamphleteers now drew attention to the heavy burdens imposed by the necessity to maintain expensive establishments and fortifications abroad. Covering these fixed costs required a high volume of turnover. Any restrictions on access to markets—such as those called for by the English weavers—would thus compromise the very survival of the East India commerce. One of the Company's advocates asked: 'What Encouragement can there be to go on with so vast a Business, if our Merchants must singly depend upon the Markets abroad? One Country, to advance their Own Manufactures, may prohibit Our Goods, The Hollanders will buy 'em up at their own Rates, when their Use is forbidden here, And they will be a Drug, and blown upon, all Over Europe. There is a great difference between a Merchants having a choice, or a Necessity to sell his Ware. In one case he may in some Measure make his own Price, in the other he must take what is offer'd.'[50]

A related line of argument could be deployed in rejoinder to the charges of the Turkey Company. Those who maintained that the Company had been laggard in its efforts to expand the geographical scope of the trade in Asia—and that 'regulated companies' would proceed more ambitiously—had misunderstood the problem. A crucial fact about operations in the East (a point which the Company's pamphleteers were at pains to emphasize) was its unique requirement of time-consuming dealings with an alien people. The Company was eager to open new trade routes whenever consistent with minimum conditions of security and it had every incentive to do so. In any event, the rate of growth in the East India commerce was not constrained by deficiencies of either skill or capital.

Similar considerations were also invoked to justify the necessity of exclusive monopoly privileges in the conduct of the East

[50] *An Essay on the East India Trade*, pp. 54–5.

India commerce. In the nature of the case, only an organization with a high degree of centrality in its direction, with access to much larger capital resources than could possibly be commanded by groups of individual merchants trading on their own account, and with assurances of reasonable prospects of continuity could pursue this sphere of commerce successfully. Expeditures on the required infrastructure in the East—including not only the obvious outlays for the construction and maintenance of ware-houses and garrisons, but also the costs incurred in negotiating treaty concessions with local rulers—were heavy and growing heavier. In 1681 a pamphleteer presenting the Company's case estimated that capital outlays for these purposes (including allowance for the cost of acquiring privileges and immunities) amounted to more than £300,000.[51] In the same year it was calculated that the annual recurring charge for the maintenance of 'forts, castles, soldiers and otherwise' amounted to more than £100,000.[52] By 1698 it was estimated that fixed capital expendi-ture for such purposes had risen to £1 million.[53]

All of this approximated to a 'natural monopoly' case for the defence of the Company's structure and its privileges. Fixed costs were not only heavy but highly indivisible and there appeared to be substantial economies of scale. The argument suggested that attempts to legislate an open competition would lead either to the extinction of English participation in the trade (in which case, the Dutch would fill the vacuum) or to the formation of a new monopoly. The mere attempt to open the trade, however, would involve major and irrecoverable costs. The treaties, under the shelter of which the trade could flourish, had been negotiated by the East India Company and were allegedly non-transferable. Should the Company be allowed to lapse, the total extinction of England's commerce with the East was predicted.

Such an outcome, spokesmen for the Company insisted, should be averted at all costs. The national interest, they main-tained, was heavily involved—and they could now invoke the findings of the new 'political arithmetic' to support that con-clusion. With the aid of Gregory King's pioneering exercises in

[51] *A Treatise Wherein is Demonstrated that the East India Trade is the Most National of all Foreign Trades* (1681), p. 36.

[52] *The East India Company's Answer* (1681), p. 14.

[53] *The Case of the Governour and Company of Merchants of London Trading to the East-Indies* (1698), p. 2.

national accounting, it could be asserted that the East India traffic was responsible for roughly 30 per cent of the increase in the 'wealth and general stock of England' in the late seventeenth century.

Growth in 'national income' was then estimated to be of the order of £2,000,000 per annum. The factors contributing to this result were identified as follows: 'From Our Manufactures and Home Product, sent to the Plantations, and from the Returns thereof, Exported to Foreign Parts: £900,000; From our Woollen Manufacture, Lead, Tin, Leather, and Our other Native Product, sent to France, Spain, Italy, Germany, etc.: £500,000; From the Net Profit accruing by the East-India Trade: £600,000; total: £2,000,000.'[54] These estimates seemed not only to demonstrate the importance of the East India commerce to the national economy; they also, as this pamphleteer emphasized, drew attention to the fact that 'but a fourth part of Our Riches, arises from the vent of Our own Commodities.'[55] The re-export commerce, to which the East India Company was still an important contributor, was thus seen as a major source of England's economic growth.

But the same mode of argument could also be employed by critics of the Company. By 1699 a spokesman for the weavers' lobby had adopted the style of 'political arithmetic' for the purpose of showing the loss to the nation arising from the East India trade. In a calculation of daring scope, these losses were computed as amounting to more than £1,700,000 per annum.[56]

V. THE UNSTABLE OUTCOME OF THE DEBATES OF THE 1690s

In controversies of the 1690s, the official rationale for the conduct and the organization of the East India commerce underwent a significant transformation. No longer was the major case built within the framework Mun had constructed with its

---

[54] *An Essay on the East-India Trade* (1696), p. 18. Though not identical in all particulars, these calculations are clearly derived from Gregory King's *Of the Naval Trade of England anno 1688 and the National Profit then arising thereby*.

[55] Ibid., p. 8.

[56] This calculation was put together as follows: 'Damage as it hinders our Exports to Holland, Germany, Portugal and our West-India Colonies, £200,000; As it hinders our Export to Turkey and Italy: £100,000; As it hinders the working up of Turkey and Italian Effects, and employment of our Poor in them: £100,000; As it hinders the Employing of our Poor, and procures the debasing of our own fine manufactures: £1,200,000; As it hinders the Consumption of our Wool, and as it tends to bring down

emphasis on the contributions to growth of the re-investment of earnings won primarily in the re-export trade. In the light of the new shape of the trade pattern, the focus of argument was shifted toward the contributions to the welfare of consumers which the trade could offer by making final consumption goods available at prices below those of their domestic substitutes. Similarly, the pattern of defence against the increasingly passionate assaults on the Company's privileges gave a new twist to some earlier themes. The suggestion that monopoly privileges were necessary to shelter the fledgling latecomer disappeared from view. In the age of commercial maturity, the monopoly arrangement of trade with the East was held to be inevitable. In its absence, England would be totally excluded from a commerce vital to the nation.

As the pattern of debate unfolded in the 1690s, it was already apparent that these new positions were not themselves highly secure. If the Company was genuinely interested in the welfare of English consumers, could not this objective be better served by an open trade which would preclude the possibility that a single supplier of goods from the East could manipulate prices to his advantage? Nor did it necessarily follow—even if the Company's arguments on the indispensability of major outlays on establishments in the East were accepted—that the burdens of these fixed costs required the perpetuation of a chartered monopoly. Certainly other arrangements were conceivable in which provision for these costs could be made compatible with a more open commerce.

Questions of this sort were raised in the controversies of the late seventeenth century. As early as 1680 a hostile pamphleteer argued that a monopolist, with power to control the volume of trade, could exercise it to produce prices to consumers which would maximize his profits. These prices, in turn, could be expected to be higher than those which would have obtained in presence of greater competition. As this critic observed: 'when the Sellers being infinite, some of them are ready, and all long for dispatch and a new adventure, whereby they work down one another to as low a price as the Commodity can be afforded

the value thereof: £116,000; Total: £1,716,000.' (*The Profit and Loss of the East-India Trade* (1699), p. 21.)

at . . .'[57] But this was not the only way in which monopoly over trade with the East tended to compromise the interests of Englishmen. Even though the volume of domestic products exported by the East India Company (as opposed to the export of precious metals) was limited, the Company's position as the sole procurement agent afforded to it an unhealthy power to depress the prices paid to English suppliers. Thus it was 'in the nature of such Companies' that 'they must be as injurious as may be to all home-Manufactures made of our own materiales, and the vent of our other exports, because by trading on a Joynt stock they make but one buyer . . .'[58] The same point could, of course, have been made with reference to the bargaining position of suppliers in India. In an argument intended to influence opinion in England, this aspect of the matter was neglected.

The Company's defence of its privileges on the grounds of a 'natural monopoly' was also vulnerable, even if two of its propositions were taken as given: i.e. that the trade depended on the maintenance of expensive establishments abroad and that the resources required for these overheads were beyond the capacity of small merchants acting independently. The overhead costs might be 'nationalized' with the state assuming responsibility for all capital charges associated with the conduct of the commerce. The trade itself could then be genuinely open to all who might be interested. On the assumption that the volume of trade would then mount, the state could, over time, more than recoup its costs through the subsequent growth in its customs revenues. Such a proposal was in fact advanced in 1680 by a pamphleteer who maintained that 'if this Trade be taken into the protection of the Government, it will have the Joint stock of the Kingdom to secure it, the same by which we are all secured . . .'[59] A variation of this scheme, proposed in the 1690s, recommended that the East India Company be stripped of its trading monopoly but that it remain in being as the 'owner-manager' of establishments in India. Under this proposal, the Company would be

---

[57] *Britannia Languens, Or a Discourse of Trade* (1680) (as reprinted by J. R. McCulloch in *Early English Tracts on Commerce*, p. 334). The authorship of this pamphlet has been attributed to Petyt.

[58] Ibid., p. 333.

[59] Ibid., p. 337.

empowered to levy charges for the use of its facilities. The scale of fees would be fixed in relation to turnover, thus affording the Company an incentive to stimulate growth in the trade.[60]

The materials for a more thorough analysis of the consequences of alternate types of market structures for the formation of prices were thus clearly at hand. They were not, however, enthusiastically seized upon. Part of the explanation for the failure of fuller analytic treatment to emerge at this stage may perhaps be found in the lingering influence of Mun's categories on the terms of debate. Attention was thus oriented primarily toward the implications of monopoly for growth, rather than toward its influence on price determination.[61] But another factor also helps to account for the arrested development of microeconomic thinking on the consequences of the East India commerce. The best-publicized critics of the monopoly mode of organization—particularly the members of the Turkey Company —were much less concerned with the demolition of monopoly shelters than with arrangements which would permit them to enjoy its privileges. In the late seventeenth century, most of those who insisted that the East India trade should be in the hands of a 'national company' did not welcome involvement by

[60] This scheme called for the financing of "forts and castles" as follows: 'The money may be raised to pay for them, either on the trade, as all impositions are in the Turkey and other regulated companies, or paid by the government out of the customs arising by the trade, which would soon more than compensate that charge by their increase.' (*A Discourse concerning the East-India Trade: wherein is shewed, by Arguments taken from a Treatise written by Sir Josiah Child, that the said trade may be carried on by a regulated Company, to much greater Advantage of the Publick, than by a Company with a Joint Stock*, as reprinted in Somers (ed.), *A Collection of Scarce and Valuable Tracts*, vol. 10 (1813), p. 645.)

[61] Moreover, Mun's framework had suggested that neither English suppliers of exports nor English consumers would have direct contact with transactions in India. Within that context, it could thus be argued that greater competition—even if it reduced the prices of Indian goods—would largely benefit the wrong parties. The bulk of the gains would accrue to buyers in third markets, not to consumers in England. This rejoinder—which could not have been made in the 1690s—was offered in 1681: 'As to Goods Imported from India, and sold in England, the multitude of buyers in India raising the Prices there, and of Sellers in England, lessening the Prices here, cannot be but very contrary to the Kingdoms Interest. And this will appear demonstratively, if you consider, That not above one part of four of the Goods brought from India into England are here consumed, the other three fourths are Transported into Forreign parts. Now if the prices of the one fourth part for the Consumption of England be lessened and brought down, the like must inevitably follow for the other three fourths that are sent abroad.' (*A Treatise Concerning the East-India Trade being a most Profitable Trade*, pp. 24–5.)

the state. They sought an organization which, though private, would have a much broader shareholding participation.

For its part, the East India Company attempted to cushion the force of these critiques by appropriating for its own purposes one ingredient of the doctrine advanced by a hostile pamphleteer in 1680. Its status as a single procurement organization in the East, it could be asserted, enabled the Company to obtain supplies at minimum prices. English consumers, the Company's spokesmen alleged, could benefit when imported goods were obtained at lower costs than would have been possible under any alternate mode of organization. The disastrous escalation of procurement prices in the East when the trade had been open to all comers between 1653 and 1657 was introduced to bolster this position. Though the term 'monopsony' was not used, advocates of the Company's exclusive privileges were in command of its central insights.

By latter-day analytic standards, this defence was far from satisfactory. But the exchanges of the 1690s did not probe seriously its inherent weaknesses. The more visible and vocal opponents of the East India monopoly—the weavers and the Turkey merchants—had little stake in pursuing the possibility that monopoly in selling (even if linked to monopsony in buying) might still produce prices higher than those yielded by greater competition in final markets. Much of the agitation of these critics arose from the perception that the prices generated by the activities of the East India Company were too low for their competitive comfort.

Other omissions from the pattern of argument in this period are also noteworthy. To a modern reader, two lines of argument often associated with the defence of monopoly are noticeably absent. The Company's spokesmen made no claims that monopoly stimulated the national economy by generating a distribution of income highly favourable to maximizing the rate of investment and re-investment. Though Mun in a different context had attached an important weight to this function, his successors were more at pains to demonstrate that the profits won from a monopoly commerce were not excessive. Nor was attention paid to the argument that the monopoly mode of organization was uniquely well suited to the performance of research and development activities. Neglect of this point in the late seventeenth century is not surprising. Consciousness of the opportunities presented by technological dynamism was to be the product of another age.

The framework within which problems of the East India commerce were discussed in this period excluded another set of considerations. Conditions in India—though the backdrop to the entire debate—rarely came to the foreground. The basic perspective of this literature was parochial. Neither the pamphleteers for the Company nor its critics were concerned about the impact of their recommendations in the East. In this age, the narrow advocacy of national interest at the expense of others was a recognized virtue. In so far as competition with trading nations within Europe was concerned, strategies which promised to enhance England's position and to diminish the wealth and power of her major rivals were regarded as self-evidently sound. In the case of the links with the East Indies, another factor helps to account for the general lack of sensitivity to the economic interests of Indians in the trading arrangements worked out there. The dominant image of India was then—and continued to be for some time—that of a richly opulent country. So long as this view prevailed, no special concern for the economic status of Indian suppliers appeared to be called for. The richer partner could well afford to be a lesser participant in the gains from trade.

CHAPTER 3

The Climax of Seventeenth-Century Development

ENGLAND'S contact with the East during the course of the seventeenth century had been associated with a remarkable transformation. The transition from commercial infancy to commercial maturity had, of course, bred new problems. It had also stimulated a substantial alteration in the structure of the English economy and spurred a notable shift in both the mode and substance of economic discussion.

Mun's insight that significant potential for economic expansion lay in the development of the long distance trades had proved to be arrestingly on target. From all appearances, a substantial proportion of the capital accumulated through overseas commerce had, in fact, been ploughed back into trade. Indeed, the bulk of the change in England's trade pattern during the seventeenth century was attributable to the re-export of commodities procured in the remoter parts of the world. Wool and woollen cloths, which had generated virtually all of England's export earnings in 1600, accounted for less than half of the total by 1700. The re-export trade, which provided about 30 per cent of England's total export traffic at the close of the century, had been the major source of growth.

The East India trade, to be sure, was not the sole source of this dynamic stimulus. Expansion in the 'plantation' trades with the Americas had also been remarkable. Between them, three commodities procured from the long-distance commerce were responsible by the close of the century for two-thirds of English re-exports to Europe: the calicoes of India, and tobacco and sugar from the Americas.[1]

It was thus clear that a significant change in the economic structure had occurred and that much of Mun's broader vision had been realized in practice. In the light of this transformation,

---

[1] These calculations are drawn from Ralph Davis, 'English Foreign Trade, 1660–1700', *Economic History Review*, 2nd ser., vol. 7 (1954–5), pp. 150–66.

one can readily concur with the conclusion that it would be appropriate to look 'with a little more favour on those historians of the past who dubbed this century with the title of "The Commercial Revolution".'[2]

The achievements of the seventeenth century also bred new realities—and ones which Mun's conceptual categories were not designed to handle. Symptoms of inadequacy in the inherited conceptual system had surfaced forcefully in the 1690s. The arguments of both the Company's defenders and its major critics lacked analytic completeness. If the dominant 'master model' could no longer effectively come to grips with the issues of the day, the times were opportune for intellectual innovation.

I. THE OPENING OF NEW ANALYTIC TERRITORY

In 1701 that opportunity was seized by the author of a remarkable document, published anonymously, under the title *Considerations Upon the East-India Trade*.[3] He was acutely aware of the confusions and passions which had been generated by recent controversies. 'What Heats and Animosities', he wrote, 'have been caus'd by this Division? What Distractions in the Publick Counsels? Our Elections are not free, neither our Debates of Parliament. The Publick Business is very often at a stand; every one is engag'd on the side of the one or the other Company.'[4]

This author was also persuaded that the categories which had shaped the earlier rounds of debate offered little guidance to an understanding of the latest dimensions of problems. The basic question remained: was the East India commerce a blessing or a curse to the nation? Mun's answer—i.e. that the trade was

---

[2] Ibid., p. 163.

[3] The authorship of this essay is still shrouded in mystery. P. J. Thomas in *Mercantilism and the East India Trade* has suggested that the most likely author is one Henry Martin, sometime contributor to such publications of the day as the *Spectator* and the *British Merchant*. Martin has also been reported as the author of 'An Essay Towards Finding the Balance of Our Whole Trade'; see G. N. Clark, *Guide to English Commercial Statistics, 1696–1782* (Royal Historical Society, Guides and Handbooks, No. 1, London, 1938). J. R. McCulloch, on the other hand, though 'sometimes . . . half, inclined to suppose that it might have proceeded from the pen of Mr. Henry Martin'. ultimately concluded that he was 'not disposed to lay much stress on this conjecture'; (Preface to a *Select Collection of Early English Tracts on Commerce* (London, 1856), p. xv). Authorship has also been attributed to Sir Dudley North. As Viner has noted, this possibility can be ruled out; North died in 1691. (See Viner, *Studies in the Theory of International Trade*, p. 105.)

[4] *Considerations Upon the East-India Trade* (London, 1701), p. 26.

BETI—C

uniquely advantageous because of its contributions to England's economic growth—had been seriously challenged by the subsequent flow of ideas and events. It was now necessary to approach the fundamental issue from a fresh perspective.

The crucial analytic insight in *Considerations Upon the East-India Trade* rested on a redefinition of the concept of national gain arising from international transactions. In the mainstream of seventeenth-century discussion, the operative notion had largely been tied to the accumulation of capital for re-investment in trade. Within that framework, the monopoly mode of organization could be challenged (and was by the critics of the East India Company) on the grounds that it suppressed commercial growth and thereby diminished the nation's profit. But it was also possible to entertain a notion of national loss—at least when expansion in international commerce was not neutral in its impact on established producer interests in England. The case of the weavers' lobby had been presented within this larger design.

Such approaches were quickly rejected by the pamphleteer of 1701. The appropriate criterion of national profit (or loss) from international transactions was whether or not the real income of the community had been enlarged. There were national gains to be won when, through trade, goods were obtained with less sacrifice than would have been required had they been produced at home. Exchange would then be on the basis of 'less for greater value'. The point was illustrated as follows:

Then to imploy to Manufacture things in England, more Hands than are necessary to procure the like from India, is to imploy so many to no profit, which might otherwise be imploy'd to profit, is the loss of so much profit.[5]

From this position, the errors of those who had sought to impose special restrictions on either the freedom to export or on the freedom to import in the conduct of the East India commerce could readily be identified. Those who had been concerned about the 'drain' of precious metals to the East had, in this view of things, misconstrued the problem. 'To Export Bullion for Indian Manufactures,' he wrote, 'is to exchange less for greater value; it is to exchange Bullion for Manufactures more valuable, not only to the Merchant, but also to the Kingdom.'[6] Similarly, advocates

---

[5] *Considerations Upon the East-India Trade* (*London,* 1701), p. 55.
[6] Ibid., pp. 12–13.

of prohibitions on the importation of Indian goods had been misguided. On this point he observed: 'the law to restrain us to use
only English manufactures, is to oblige us to make them first, is
to oblige us to provide for our consumption by the labour of many,
what might as well be done by that of few, is to oblige us to consume the labour of many when that of few might be sufficient.
Certainly we lose by being restrained to the consumption of our
own, we cannot be so much impoverished by the free and indifferent use of any manufactures.'[7]

It was recognized in this argument that the free importation
of Indian manufactured goods, though a boon to consumers in
England, would not necessarily be regarded as a blessing by
English producers whose markets were challenged by imports.
Nevertheless, this author resolutely insisted 'that the East India
trade cannot destroy any profitable manufacture, it deprives the
people of no business which is advantageous to the kingdom;
contrary, it is the most likely means to make full employment for
the people . . . It deprives the people of no employment, which we
should wish to be preserved.'[8]

Participation in international commerce, without artificial
impediments, was thus the course consistent with maximization
of the nation's 'profit' (as that notion was now construed). For a
country in England's situation, it was the natural strategy. 'Why',
he asked, 'are we surrounded with the Sea? Surely that our Wants
at home might be supply'd by our Navigation into other Countries,
the least and easiest Labour. By this we taste the Spices of
Arabia, yet never feel the scorching Sun which brings' them forth;
we shine in Silks which our Hands have never wrought; we drink
of Vinyards which we never planted; the Treasures of those
Mines are ours, in which we have never digg'd; we only plough
the Deep, and reap the Harvest of every Country in the World.'[9]

But the full benefits obtainable from international commerce—
and particularly from trade with the East Indies—were obtainable only when the commerce was thoroughly competitive. A
market structure in which two companies contested with one
another was preferable to a monopoly, but it was still far short of
the ideal. The situation to be sought was one in which all who
chose to enter the trade could freely do so. The result, it was
recognized, would be the reduction in the profit won by individual

[7] Ibid., p. 48.   [8] Ibid., pp. 49–50.   [9] Ibid., pp. 58–9.

merchants. But, as this author observed, 'to such merchants should be told, that the East India trade is not carried on for his sake, but for the kingdom's.'[10]

If a competitive trade with the East was to become a practical reality, it was recognized that suitable arrangements to cover the fixed costs of permanent establishments in India would be required. The author accepted the necessity of such installations, but rejected the 'natural monopoly' arguments for the *status quo* propounded by the East India Company. Developing more fully the suggestions which had been advanced in 1680s and 1690s, he recommended state ownership of these installations. If the trade were then opened freely to all comers, gains in customs revenue would be more than sufficient to cover the costs involved in taking over the factories and fortifications of the old East India Company.[11]

Free entry into the East India trade would, in turn, set in motion important mechanisms of adjustment, both abroad and at home. Competition could be expected to bid up procurement prices in India but would still yield lower prices in England than would have prevailed under monopoly. Producers in India and consumers in England thus stood to benefit. Meanwhile the merchant's rate of profit would be squeezed.[12] Ultimately, a fully competitive system would produce an optimal division of labour between nations and within them. The day might conceivably come when manufactured goods imported from India could not undersell home-produced substitutes. If it arrived, 'our End is gain'd; we have reap'd the utmost Profit that is to be obtain'd by that or any other Trade; our Manufactures will then be quiet; they will not be disturb'd by the cheaper Indian Manufactures; these will not rule the price of ours, neither in our own nor foreign Markets . . . The East-India trade the more open and closer driven, will less disturb the English Manufactures . . .'[13]

[10] *Considerations Upon the East-India Trade* (London, 1701), pp. 24–5.

[11] The author treated this matter as follows: 'The necessary forts and castles may be as well maintained at the public charge; and this may be better paid by the greater gain of an open trade. The want of factories can be no complaint: a greater trade must needs increase these; it has done so in every country; the reason is like in all; our factories must be as well secured by forts and castles, under the immediate care of the government, as if the same were maintained by the joint stock of a company.' (Ibid., p. 28.)

[12] The author assumed, however, that the relevant elasticities would be such that the profit of the merchant, though 'less in proportion to the Bulk of the Trade' would still be 'more in quantity'. (Ibid., p. 24.)   [13] Ibid., p. 25.

In all its essential particulars, the analysis the nineteenth century was to know as the theory of comparative advantage can be found in the pages of an obscure tract produced by a man who sought to unravel the mysteries of the East India trade in 1701.

II. TRADE AND GROWTH IN A NEW PERSPECTIVE

While the micro-economic questions of efficient resource allocation achieved a new prominence in *Considerations Upon the East-India Trade*, the broader questions of long-term economic growth did not totally disappear from view. These issues, however, were approached from another direction. The East India commerce had a vital part to play in stimulating economic expansion in England, but its role was quite different from that which Mun had assigned to it.

In the first instance, competition provided through a free trade with India would spur improvements in productivity in England. It was expected 'to introduce more Artists, more Order and Regularity into our English Manufactures' and 'put an end to such of them as are most useless and un-profitable . . .' But the victims of such displacement could readily be absorbed elsewhere if work patterns were sub-divided and specialized. As this commentator saw the matter, 'for plain and easie work is soonest learn'd, and Men are more perfect and expeditious in it: And thus the East-India trade may be the cause of applying proper Parts of Works of great variety to single and proper Artists, of not leaving too much to be perform'd by the skill of single Persons; and this is what is meant by introducing greater Order and Regularity into our English Manufactures.'[14] Long before Adam Smith was to spell out the opportunities for economic expansion latent in the efficiency gains attainable through specialization and the division of labour, this anonymous pamphleteer had developed the same insight.

Similarly, it was expected that the East India commerce, if conducted on the basis of *laissez-faire* principles, would stimulate technological innovation in England. Precisely because the East India trade 'procures things with less and cheaper labour than wou'd be necessary to make the like in England', it was also 'very likely to be the cause of the invention of Arts, and Mills, and Engines, to save the labour of Hands in other Manufactures. Such things are successively invented to do a great deal of work with

14 Ibid., pp. 67–8.

little labour of Hands; they are the effects of Necessity and Emulation . . .'[15]

But this was not all. A fully competitive system for the conduct of the East India trade would tend to shift investment patterns in ways which, ultimately, would restructure the English economy. Free trade, it was maintained, would reduce rates of return on capital invested in overseas commerce. As this occurred, it was reasonable to expect money to 'be drawn out of trade' and placed in activities promising higher yields. Ultimately, 'when the plenty of money shall be as great as among any of our Neighbours, some of their Manufactures may be attempted . . .'[16] Though this matter was not fully elaborated, the author concluded that 'the East India trade, by inlarging the business of the Old, by setting on foot new Manufactures, is the most likely way to make most imployment for the people . . .'[17]

This was a far cry from Mun's model which had charted a course of economic growth through the re-investment in overseas commerce. Now it was suggested that profits accumulated in trade would, under competitive conditions, tend to flow increasingly into manufacturing at home. Clearly a major change in the conceptual framework had been accomplished. Mun's case for special privileges for the infant commercial enterprise had now been totally rejected. The infant had reached maturity and, like the woollen industry at home, should be able to hold its own in a competitive environment if it deserved to survive. The East India commerce was still of strategic importance in stimulating technical dynamism in the home economy. If organized competitively, the Indian trade would re-direct capital to broaden the industrial base in England.

This vision of economic expansion pointed toward an industrial revolution, rather than toward a commercial revolution. It also took into account two factors which had generally been neglected in the mainstream of seventeenth-century discussion. Technical progress was now introduced as a relevant consideration. In addition, the impact of the East India monopoly on producers in India had at least begun to emerge from the shadows, even though the implications of the trade for England remained at the centre of attention.

[15] *Considerations Upon the East-India Trade* (London, 1701), p. 66.
[16] Ibid., p. 74.   [17] Ibid., p. 75.

III. THE SEEDS OF A SCIENTIFIC REVOLUTION

Considerations Upon the East-India Trade was a remarkable analytic performance. Its pages offered a perspective well in advance of anything that had come before. Some of the arguments presented by this anonymous pamphleteer had, to be sure, been articulated by earlier commentators. One of the striking features of his perspective—the case for free trade—had, for example, been cogently presented a decade earlier. Sir Dudley North, writing anonymously in 1691, had then set out the general proposition in a tract entitled *Discourses Upon Trade*. North's statement was primarily a deductive demonstration of the mechanisms tending to generate equilibria in commercial and monetary affairs and of the unhappy consequences which resulted from attempts by governments to regulate these processes.[18] While North's tract deserved commendation for its perceptiveness, his performance fell short of the level reached in 1701. Unlike the author of *Considerations Upon the East-India Trade*, he did not offer a clear statement of the doctrine of comparative advantage, nor did he inquire into the implications of commercial freedom for technical innovation. But then more than a century was to elapse before an analysis of international commerce with a sophistication equivalent to that displayed by the unidentified pamphleteer of 1701 was to be produced.

The arresting insights emerging from *Considerations Upon the East-India Trade* have, in some measure, been appreciated by historians of economic analysis. Schumpeter credited this author with the major analytic accomplishment of the period and with a 'technically superior formulation of the benefits from territorial division of labour.' He further described him as 'a predecessor of Ricardo, though possibly a quite uninfluential one'.[19] In Jacob Viner's judgement, this unknown author had been 'rightly praised' because his work revealed 'almost no trace of the mercantilist or protectionist fallacies'.[20] J. R. McCulloch, writing from the vantage-point of the mid-nineteenth century, observed

[18] Despite long experience as a merchant with the Turkey Company (which included participation in drafting one of its manifestos denouncing the exclusive privileges of the East India Company), North did not address specifically the controversies then raging over the East India commerce in his *Discourses*.

[19] Schumpeter, *History of Economic Analysis*, pp. 373, 374.

[20] Viner, *Studies in the Theory of International Trade*, p. 104.

that this tract had 'set the powerful influence of the division of labour in a very striking point of view, and had illustrated it with the skill and felicity which even Smith has not surpassed, but by which he most probably profited'.[21]

Yet there is an air of puzzlement surrounding the appraisals of this document offered by latter-day commentators. Had such arguments been advanced a century later, their appearance would present no significant interpretative problems. Publication in 1701, however, seems not to mesh with the standard image of the intellectual environment of that phase of mercantilist discussion. *Considerations Upon the East-India Trade* can thus appear to be not of its time, but ahead of it.

Against the background of the dynamics of seventeenth-century debate over the East India trade, the timing of the formulation of this argument is much easier to comprehend. The author's achievement can, in fact, be best understood as a logical outgrowth from the controversies of his age. The initial phases of argumentation about the East India Company had been focused on justifying a freedom to export (i.e. of precious metals). A later phase—which began to take shape in the last quarter of the seventeenth century—shifted the emphasis to a freedom to import (i.e. of final consumer goods from India). Simultaneously, new momentum developed behind the position that the monopoly character of the commerce was unfortunate and that freer entry into the trade should be permitted.

Viewed purely as an intellectual exercise, it was only a short step beyond this to a case which linked the freedom to export and the freedom to import with an argument for complete freedom of entry into the commerce itself. In fragmented form, these notions were already current. The achievement of the author of *Considerations Upon the East-India Trade* was to wrap all of these ingredients into a coherent package.

IV. THE SUPPRESSION OF INTELLECTUAL INNOVATION

Considerations Upon the East-India Trade was very much a product of its day. The more interesting question remains: why should this ingenious analysis have been so ignored by contemporaries?

Part of the answer must lie in the structure of economic dis-

[21] J. R. McCulloch, *Early English Tracts on Commerce*, Preface, p. xiv.

course in that age. The prominent polemicists—and the only ones in a position to sponsor and disseminate tracts—were the organized interest groups: among them, the textile lobbies, the commercial rivals of the old East India Company (e.g. the Turkey Company and later the 'new' East India Company), and the old East India Company itself. The argument of *Considerations Upon the East-India Trade* offered no comfort to any of these parties. Each had able lobbying pens at its disposal. It was to the interest of none of them to draw attention to this publication. Such advanced doctrine undercut the protectionist position of the English textile interests and threatened the privileges of the East India Company. Nor were rival claimants to the East India trade prepared for this message. Their attacks on the iniquities of chartered monopoly were complaints that prevailing arrangements—at least in law—excluded them from sharing monopoly gains. The promotion of unbridled *laissez-faire* was not their objective.

While *Considerations Upon the East-India Trade* contained the insight required for a model of a new age, events themselves were being played out within an older framework. In 1700 English textile interests won a Parliamentary victory in legislation which prohibited the use or wearing in England of 'all wrought silks, Bengalls, and stuffs mixed with silks or herba, of the manufacture of Persia, China, or East India, and all calicoes painted, dyed, printed or stained there'.[22] These goods could still be imported—so long as they were soon thereafter re-exported. Though finished textiles procured through the East India trade were now prohibited in the English market, the importation of materials which required further processing in England—e.g. raw silks and plain calicoes—was still permitted.

Only a year was to pass following the publication of *Considerations Upon the East-India Trade* before members of the 'Old' and the 'New' companies concluded that their rivalry was a destructive form of competition. The attempt of each to outbid the other for official favour—whether through loans to the state or through outright bribery—had become an unacceptable drain on resources. In 1702 effective steps to merge the two organizations were set in motion. Formally, the formation of a United Company

---

[22] William Foster, *The East India House: Its History and Associations* (London, 1924), p. 74. Pressure on Parliament for such action had mounted forcefully following the riots of the silk weavers of Spitalfields in 1696–7.

of merchants trading in the East Indies was deferred until 1708. The new charter was not an instrument designed to encourage freedom of entry into the trade. Instead, the 'United Company' acquired the full set of monopoly privileges for the conduct of English trade to the East which its seventeenth-century predecessor had enjoyed.

Over the long run, Keynes's judgement that 'the power of vested interests is vastly exaggerated compared with the gradual encroachment of ideas' may well be correct. In the short run, his conclusion is less persuasive.

PART II

Problems in the Political Economy of Governance of East India Affairs: 1770–1813

SEVENTEENTH-CENTURY developments associated with the East India trade had stimulated change in England's economic structure and in the analytic categories available to comprehend it. By contrast, the first half of the eighteenth century was largely a period of consolidation and regrouping.

With the Godolphin award of a new charter to the 'United Company of Merchants Trading to the East Indies' in 1708, much of the internecine warfare between rival English claimants to the prizes of the East was brought to a close. One of the factors which had raised the political temperature in the late 1600s thus vanished from the scene. But the price of peace was heavy. Monopoly privileges in the English trade to the East had been conferred on the United Company on condition that the sum of £3,200,000 would be lent to the state. This requirement committed all of the equity capital of the newly constituted East India Company to the financing of government; none remained to support commercial operations. Faced with this extraordinary situation, the Company was obliged to rely on the London capital market to finance regular business. Its own debt issues (typically at short-to intermediate term) provided the working capital for commerce. East India bonds—subject to a statutory ceiling of £5 million until raised to £6 million by legislation in 1744—soon established themselves as prime gilt-edged paper in the growing London money market.[1]

Despite the strains imposed by its function as a financial intermediary and underwriter of government debt, the commercial operations of the East India Company continued to expand. The dramatic rate of growth of the late seventeenth century was not, however, sustained. Nevertheless, trade with the East—as measured both by the value of exports from England and by the

---

[1] See Lucy S. Sutherland, *The East India Company in Eighteenth Century Politics* (Oxford, 1952), p. 32.

value of Asian goods disposed of at the Company's sales—more than doubled in the first half-century of the life of the 'United' Company. Meanwhile, one of the significant structural characteristics of the commerce persisted: English exports to the East were still dominated by the shipment of silver. This category of exports typically accounted for about three-quarters of total export values.[2]

Though the composition of the East India Company's exports to the East remained in a familiar mould, significant changes began to emerge in the commodity pattern of imports from Asia. Some adjustment in the trading pattern was necessitated by the legislation which had banned the sale to English consumers of finished textile products made in the East. The Company responded to this challenge by pressing these 'prohibited goods' in Continental markets and by increasing its shipments of plain white calicoes to England where they were welcomed by the printers and dyers of fabrics. These expedients sustained the volume of traffic in calicoes with little change during the first half of the eighteenth century. The company was obliged to look elsewhere, however, for a source of dynamic momentum in the commerce. The commodity which was to supply this boost was tea. Whereas tea procurement had amounted to less than 200,000 pounds per annum in the years 1711–17, the volume of the Company's dealings rose to an annual rate approaching 3 million pounds in the years 1748–57.[3] By 1760 tea had well surpassed

[2] The general pattern of the Company's trade with India in this period has been reported as follows:

Decenniel Period	Imports into India from England:			Sale Proceeds in England of East India Goods
	Merchandise	Bullion	Total	
1708/09– 1717/18	1177	3816	4993	9786
1718/19– 1727/28	1120	5663	6783	14 669
1728/29– 1737/38	1390	5135	6525	16 026
1738/39– 1747/48	1896	5228	7124	18 063
1748/49– 1757/58	2767	7669	10436	21 453

Source: Milburn, Oriental Commerce, vol. 1 (as quoted by I. Darga Parshad, Some Aspects of Indian Foreign Trade, 1757–1893 (London, 1932), p. 208).

[3] Calculated from Bal Krishna, Commercial Relations between India and England, 1601–1757, p. 195.

calicoes as the most important item in the Company's list of trade goods.[4]

With the rising prominence of tea, the East India Company had at last found a commodity with a relatively high price and income elasticity of demand which was also complementary to (rather than competitive with) England's domestic production pattern. While the growing weight of tea in the total trade solved one set of long-standing problems, it also created new ones. In this period, the source of tea was China, rather than India. The geographical focus of the Company's trade thus tended to shift. This turn in commercial affairs further complicated the intricate relationships between Company and state. Tea was a highly tax-eligible commodity and, as the fiscal requirements of government increased, the rates of duty assigned to it were revised sharply upward. The Company's enthusiasm for expanding the market for tea and the state's insatiable demands for revenue were at odds with one another. The state's first attempt to widen space for the Company's commerce in this commodity produced an unexpected result. Legislation of 1773, which waived the duty on tea for re-export, provoked a group of Americans (who were unwilling to accept evaporation of the profits from tea smuggling) to dump the Company's shipments into Boston harbour. This action might be described as a demand for 'no tax reduction on smuggled items without representation'. Later, after political events had effectively closed the American market, the Company was afforded relief at home. The 'Commutation Act' of 1784 (so designated because a supplementary window tax was levied to offset the revenue lost from a major reduction in tea duties) gave fresh impetus to this branch of the Company's trade.[5]

Though adjustments in the commodity pattern of trade minimized conflicts with producer interests in England, not all of the Company's critics were silenced. Protests about the Company's exclusive character and about its corrupting influence on English life were nearly as frequent after 1708 as they had been before. But while these challenges persisted, the East India Company had perfected techniques for parrying them. With the financial inter-

---

[4] Measured at 'official values', tea imports in 1760 came to £291,000 and calicoes to £184,000. (Ibid., p. 195.)

[5] Under the terms of the Commutation Act of 1784, the *ad valorem* duty on tea was reduced from 112 per cent to 25 per cent.

dependence between Company and state now closer than ever, the state became a more reliable ally. In addition, valuable alliances were forged with certain private groups in England. Shipbuilders and seamen—whose livelihood was closely tied to the fortunes of the East India trade—could readily be persuaded to champion the Company's cause.[6] One component of the textile industry (that which prospered by printing and dyeing imported textiles) could be mobilized to oppose the restrictionist petitions of the weavers. Similarly, the silver merchants of England— whose skills were heavily committed to procuring and preparing precious metals for shipment to the East—were alert to their stake in the Company's fortunes.

But perhaps the most effective strategy for protecting monopoly privilege in this period was a discriminating use of patronage. The directors of the East India Company had at their disposal a sizeable number of attractive posts. The stipends attached to them were modest, but the appointments themselves afforded considerable scope for the accumulation of private fortunes.[7] It was regarded as a legitimate part of the system for men employed as factors and 'writers' in the Company's service to devote part of their time to commercial ventures of their own. The 'indulged trade' which had developed in the seventeenth century had now been extended. While the Company continued to reserve cargo space for goods shipped on the private account of its directors and employees, a 'private trade' within India was also tolerated, if not encouraged.[8] Access to these plums was within the jurisdiction of the chairman and directors of the Company and they were not averse to distributing them with an eye to the Company's political advantage. A few of the appointments might

[6] At times, however, the Directors of the Company regretted the closeness of these ties. Their contractual relationships with shipbuilders and ship-captains came to be regarded as commitments to 'permanent bottoms' and 'perpetual commands'—i.e. that the Company was obliged to ensure continuity in employment, without regard to its current requirements for shipping. See Sutherland, op. cit., p. 38.

[7] It was reported that a junior appointment as a 'writer' (i.e. as a clerk) had a market value of £1,500 to £2,000. See J. Steven Watson, *The Reign of George III, 1760–1815* (Oxford, 1960), p. 157.

[8] With expansion in the territorial jurisdiction of the East India Company in the later eighteenth century, these opportunities were greatly increased. Cornwallis, newly arrived as Governor-General in 1787, could then report the case of a collector with a salary of 1,000 rupees per month (about £100) whose private trading activities brought his annual income to at least £40,000. See J. C. Sinha, *Economic Annals of Bengal* (London, 1927), p. 201.

have been sold to line the pockets of directors; the more usual practice—and the more significant one—was the allocation of patronage to strengthen the Company's position in influential quarters.

Though the Company's affairs at home tended to stabilize in the first half of the eighteenth century, this was not the case abroad. Rivalry with the French (who had now displaced the Dutch as the major competitors of the English East India Company) intensified. At the same time, the waning authority of the Mogul Empire within India generated fresh uncertainties about the security of outposts in the East. Increasingly, both Englishmen and Frenchmen sought to strengthen their respective positions by striking deals with local rulers. Violent confrontation was latent in such situations and its prospects were maximized by the freebooting behaviour of Europeans (whether English or French) on the spot. Few effective restraints on their activities could be exercised from either London or Paris. The headquarters in the home countries could expect, for example, to learn the consequences of decisions of its officers in India long after the crucial event had occurred. Few practical means were available to those at the top to control the course of events from which they were removed by half the circumference of the globe.

Decisive change in the relationship between England and India and in the character of the East India Company followed Clive's military initiative at Plassey in 1757. The rules of the game from that point onward were radically transformed. The escalation of armed intervention in India might, at first, have been understood as an application of the doctrine of Sir Josiah Child who had insisted in the 1680s that the Company's trade would be secure only when it had become a territorial power in the East. The acquisition of territorial power, however, introduced a new range of problems. When Clive completed the conquest of Bengal by claiming the *diwani* (or taxing authority) in 1765, the East India Company was as much a sovereign as a trader.

How well could received categories of interpretation be adapted to this unprecedented situation? It was, of course, tempting to regard the new state of affairs as simply another phase in the diversification of the Company's business ventures. In this view of matters, no sharp break from the pattern of the past had occurred: tax-gathering was merely an extension of the Company's range of service activities. But there was also ample justification for asking a different set of questions about the state of affairs Clive had created. Were trade and governance genuinely compatible? If it was not self-evident (and to many it was far from being so) that a merger of these functions was desirable, what arrangements would be more satisfactory? These questions became the central ones for the leading economic thinkers of Britain (for the Scots had now joined the mainstream of these controversies) who grappled with the perplexities of the East India connection in the late eighteenth and early nineteenth centuries.

CHAPTER 4

Trade, Governance, and the Monetary System: Sir James Steuart and the Materials for a New Official Model

T H E initial reaction of most Englishmen to the events of the 1760s in Bengal was that they presented new opportunities, not new problems. Clive's command over the territorial revenues appeared to mean that an asset of enormous value had been added to the Company's estate. Income from this source was confidently expected to overshadow by far the profits won in conventional commerce. Prosperity seemed to be assured.

To the Directors of the East India Company, the windfall in Bengal had a further significance. Commercial operations could now be reorganized. The trade pattern of the past—which had depended on the export of silver from England to purchase the 'investment' in the goods of the East—could largely be scrapped. With the tax revenues of Bengal at the Company's disposal, liquid funds for the purchase of Asian goods were available locally. The 'drain' of precious metals to India could thus be restrained. Not only would some of the noisier critics be silenced; the Company would also be spared the expense involved in purchases of bullion. Accordingly, further shipments of silver to India were suspended, though silver exports to finance the China wing of the commerce continued.

In the euphoria of the 1760s, prices of the Company's shares were bid to record levels. Dividends were increased to 10 per cent in 1767 and raised again—to $12\frac{1}{2}$ per cent—in 1769. But members of the East India Company were not the only ones to entertain buoyant expectations. Pitt saw no reason why the wealth of Bengal should be privately appropriated. In 1767 the state claimed £400,000 per year as its share. When this arrangement was reviewed in 1769, the annual payment of £400,000 was renewed for a further four years.[1]

---

[1] Some commentators took a more ambitious view of the possibilities. If the British government assumed responsibility for the territorial domain in the East, it was ex-

But by 1772 it was clear that something had gone wrong. The Company was unable to honour its commitments, either at home or abroad. Deficits were reported on the territorial account in Bengal. To purchase the 'investment', borrowing in India had been required. Nor was the Company in a healthy position in England. Though it had undertaken to redeem in London the bills of exchange issued in the East, it was unable to do so. The Company faced a liquidity crisis on all fronts. In England it appealed for relief from the scheduled payments to the State and petitioned for financial assistance from the government; both requests were acted on favourably and the state advanced £1,400,000. Within a remarkably short span of time, the golden goose had taken on the appearance of a 'lame duck' (to borrow a latter-day idiom to describe the condition of major private enterprises which have turned to the state for financial support).

As expectations were shattered by events, the complexity of the problems created by the post-1757 dispensation in Bengal became more visible. Initially, the Company's behaviour as a sovereign had been guided by categories supplied by its commercial tradition. Within that framework, it was natural to appropriate the territorial revenues as substitutes for imported silver. Not only did this tactic appear to make good business sense; it had political recommendations at home as well. By 1770, however, this operation no longer seemed as simple as it had earlier been thought to be. Officials resident in Bengal were reporting with alarm that taxes could not be collected because of the shortage of coin. The strategy of tax collection as a reinforcement to commerce was in jeopardy. If local revenues failed to reach the targeted levels, the new scheme for the procurement of the investment could not be implemented, nor could the expected commercial profits be realized. Monetary derangement in Bengal threatened the viability of the entire system.

At this point, the Directors of the Company sensed the need for expert guidance on the monetary difficulties which confronted their territorial enterprise. The man to whom they turned was Sir James Steuart (1712–80), a political economist whose stature

---

pected that the national exchequer would soon enjoy an increment in its net receipts of some £2 million per year. These sums could be allocated to the retirement of the national debt. See, for example, *An Attempt to Pay off the National Debt by Abolishing the East-India Company of Merchants* (London, 1767).

as a major thinker on monetary questions had been established with the publication of his *Inquiry into the Principles of Political Economy* in 1759. Steuart was assigned the task of investigating the monetary system of Bengal and encouraged to recommend reforms to improve its operations. In fact, he construed his mandate more broadly. Not surprisingly, his approach reflected the intellectual position he had worked out when preparing his major treatise. In that work, he had argued that money was of little theoretical or practical interest for its own sake. The issue which demanded attention was the relationship of money to economic expansion. Mismanagement of the monetary system could stifle healthy development and skilful monetary organization could spur economic growth by stimulating improvements in productivity. Ultimately, however, a country's economic well-being depended, not on its stock of precious metals, but on the energies and talents of its population.

I. THE DIAGNOSIS OF THE PROBLEMS IN BENGAL

Steuart reported his findings on Bengal's monetary problems to the East India Company in 1772. Though he did not visit the East in connection with this assignment (nor had he had any prior direct contact with India), he had no doubts about the seriousness of the problem created by the Company's decision to procure the 'investment' from the territorial revenues. He was amply satisfied that Bengal's situation was one of genuine distress. 'The complaints of a scarcity of coin in Bengal', he wrote, 'once so famous for its wealth, are so general that the fact can hardly be called in question.'[2]

What accounted for this reversal from past form? In Steuart's judgement, the basic difficulty could be traced to the transformation in the Company's role when it mixed governance with trade. Formerly, exporters in India had been compensated in silver supplied from England. The new arrangement meant, however, that 'the industry of the workman' who supplied export goods 'was paid for with the money of his own country'.[3] But this was not the only effect of the decision to finance the Company's investment through the Bengal tax system. The Company's government now had a prior claim on the exportable commodities

---

[2] Sir James Steuart, *The Principles of Money Applied to the Present State of the Coin of Bengal* (London, 1772), p. 56. [3] Ibid., p. 57.

of the territory. The consequence, as Steuart saw it, 'was to diminish greatly, if not quite to absorb that fund of domestic industry, from the exportation of which the country drew every year new treasures from foreign nations'.[4]

Bengal had thus been doubly disadvantaged. In the first instance, acquisition of the *diwani* had led to the cessation of fresh inflows of silver from England. In addition, the country's capacity to replenish its coinage by running export surpluses in its trade with third parties had been compromised. The Company's status as a pre-emptive buyer had restricted Bengal's ability to earn silver elsewhere. It was thus not surprising that the country should suffer from a shortage of coin.

Though this distressing outcome was the result of the East India Company's use of sovereign powers, its intervention had produced one change with happier consequences for the monetary system. From the information at his disposal, Steuart concluded that much of Bengal's silver stock had formerly been transferred as tribute to the Mogul's court at Delhi.[5] The government supplied by the East India Company had at least 'retrenched' much (though not all) of this drain. On balance, Bengal's monetary circumstances had still been weakened by the merger of commerce with sovereignty. The problem was not only real: it was urgently in need of attention.

II. THE CHALLENGE TO COMPANY GOVERNMENT

In light of his diagnosis of the monetary difficulties of Bengal, Steuart might have recommended that the links between commerce and sovereignty should be severed and the earlier pattern of trade between England and India restored. He did not do so: presumably his terms of reference precluded such advice. If the flow of silver from England was not to be resumed, it was incumbent on the Company to use its new powers imaginatively. Sovereignty and commerce could be successfully married, but

[4] Sir James Steuart, *The Principles of Money Applied to the Present State of the Coin of Bengal* (London, 1772), p. 57.

[5] In support of this point, Steuart cited a letter of a Mr. Mandeville, dated 27 Nov. 1750, in which it was observed: 'As the King's revenues, and other money, are annually sent to the Mogul's court at Delhi . . . this sweeps away almost all the silver, coined or uncoined, which comes into Bengal; it goes to Delhi, from whence it never returns to Bengal . . . there is hardly currency enough left in Bengal to carry on any trade, or even to go to market for provisions and necessaries of life, 'till the next shipping arrives to bring a fresh supply of silver' (as quoted ibid., pp. 62–3).

only when those in control were prepared to implement com-
pensatory strategies for Bengal. As Steuart defined the task: 'we
must endeavour to indemnify it for the gratuitous exportation of
the many manufactures, which we formerly bought with this
silver sent thither.'[6]

Steuart entertained no illusions that the steps required would
win instant applause. Some of them, he recognized, were likely to
run counter to the perceived interests of the East India Company
—and even of Great Britain. Should that be the case, he urged
that the economic health of Bengal should be the dominant consideration. On this point, Steuart spoke unambiguously: '. . . it is
in vain to think of a remedy without sacrificing the interest of
Great-Britain, and of the Company itself to that of Bengal. All
therefore that can be done in this particular, is to carry on the
trade to the best advantage of the Company and for this nation,
consistently with the permanency of it. Not to kill the hen which
lays the golden eggs, but to feed her and preserve her.'[7]

How was the economy of Bengal best to be nurtured? Given
Steuart's cast of mind, the natural path toward economic growth
for any country involved the achievement of a favourable
balance of trade. This course, after all, was the one on which
England had embarked at an earlier moment in its history. In the
case of Bengal, however, an important qualification was necessary. As a 'general maxim', Steuart accepted that 'exportations
enrich a country, and that importations impoverish it'. But he
added: 'the exportations made from Bengal by the East-India
Company do not enrich it, any more than the importations of the
spoils of the world impoverished ancient Rome.'[8] This was clearly
a special case. The exports organized by the Company in its dual
role as a trader and sovereign fell outside the normal pattern of
commercial transactions. If one accepted the political structure
as given, it was all the more urgent to ensure that the rest of
Bengal's international transactions were to her advantage.[9]

The task of organizing Bengal's 'normal' commerce to promote

---

[6] Ibid., p. 64.   [7] Ibid.   [8] Ibid., p. 81.

[9] As Steuart summarized his position: '. . . when we consider Bengal to be a country
belonging to the Company, exposed to many drains in consequence of this property, and
to one among the rest, not inconsiderable, viz. the price paid for the raw materials of all
the goods exported by the Company without any profit *to Bengal*; it will appear expedient to encourage as much as possible the sale of all that is over the investments of the
Company, in such a way as to increase the demand of strangers . . .' (Ibid., pp. 82–3.)

economic expansion would require the East India Company to
impose severe disciplines on its own activities. In the days when
the Company had existed solely as a society of merchants, 'it was
their interest, and that of the mother country, to export thither
every article of British luxury, as well as manufactures.' That
situation no longer obtained. A different strategy was called for
'now that this very country is in a manner our own'. Imported
luxuries—which claimed scarce supplies of silver—should be discouraged. The Company should instead 'fall upon every expedient,
to procure for them articles of raw productions from every part
of the world'.[10] The foreign trade which mattered most to the improvement of the condition of Bengal consisted of 'raw materials
for their manufactures, and in that part of such manufactures as
is sold for money brought into the country'.[11] Trade in intermediate goods, Steuart insisted, should be 'left entirely in the
hands of the natives, and every protection and encouragement
should be given to those who are concerned in it'.[12]

This counsel had much in common with that which Mun had
offered to England roughly a century and a half earlier. A
country in search of growth stimuli through foreign trade should
avoid the importation of luxuries and should concentrate its import bill on intermediate goods, particularly on those which could
be processed for export. In a new incarnation, these recommendations were being made available to a part of India ruled by the
East India Company.

Uplift for Bengal called for yet another change in the Company's
behaviour. In its recent practice, the Company had appropriated
part of the silver collected through the revenue system to finance
tea purchases in China. Steuart held this drain to be totally in-
defensible: the sooner it stopped, the better. Such a burden was
not one which Bengal could legitimately be asked to bear. Silver
required for the China wing of the trade should instead be found
entirely in Europe. Steuart was alert to the importance of tea to
the Company's over-all operations and he urged that the handicaps imposed on its re-export by British customs regulations be
removed.[13] The lively sale of tea in third markets would, he argued,

[10] Sir James Stueart, *The Principles of Money Applied to the Present State of the
Coin of Bengal*, (London, 1772,) p. 64.   [11] Ibid., p. 82.   [12] Ibid.
[13] In the year following the publication of Steuart's report, the British government
waived duties on tea which was re-exported.

augment the Company's capacity to acquire silver to finance direct dealing with China.

Steuart was sharp in his criticism of another set of practices which contributed to leakages from Bengal's limited stocks of silver: the behaviour of servants of the Company when repatriating the proceeds from 'moonlighting' in private trade in India. These activities were reprehensible on two counts. In the first instance, the participation of officials (though acting in unofficial capacities) in the internal trade was an unfair form of competition with local traders. In addition, the transfer of these gains to England had often taken an unfortunate course. Frequently, silver had been lent to non-British companies trading in the East on the understanding that repayment would later be made in Europe. Steuart called for restraints on the private trade of the Company's employees. He further recommended that alternative channels be provided for the transfer of the legitimate earnings of Company servants to England. By developing a local capital market which offered bills of exchange on London, more of Bengal's silver could be retained for local use. Such arrangements would have the further advantage of cutting off sources of finance to the Company's commercial rivals.[14]

Steuart had charted an ambitious course for the Company's government. He did not pretend that the Company's commercial interests and its responsibilities as a sovereign were automatically compatible. On the contrary, they might frequently be in conflict with one another. The system, however, could be workable if the Company raised its sights. In the long view, the Company's success as a business was closely linked with the prosperity of its territorial dependency. But the prospects of prosperity in Bengal would be considerably darkened unless Englishmen could be persuaded to forgo maximization of their short-run gains.

[14] Steuart took note of two other factors which made claims on Bengal's supplies of silver: outlays in support of military operations in neighbouring territories and transfers to the court of the Mogul in Delhi (which, though sharply reduced under Company government, had not ceased altogether). On these matters, he recognized that the competence of economists to comment was restricted. He suggested, however, that part of the loss of silver through transfers to the Great Mogul might be reclaimed by 'introducing the trade of European luxuries into his court'. (Ibid., p. 67.) Whereas the importation of luxury commodities was to be discouraged in Bengal, it was readily admissible in areas which absorbed its coin.

III. PROPOSALS FOR MONETARY REFORM IN BENGAL

Steuart's prescriptions for conserving Bengal's supplies of silver or for enlarging them through export promotion were but the first steps in the larger strategy. He also sought to stimulate the economy through monetary innovation. Two lines of approach, in his judgement, were appropriate in the circumstances: one involved measures to increase the velocity of circulation of the existing money supply; the other called for enlargement of the money supply itself.

Steuart did not use the term 'velocity' in his discussion of Bengal's monetary difficulties, though he was well aware of its significance. 'By accelerating the circulation of the coin you have', he wrote, 'you *virtually* increase the quantity of it; that is to say, a less quantity will be necessary for performing the same purpose.'[15] The money supply could be used much more efficiently, he argued, if institutional changes—which, in any case, were desirable on their merits—could be accomplished. Much could be gained, for example, by instituting a uniform coinage system to displace the multiplicity of silver rupees which presently passed in circulation. Standardization in the coinage would have a further significant effect. Much of the livelihood of the shroffs (the traditional money changers and money lenders) would be destroyed. The shroffs, in Steuart's view, were parasites whose activities in weighing, measuring, and assaying slowed the velocity of circulation. The results would be even healthier if accompanied by the elimination of intermediaries from the collection of land revenues. This could be done if the Company established a 'sort of quit rent which may be payable by the whole district to some man of consequence . . . without giving him any jurisdiction which may enable him to oppress the people, or interrupt the settled plan for levying the revenue.' Such a reform would mean that 'the rents of the lands will pass directly from the occupier into the hands of the Company; the circulation of money will be quicker . . .' In addition, the wealth of the country would no longer be 'swallowed up' by the shroffs.[16]

But Steuart had even more radical departures in mind. Pressure on the monetary circulation, he noted, could be relaxed by allowing some taxes to be paid in kind, rather than in cash.

[15] Sir James Steuart, *The Principles of Money Applied to the Present State of the Coin of Bengal* (London, 1772), p. 71.   [16] Ibid., p. 73.

Thus: 'In the proximity of great cities, and in very populous districts, granaries might be established, and part of the rents might be received in grain for the supply of markets, at a price proportionate to the plenty of the year.'[17] Manufactured goods should also be acceptable to discharge tax obligations so long as government officials maintained quality controls to ascertain 'their being made without defect'.[18]

Even more arrestingly, Steuart broke with conventional thinking in his proposals for enlargement in the money supply. Part of Bengal's requirements for a circulating medium should be satisfied with a paper currency. Such additions to the money supply could be created by a note-issuing bank, rather than by the Company itself. This innovation would also reinforce the broader strategy of economic uplift. The bank could issue bills to absorb funds which Company employees might otherwise transfer abroad in silver. It could be the vehicle for rationalizing and standardizing the coinage—and its doors should be open to the participation of traditional money changers. Steuart expected that the shroffs would 'naturally become proprietors' in the banking organization and would thus 'be employed in a trade something like what they now carry on; but it would be so fenced in by proper regulations, that it will have every advantage and none of the inconveniences of the present practice'.[19] The notes of the bank might also be thought of—at least in part—as a commodity-reserve currency should the bank become the agent for collecting taxes in kind.

But there were other tasks which a note-issuing bank might usefully be assigned. It could, for example, facilitate prompt collection of land revenues by denying credit to districts which were in arrears. Its central mission, however, should be defined as the stimulation of economic expansion. As Steuart stated his objective: 'I have endeavoured to find out a method for conducting those resources which proceed from herself (namely, the money that she at present possesses) into a channel which may set new engines to work in order to augment circulation and encourage her manufactures; instead of serving as a bare equivalent for those at present produced.'[20] What had been commissioned as a limited investigation of an immediate practical problem thus emerged as a much broader vision of the potential for economic growth in Bengal.

[17] Ibid., p. 74.   [18] Ibid., p. 73.   [19] Ibid., p. 79.   [20] Ibid., p. 80.

IV. THE SIGNIFICANCE OF STEUART'S MESSAGE

Steuart's report had offered an agenda for economic policy in Bengal—but it had also done more. By assigning a set of policy functions, it had provided a rationale for an alien government. Some of the tasks of Company government had to be performed as solutions to problems it had itself created. But the mission of a British authority in India went well beyond that. Steuart called also for structural change in the institutions of the local economy to improve conditions for the Indian population. These reforms— which he regarded as desirable on their merits—could most readily be accomplished under the guidance of outsiders.

Company government had a challenge set before it. But neither its Directors nor its officials in Bengal (who received Steuart's recommendations in 1774) rose fully to it. A few of his proposals did find their way into practice, though not always in the form Steuart would have preferred. Preliminary moves toward standardization in the coinage were made by the government of Bengal with the decisions of 1775 to confine the coinage to a single mint. By 1780, the possibilities of a paper currency had captured the attention of Warren Hastings, the Governor-General. It was not until 1787, however, that a note-issuing bank (the General Bank of India) began to function. Though its notes were declared acceptable in payment of obligations to the government, this institution did not survive beyond 1791.[21]

Steuart's imaginative package of measures to link monetary innovation with uplift of the local economy received even less attention. Some of his suggestions, to be sure, were acted upon, though on a piecemeal basis. Cornwallis's reform of the land revenue system in 1793, for example, adopted one of Steuart's goals: minimization in the number of intermediaries in the collection chain. The Company's government did not intervene vigorously, however, to stimulate expansion in production and in exports. Following the declaration of a government monopoly in the opium trade in 1773, a substitute for Bengal's silver in financing the tea 'investment' in China began to take shape. It is not clear, however, that Steuart would have assigned priority to this form of export promotion.[22]

[21] See J. C. Sinha, *Economic Annals of Bengal* (London, 1927), esp. pp. 154, 238–9.
[22] The Company did encourage the production of indigo for export. This was done through contracts with Europeans. Indigo—which had been of some importance in the

Nor did Steuart's larger message leave much imprint on opinion in England. One strand of thought there quickly dismissed his findings on the ground that he had proceeded from a mistaken premiss. Steuart's report had accepted the constraints inherent in Company government. In the 1770s and 1780s—particularly after Adam Smith's denunciations of the East India Company both as a commercial monopoly and as a sovereign authority—the future of the entire Bengal system was very much in question. The relevance of Steuart's argument was thus highly suspect.

But doubts about the stability of the East India Company's position were not in themselves sufficient to explain the failure of Steuart's general strategy to receive a more sympathetic hearing. The new wave of thinking in political economy had brought to ascendency the quantity theory of money. With the aid of this doctrine, it could be argued that changes in the money supply would necessarily affect price levels and that price adjustments, in turn, regulated the flow of precious metals between countries. According to this line of reasoning, a country suffering losses in its supply of precious metals—as Bengal allegedly was—would soon experience reductions in its price level. This situation would prompt expansion in its exports and would encourage the substitution of home production for imports. Its international balances would thus be corrected and its stock of precious metals would find its natural level. This doctrine further implied that artificial attempts to broaden the monetary base—such as the issue of paper currency—would be self-defeating. Consequent price adjustments at home would only aggravate the drain of precious metals.

This mode of argument dismissed the concerns expressed by Bengal administrators in the 1760s and 1770s about a shortage of coin as ill-founded and ill-informed. On such grounds, James Mill—writing in 1817—rebuked those who had insisted that Bengal had then experienced a shortage of silver. In his view, 'the absurdity of the theory which they invented to account for

---

seventeenth-century trade pattern—had later lapsed when a superior product could be obtained in the West Indies and in the American colonies. By 1779, two events created a new market opportunity in England for Bengal indigo: much of the West Indian production had been abandoned in favour of the more profitable planting of sugar and coffee; and the American Revolution had cut off the alternate source of supply.

the want of money . . . is shown by this fact; that the price of commodities all the while, instead of falling had immensely risen.'[23] This judgement amounted to saying that the problem which Steuart had been invited to analyse had never, in fact, existed.

Steuart had anticipated such criticisms. As early as 1759, he had disputed the quantity theory of money as it had been formulated by David Hume. In particular, he had challenged its applicability to predominantly agrarian economies. The quantity of money, he maintained, could affect prices only to the extent that transactions were conducted in money. In a poor country, monetized transactions accounted for only a part of the exchange of goods and services, and often for an even smaller fraction of total output. Attempts to generalize about the impact of a change in the quantity of money on the general level of prices were thus subject to grave misinterpretations. He handled this point in his *Principles of Political Economy* as follows: 'In all countries where there is little industry; where the inhabitants are mostly fed directly from the earth, without any alienation of her fruits taking place; where agriculture is exercised purely as a method of subsisting; . . . the demand for grain in the public markets must be very small, consequently, prices will be very low, whether there be little or whether there be much money in the country. The reason is plain. The demand is proportioned here, not to the number of those who consume, but of those who buy: now those who consume are all the inhabitants, but those who buy, are the few industrious only who are free, and who gain an independent livelihood by their own labour and ingenuity.'[24]

Steuart was even prepared to argue that quite perverse effects —if perversity were judged against the expectations of a quantity theorist—might follow a reduction in the quantity of money. Whereas an orthodox classical monetarist would expect prices to fall following such an event, Steuart saw no reason to rule out the possibility of a rise in the prices of goods exchanged against money. This result could occur if sellers of goods responded to a contraction in the circulating medium by shrinking their offerings to the monetized market in order to conduct barter transactions.

In the terminology of mid-twentieth-century controversies,

23 James Mill, *History of British India* (London, 1817), vol. 2, p. 262.
24 *The Works of Sir James Steuart* (London, 1805), vol. 2, p. 91.

Steuart might be described as a 'structuralist' in his basic approach. He raised questions held to be irrelevant or inadmissible in the 'monetarist' orthodoxy. Within his analytic scheme, it could plausibly be argued that an expanding money supply—fed by a paper currency—could stimulate production and hasten the transition from a predominantly subsistence to a cash economy. Nor were fears justified that such action would necessarily jeopardize a country's position in international transactions. The links between changes in the money supply and the behaviour of the general price level were far from close. In any event, Steuart maintained that the very notion of a general price level had little practical meaning. What mattered in international transactions was particular prices, not general ones. The former were determined in specific markets and moved with the state of 'demand and of competition'. The quantity of money was a remote and unpredictable influence on the prices of specific goods entering foreign trade.

Steuart's report on Bengal had been formulated for the purpose of dealing with a novel and unorthodox reality. Contained within it were the materials for an official model of a new age. Steuart invited the leadership of the East India Company to transcend a narrowly commercial approach to its affairs in the East. Sovereignty and commerce could be mixed successfully, but only when the Company in its governing capacity gave paramount attention to economic improvement for its subjects. Any other course would prove to be bad business. In the longer run, the Indian domain would be an attractive site for trade to the extent that growth in the local economy was nurtured. The East India Company had before it an opportunity to chart new paths in corporate responsibility.

This vision of a fresh strategy failed to capture the official imagination. Meanwhile, intellectual developments outside the orbit of the East India Company were producing doctrines hostile to much of Steuart's position. As a new set of ideas acquired the status of an orthodoxy, its categories dominated the agenda of debate.

CHAPTER 5

India in the Classical Analytic Perspective: Adam Smith's Formulation of the Problem

In Bengal in the 1760s, events had moved ahead of ideas. The East India Company faced a novel situation but lacked the categories adequate to its interpretation. Steuart's report of 1772 had attempted to fill the vacuum. His analysis, however, had gone largely unheeded.

By the mid-1770s, critics of the Company were much better prepared. A new mode of analysis—in the form of what was to become classical political economy—had then begun to take clear shape. Its conceptual scheme had not been formulated with a particular eye to East India affairs. Yet it provided an interpretative framework within which these issues might be fitted and, at one remove, it was to have a significant impact on perceptions of the realities of India and on the strategies which were to alter them.

I. CENTRAL PROPERTIES OF THE CLASSICAL ANALYTIC PERSPECTIVE

The organizing theme of classical political economy was the analysis of the causes of economic growth. How, it was asked, could one account for the differential rates of economic expansion —and, for that matter, for conditions of economic stagnation or even of decline—which appeared to prevail in various parts of the world? Not unnaturally, British contributors to this stream of thought were, in the first instance, interested in improving the understanding of economic life in their home country. But they also transcended, at least in part, the parochialism which had dominated the bulk of seventeenth-century economic discourse. Classical analysis was global in its aspirations. It was no accident that Adam Smith regarded his task as the study of the wealth of *nations*, rather than an investigation of the wealth of *the* nation.

Within the classical perspective, a large part of the answer to this primary question was identified as depending on the ability and the will of differing societies to generate surpluses (or 'net revenues') and to use them to enlarge productive capacity. In this view of matters, some segments of society—particularly wage earners—could not reasonably be expected to save. All of their income would be required to sustain a minimum level of consumption. The circumstances of large landowners—at least in England—were quite different. Their income was more than adequate, but it was far from clear that they were seriously disposed to save. In the classical imagery, those who lived on agricultural rents were more likely to maintain luxurious domestic establishments than to channel resources into productive capital formation. The main responsibility for society's savings was thus expected to fall on a small but growing group: the ambitious capitalists and entrepreneurs. In the seventeenth century, membership of this class had been dominated by the merchants and traders by sea. By the late eighteenth century, the industrialists at home provided its main strength.

This view of the behaviour of various economic groups within society supported the conclusion that the rate of economic growth was closely related to the distribution of the national income among the shares of wages, rents, and profits. In particular, much depended on the share received by members of the capitalist class. Only the recipients of profits could be relied upon to forgo opportunities for consumption and to advance funds to enlarge the community's productive capacity.

But the goal of economic growth was not to be reached solely through the creation of additional productive resources. It was also important to ensure that the productive potential available at any moment in time was fully and effectively used. Within the classical framework, the best guarantee of this outcome was to be found in a regime of free and open competition. Producers would then be obliged to be efficient. In such an environment, their receptivity to technical innovation would also be enhanced.

These healthy stimuli to the 'progress of improvement' (as Adam Smith phrased it) would be denied to a country which tolerated artificial impediments to the free flow of market forces. Moreover, governmental shelters to private interest groups—of which chartered monopolies presented a prime example—necessarily promoted unjust privileges. Free markets were thus desirable as social levellers as well as for their contribution to economic progress and efficiency. The outlines of this *laissez-faire* doctrine had been provided by the author of *Considerations Upon the East-India Trade*. The fate of such ideas in 1701 had been that of the flower in Gray's country churchyard—'born to blush unseen'. By the last quarter of the eighteenth century, the message reached a more attentive audience.

An important non-economic assumption underlay the approach of the early classical economists to their analytic tasks. Their argument asserted that the freedom of each man to pursue his self-interest was not only consistent with the welfare of the community as a whole, but in fact promoted it. Confidence in this conclusion rested on a faith that two conditions were satisfied: that market participation was not concentrated, but broadly diffused (i.e. that conditions of free competition genuinely prevailed); and that the rival interests to be adjudicated in a market context could be clearly specified. The scheme was not well suited to circumstances in which the central interest of the main social actors was ambiguous.

Adam Smith's *Wealth of Nations*, published in 1776, must be reckoned as one of the most influential works in the new genre of political economy. Smith (1723–90) intended his treatise to be a general study of the factors which might accelerate (or, alternatively, arrest) the rate of economic growth. Though comment either on the East India Company's activities or on conditions in India was not his primary purpose, these matters nevertheless received considerable attention. An analyst who proclaimed the virtues of a regime of competition could not easily ignore the most prominent exhibit of monopoly power visible in his day. Nor could a theorist ambitious to formulate laws of economic progress with universal applicability omit inspection of that part of Asia about which the European world was best informed.

Though Smith had no direct personal contact with East India, he sought enlightenment on its affairs from the best sources available. At one point in his career, however, he narrowly missed an appointment with the East India Company. In 1772 the Company had under consideration the formation of a 'Commission of Supervision' to inquire into the details of administration in Bengal. The assignment of this group was to be quite distinct from the one given to Sir James Steuart; it would be charged to investigate allegations of irregular conduct by Company officials in Bengal and empowered to punish offenders. Smith was an enthusiastic candidate for membership of the proposed Commission. On 5 December 1772 he wrote to his sponsor, William Pulteney: 'I think myself very much honoured and obliged to you for having mentioned me to the E. India Directors as a person who would be of use to them. You have acted in your old way of doing your friends a good office behind their backs, pretty much as other people do them a bad one.'[1] The Commission for which he had been considered encountered Parliamentary opposition and was never dispatched.[2] One can only speculate about how the contents of The Wealth of Nations might have differed had events at this point taken a different course.

II. THE APPRAISAL OF THE ECONOMIC CONDITION OF HINDUSTAN

Within Smith's analytic scheme, the condition of India was of interest in the first instance as an intellectual problem. How was this part of the world to be categorized: as an example of an expanding, stationary, or declining economy? The question had obvious pertinence to the study of the general causes of economic development. At the same time, it touched on a matter which had troubled many late eighteenth-century men.

Since the earliest days of European contact with the East, India had generally been regarded as a richly opulent country. How else could one account for the lack of demand in that part of the world for products of European manufacture and for the persisting flow of silver to the East? Only in a rich country where the demand for goods had already been satiated did this characteristic of the trade seem to be readily comprehensible. Moreover, the

---

[1] As quoted by John Rae, Life of Adam Smith (London, 1895), p. 254. Edmund Burke had also been offered a seat on this Commission, but had declined after being persuaded that his political talents could not be spared in England.

[2] In 1769, a Commisssion with a similar charge had been appointed. The vessel carrying this party was lost en route to the East. The urgency attached by some observers to the appointment of a new commission may be conveyed in the words of a Company Shareholder. The failure to act would mean that 'the Provinces and Wealth of India would thereby by virtually surrendered to the rapine and tyranny of the Company's Servants.' Unless the behaviour of officials in the East was rapidly brought under control, the further consequences would be: 'More rapacity abroad; decrease of Funds at home; reduction of Dividend; rage of the Public; dissolution of the Company; and an enormous encrease of the King's Prerogative' (A Letter to the Proprietors of East-India Stock on the Subject of Sending Supervisors with Extraordinary Powers to India, by a Friend to Fair Discussion (London, 1772), p. 32).

commodity composition of Europe's imports from India seemed to reinforce this impression. The East India trade was the source of exotic primary commodities which could not be produced in harsher climates and of impressively expensive manufactured luxuries. The affluence of returning 'nabobs' did nothing to correct a popular impression of the wealth of the East.

A puzzle then needed to be explained. How could it come to pass that lands, apparently so richly blessed, could be taken over by a handful of expatriate merchant adventurers? To Smith, this question presented a special challenge. In his view, India had once been among the world's richer societies.[3] Moreover, the Indian sub-continent seemed to be remarkably endowed with agricultural riches—at least by comparison with the harsh climates of Northern Europe. Rice countries—where two or three crops could be taken each year—had the capacity to support much larger populations than had those parts of the world which lacked such natural advantages. In turn, this state of affairs would appear to have provided an environment favourable to the accumulation of capital. As Smith saw matters there: 'the rich, having a greater super-abundance of food to dispose of beyond what they themselves can consume, have the means of purchasing a much greater quantity of the labour of other people.'[4] Resources should thus have been amply available to provide the 'advances' (in the classical terminology) required to engage labour in productive capital formation.

But this was not the only promising feature of the situation. The traditional form of government in India (as Smith understood it) appeared to have been well structured to encourage economic expansion. A land tax—which, according to his account, absorbed about one-fifth of the gross agricultural product—was the basic source of the sovereign's revenue. Local rulers should, therefore, have been inclined to promote agricultural expansion—and, further, to encourage growth outside the agricultural sector to stimulate increased demand for agricultural output. The structure of his revenue base meant that the traditional sovereign had a natural interest in widening the market.

[3] For example, he wrote: 'The improvements in agriculture and manufactures seem likewise to have been of very great antiquity in the provinces of Bengal in the East Indies . . .' (Smith, *An Inquiry into the Nature and Causes of the Wealth of Nations*, ed., Edwin Cannan (London, 1904), vol. 1, p. 22.)

[4] Ibid., vol. 1, p. 205.

Yet these favourable conditions for a 'take off' seemed not to have been fully exploited. How was the outcome to be explained? In view of Smith's analytic presuppositions, one might have expected him to seek evidences of restraints on competition to account for the apparent result. Market imperfections, he suggested, must have played some part—particularly the institution of castes which imposed unnatural restrictions on occupational mobility.[5] Nevertheless, this institutional factor was insufficient as an explanation for international differentials in economic performance. Rigidities in the labour market were by no means unique to India. In Europe, the guild system and its remnants were at least equally reprehensible.[6]

In the Indian environment, inhibitions to the free play of market forces were not without some compensating features. When institutional constraints kept wages below their natural levels, prospects for capital accumulation should have been correspondingly brighter.[7] The distribution of income was thus slanted in favour of the non-wage shares of income from which productive saving could more easily arise. Smith held that this conclusion had been amply demonstrated: 'The great fortunes so suddenly and so easily acquired in Bengal and the other British settlements in the East Indies, may satisfy us that, as the wages of labour are very low, so the profits of stock are very high ...'[8] The lower the wage share of the national income, the higher would be the proportion of the national product potentially available for accumulation and re-investment.

Within India, the principal recipients of the non-wage shares

[5] As Smith observed: 'The police must be as violent as that of Indostan or antient Egypt (where every man was bound by a principle of religion to follow the occupation of his father, and was supposed to commit the most horrid sacrilege if he changed it for another), which can in any particular employment, and for several generations together, sink either the wages of labour or the profits of stock below their natural rate.' (Ibid., vol. 1, p. 64.)

[6] On this point, he wrote: 'How much the lower ranks of people in the country are really superior to those of the town, is well known to every man whom either business or curiosity has led to converse much with both. In China and Indostan accordingly both the rank and the wages of country labourers are said to be superior to those of the greater part of artificers and manufacturers. They would probably be so everywhere, if corporation laws and corporation spirit did not prevent it.' (Ibid., vol. 1, p. 129.)

[7] Smith was confident that real wages were indeed considerably lower in the East than in Europe. 'But the real price of labour, the real quantity of the necessaries of life which is given to the labourer, ... is lower both in China and Indostan, the two great markets of India, than it is through the greater part of Europe.' (Ibid., vol. 1, p. 206.)

[8] Ibid., vol. 1, p. 96.

were those who derived their income from agricultural rents. Smith had little confidence in large landowners anywhere to be socially useful accumulators. On this count, his indictment of the English landowning class was severe. He treated their behaviour as socially parasitic. Landlords—'those who reaped where they had never sowed'—diverted income from potentially productive purposes to gratify their personal tastes. Resources which could have enlarged the national stock of capital tended to be squandered in support of personal retainers. Practices in the East by members of this group were not totally dissimilar: 'The retinue of a grandee in China or Indostan accordingly is, by all accounts, much more numerous and splendid than that of the richest subjects in Europe.'[9]

Nevertheless, an important distinction needed to be drawn between the status of recipients of land rents in India and in Europe. In India, Smith maintained, revenues from land accrued primarily to the sovereign, rather than to private individuals (as was generally the case in Europe). There was thus a greater likelihood in Indian circumstances that some portion of the rental income would flow into productive channels. The revenue system linked the interests of the sovereign with expansion in agriculture. Thus investments designed to widen the market and to promote agricultural uplift—e.g. in road building and irrigation works— were likely to be made. In Europe, on the other hand, such functions could not safely be left in the hands of the state.[10] These considerations, however, failed to yield a fully satisfying explanation for the apparent failure of the Indian economy to grow at the rate justified by its resource endowments. The mystery largely remained.

Smith's further search for a solution to this paradox led him to the view that, at some crucial stage in its history, the Indian economy must have missed an opportunity to reap the full benefit from participation in international commerce. England had transformed its economic structure in the seventeenth century by organizing long-distance trades on a considerable scale. The Indian sub-continent had not. Part of the absence of a national initiative could be accounted for by India's geographical situation. The very scale of the land mass of the sub-continent

---

[9] Smith, *An Inquiry into the Nature and Causes of the Wealth of Nations*, ed., Edwin Cannan (London, 1904), vol. 1, p. 205.   [10] Ibid., vol. 2, pp. 181, 221–3.

permitted the division of labour to proceed some distance in less hazardous trade closer to home. Yet, in the absence of significant technological change, the potential for further specialization and exchange within the confines of a landlocked market area (extensive though it was) must have reached its limits. The moment at which Indian merchant adventurers embarked to trade beyond their own shores seemed not to have arrived. Smith's explanation for the failure of a new momentum for economic expansion to assert itself rested heavily on a curious factor: that the Hindu religion (or, in his terms, 'Gentoo') did not 'permit its followers to light a fire, nor consequently to dress any victuals upon the water, it in effect prohibits them from all distant sea voyages'.[11] The opening of distant markets was thereby precluded, and the stimulus which might otherwise have spurred the development of further specialization in the economic pattern was blunted. Adherents to the 'Gentoo' religion did not spurn participation in international commerce completely. But that in which they became involved had been organized by foreigners. Thus, the Indian sub-continent 'depended almost altogether upon the navigation of other nations for the exportation of their surplus produce; and their dependency, as it must have confined the market, so it must have discouraged the increase of this surplus produce.'[12] Potential growth had thus been arrested and, presumably, a disproportionate share of the gains from trade had leaked abroad.

This line of argument hinged fundamentally on a finding about the characteristics of the 'Gentoo' religion which was incorrect. It is not clear how Smith acquired the notion that cooking on shipboard was doctrinally proscribed.[13] This example, of course, is not the only instance in the history of economic literature in which analytic utility and factual accuracy have failed to coincide.

Smith invoked another peculiarity of the East in his quest for an understanding of economic stagnation in pre-British India.

[11] Ibid., vol. 2, p. 180.   [12] Ibid., vol. 2, p. 180.

[13] His library contained a work entitled *A Code of Gentoo Laws or Ordinations of the Pundits*, published in London in 1776. This document makes no reference to such a prohibition. The closest approximation to be found within it occurs in a discussion of ordinances to magistrates which indicates that they are directed to ensure that no untended fires were lit on land during the dry season. It was, however, the case that the long-distance sea trades initiated in the Indian sub-continent—which had been carried on for centuries throughout the Indian Ocean—had been organized by Muslim rather than Hindu navigators. Smith appeared to be unaware of this phase in the history of international commerce.

Part of its potential for accumulation had, he suggested, been diverted by unproductive hoarding. How else could one account for the sustained inflows of silver which—at least until Clive's assumption of the *diwani* in Bengal—had proceeded without interruption for a century and a half? Had this massive influx of precious metals flowed entirely into the domestic expenditure stream, its impact on the Indian price structure would certainly have been visible. From the observable facts, it seemed reasonable to infer that much of the imported silver had been trapped in idle hoards. Smith, of course, was an outspoken opponent of the view that wealth could be identified with a stock of precious metals. Nevertheless, he was more sympathetic toward Indians who held precious metals as a store of value than he would have been to-ward Europeans. As he saw matters, 'where men are continually afraid of the violence of their superiors, they frequently bury and conceal a great part of their stock, in order to have it always at hand, to carry with them to some place of safety, in case of their being threatened with any of those disasters to which they con-sider themselves as at all times exposed. This is said to be a com-mon practice in Turkey, Indostan, and, I believe, in most other governments of Asia.'[14] Conditions of physical insecurity might thus be sufficient to justify behaviour which, in different circum-stances, would be indicted as irrational and socially irresponsible.

Smith's discussion of arrested development in traditional India was a striking comment on his perception of an intellectual prob-lem. His struggle to solve it was less than successful. Others were to puzzle over the same question with quite different results. If Smith failed to unravel the mystery of economic stagnation in pre-British India, he at least felt able to speak with confidence on a separate, though related, issue: the deterioration of the Indian economy following its sustained contact with the East India Company.

III. THE ECONOMIC IMPACT OF THE EAST INDIA MONOPOLY

At the date of writing *The Wealth of Nations*, Smith regarded the portion of India under the control of the East India Company as a prime example of a declining economy. He described 'the present state of Bengal, and of some other of the English settle-

14 Smith, *An Inquiry into the Nature and Causes of the Wealth of Nations*, ed., Edwin Cannan (London, 1904), vol. 1, p. 267.

ments in the East Indies' as follows: 'Many would not be able to find employment even upon these hard terms, but would either starve, or be driven to seek a subsistence either by begging, or by the perpetration of the greatest enormities. Want, famine, and mortality would immediately prevail in that class, and from thence extend themselves to all the superior classes, till the number of inhabitants of the country was reduced to what could easily be maintained by the revenue and stock which remained in it, and which had escaped either the tyranny or calamity which had destroyed the rest.'[15] At that moment in history, responsibility for such a stark state of affairs was not assigned to indigenous causes. It was to be traced primarily to the mismanagement of an expatriate monopoly which had assumed powers of government.

What were the prospects for economic improvement in the territories governed by the East India Company? In the absence of structural change, Smith regarded the outlook as bleak. Government directed by a private monopoly of alien merchants compounded the obstacles to sustained economic expansion. The merger of commercial monopoly and sovereignty would inevitably frustrate the natural flow of economic forces. As Smith put it, 'It tends to make government subservient to the interest of monopoly, and consequently to stunt the natural growth of some parts at least of the surplus produce of the country to what is barely sufficient for answering the demand of the company.'[16] It was now no longer simply a matter of foreigners holding a bargaining advantage in international transactions because of their control over shipping. The new state of affairs, in which private monopoly had become a territorial sovereign, had also deranged the internal production pattern.

Major dislocation in the normal pattern of production had been one of the immediate consequences of the Company's new practice of procuring its 'investment' through the territorial revenues of Bengal. The trade in opium—which had been organized as a state monopoly in 1773, largely for the purpose of supplying an alternative to silver for the procurement of tea from China—was a conspicuous example. Smith noted that when the Company's inventories were large, cultivators had been ordered to destroy their poppy fields. Conversely, when its stocks were low, rice was ripped out and the poppy planted.[17] At least equally

15 Ibid., vol. 1, p. 75.   16 Ibid., vol. 2, p. 137.   17 Ibid., vol. 2, pp. 135–6.

disastrous were the consequences of the unrestrained behaviour of the Company's employees in freelance trading. These activities touched not just foreign trade, but cut deeply into the fabric of the internal commerce of Bengal. Private fortunes had been accumulated quickly by individual Europeans who had claimed immunity from the inland duties levied by local rulers. This abuse had brought ruin to many native tradesmen.[18] Smith concluded that the 'moonlighting' of the Company's servants had tended to 'stunt the natural growth of every part of the produce in which they chuse to deal, of what is destined for home consumption, as well as of what is destined for exportation . . .'[19] He even held the Company responsible—through the imposition of 'improper regulations' and 'injudicious restraints' on the rice trade—for aggravating the famine of the early 1770s.[20]

A country subjected to such treatment could not be expected to prosper. The healthy stimulus of competition had been suppressed. Similarly, the prospects for mobilizing surpluses for reinvestment in the home economy had been blighted. Resources which—under different arrangements—might have found their way into the expansion of the productive capacity of the economy were now more likely to be transferred abroad. The unofficial misbehaviour of the Company's servants and the official behaviour of the Company had combined to produce these unfortunate outcomes. A shareholder in the East India Company, Smith contended, had 'a share, though not in the plunder, yet in the appointment of the plunderers of India'.[21]

Though Bengal bore the heaviest burden, the costs of this misguided system were widely distributed. In Smith's judgement, the potential gains to the entire world from the East India commerce were enormous. 'The East Indies', he wrote, 'offer a market both for the manufactures of Europe and for the gold and silver as well as for several other productions of America, greater

---

[18] When one of the local Nawabs, Mir Kasim, responded by abolishing inland duties within his territory, a military action obliged him to reimpose them in 1763. The commercial advantage of Europeans (who retained their extra-territorial privileges) over traders (who remained subject to taxation) was thus maintained. On this point, see J. C. Sinha, *Economic Annals of Bengal*, esp. pp. 70–3.

[19] Smith, op. cit., vol. 2, p. 138.

[20] Ibid., vol. 2, p. 28. J. Steven Watson has estimated that one-sixth of the population of Bengal died in the famine of 1770–2. See *The Reign of George III, 1760–1815* (Oxford, 1960), p. 166.

[21] Smith, op. cit., vol. 2, p. 243.

and more extensive than both Europe and America put together'.[22] Yet these opportunities had not been exploited. Had entry into the East India commerce been free, the resources committed to its development would have been much greater. Not only had growth been stifled; the absence of competition had also sheltered gross mis-management of the trade. Monopoly had generated 'extraordinary profits' and 'extraordinary waste which the fraud and abuse, inseparable from the management of the affairs of so great a company, must necessarily have occasioned'.[23]

Much of this line of criticism of commercial monopoly had been lodged by others, long before the East India Company assumed a governing role. Smith could now add an item to the general charge. The combination of monopoly with government, he noted, was likely to restrict the free flow of labour and particularly to discourage colonization. Members of an exclusive company were disposed to protect their privileges in territories overseas. Once they had acquired the powers of government, they could more readily exclude those who might have been inclined, not only to stimulate trade, but also to undertake direct investment in India.[24]

Smith conceded that there once might have been some merit in the 'natural monopoly' argument deployed by the East India Company to defend its exclusive privileges. He noted that special concessions could be justified for the pioneers in a 'new trade with some remote and barbarous nation'.[25] Even among 'that mild and gentle people'[26] of Hindustan, overhead expenditures on fortifications might initially have been legitimate. But the East India Company could no longer plead its case on such grounds. Smith insisted that such unusual arrangements should be treated as analogous to patents or copyrights and automatically terminated at the end of a specified period.

IV. THE INCONGRUITY OF TERRITORIAL SOVEREIGNTY AND COMMERCIAL MONOPOLY

Monopoly was inherently bad—but its results were far worse when monopoly was combined with governance. Smith stated his view of this matter bluntly: 'It is the interest of the East India company considered as sovereigns, that the European goods

---

[22] Ibid., vol. 2, p. 131.   [23] Ibid., vol. 2, p. 130.
[24] On this point see ibid., vol. 2, p. 134.
[25] Ibid., vol. 2, p. 245.   [26] Ibid., vol. 2, p. 223.

which are carried to their Indian dominions, should be sold there as cheap as possible; and that the Indian goods which are brought from thence should bring there as good a price, or should be sold there as dear as possible. But the reverse of this is their interest as merchants. As sovereigns, their interest is exactly the same with that of the country which they govern. As merchants, their interest is directly opposite to that interest.'[27]

A rational sovereign ought properly to identify himself with the well-being of the governed and with their economic improvement. This objective called for the promotion of open competition and for the removal of obstacles to economic expansion. A government linked with commercial monopoly could not rise to these tasks. Smith asserted that a private company of merchants would find it impossible to consider themselves as sovereigns, 'even after they [had] become such'.[28] He could conceive of no other situation in which those exercising sovereignty could be 'so perfectly indifferent about the happiness or misery of their subjects'.[29] To this point he added: 'It is a very singular government in which every member of the administration wishes to get out of the country . . .'[30] His final judgement on such arrangements could not have been more scathing. 'The government of an exclusive company of merchants', he wrote, 'is perhaps, the worst of all governments for any country whatever.'[31]

Smith moderated his condemnation of the existing state of affairs in British India with one qualification only. He wished his readers to understand that his denunciations were not directed to specific individuals responsible for the management of the East India Company's affairs. Many of them were honourable men with genuine feelings of concern for the welfare of the peoples in their charge. The problem was the system itself. Government in the hands of an unregulated private monopoly involved interests which were both incompatible and irreconcilable.

V. THE WIDER SIGNIFICANCE OF THE ARGUMENT

Smith's attempt to fit India into a general model was to have a formidable impact. His interpretation appeared to yield a valuable insight into those aspects of the Indian connection which had

---

[27] Smith, *An Inquiry into the Nature and Causes of the Wealth of Nations* ed., Edwin Cannan (London 1904), vol. 2, p. 137.   [28] Ibid., vol. 2, p. 136.   [29] Ibid., vol. 2, p. 243.   [30] Ibid., vol. 2, p. 140.   [31] Ibid., vol. 2, p. 72.

puzzled Englishmen. The apparent weakness of India (despite its vast productive potential) was now easier to comprehend. Similarly, there could no longer be any mystery about the commercial failures of the East India Company (despite repeated assurances that massive profits were just around the corner). The monopoly mode of organization was calculated to produce inefficiency and corruption. Its results had been disastrous for both Englishmen and Indians.

The new doctrine also offered a design for improvement in the future. It could be realized only after the East India Company had been dismantled. The first step toward constructive change was obvious: its commercial monopoly should be liquidated. This proposition was hardly original: it had been in circulation for more than a century and a half. Never before, however, had it been supported with arguments so fully elaborated.

With commercial monopoly extinguished, what disposition should be made of the government of Bengal? Smith's line of reasoning might easily have supported the conclusion that British involvement in governance there should also be terminated. He did not propose this course. Trade with the East—if organized on competitive lines—was still important. So long as other European nations threatened to pre-empt it, a British official presence might still be required. But the form it took should be radically changed. The territories and the revenues claimed in the name of the East India Company were, in his view, 'the undoubted right of the crown, that is, of the state and people of Great Britain'.[32] With governance as a public—rather than private—British responsibility, the interests of the ruler and the ruled would more readily converge. Government could then turn attention to the measures most urgently needed to stimulate economic uplift. Tax reduction and reform in the fiscal administration, he suggested, should be at the top of agenda. The territories of the East India Company were already 'more than sufficiently taxed' and the 'embezzlement and misapplication' of their payments should no longer be tolerated.[33] In this sketch of priorities, there was no room for monetary experimentation to speed economic expansion. Steuart's heterodox views were not mentioned in *The Wealth of Nations*, though Smith was far too well read to be unaware of them.

[32] Ibid., vol. 2, p. 431.   [33] Ibid., vol. 2, p. 431.

The East India Company was not unfamiliar with attacks on its privileges and position. But the new round of critiques differed from the old. In an earlier day, most of the polemical artillery had been fired by manufacturing and commercial interests threatened by the activities of the Company. The charges set off by practitioners of the new political economy, on the other hand, were the product of detached observers who disclaimed any personal stake in the issues in controversy, apart from their concern as citizens. It was to a wider public audience that they appealed.

CHAPTER 6

The Official Brief of 1793

In the 1770s and 1780s, the East India Company was again on the defensive. The intellectual critiques of its structure generated by the *avant-garde* theorists had merged with a rising public concern over the apparent irregularities of its servants abroad. In consequence, East India affairs were closer to the centre of national attention than they had been since the late seventeenth century.

Though many familiar voices could be heard in the chorus of critics, there were also some fresh ones. British mercantile interests, which had long been outspokenly opposed to the Company's exclusive privileges, continued to be so. They were now joined by citizens inspired by an aroused social conscience. The Company's position as a territorial sovereign, they maintained, had tended to victimize innocent peoples in India. Moreover, private wealth acquired by dubious means in the East was potentially dangerous for England. The position of thirteen of the Company's twenty-four directors as Members of Parliament between 1768 and 1774 had not passed unnoticed, nor had it escaped public attention that the number of Members of Parliament with experience in India rose from twenty-two in 1774 to thirty-six in 1784.[1]

If the East India interest in fact lacked the power to make the English state do its bidding, it still threatened to create a state within a state. There could be no question that part of the market for East India Company shares was made by persons more interested in the distribution of the Indian patronage than in

---

[1] P. J. Marshall, *Problems of Empire: Britain and India, 1757–1813* (London, 1968), pp. 29, 37. A contemporary observer saw matters as follows: 'The East has long been a plentiful source of wealth, and lately of *titles*, not all, indeed, *Right Honourable*, especially that of *Nabob*; which being entirely exotic, is observed to consume like a rotten cheese, particularly at the time of a general election; I should not, however, be more surprised at seeing honours and titles produced in plenty, by proper cultivation at the East India House, than at a plentiful crop of mushrooms, produced from invisible seeds, strewed occasionally on a common dunghill.' (Keane Fitzgerald, *A Letter to the Directors of the East India Company* (London, 1777), pp. 4–5.)

prospective dividends. Normal financial calculations were insufficient to explain the vigour with which elections to the Company's Board of Directors were contested and the expenditures poured into the 'proxy' battles which accompanied them.[2] When such influence on affairs of major public importance could be privately purchased, there was little basis for confidence that the results would be healthy, either for India or for England.

Precedent for direct governmental intervention in the internal affairs of the East India Company had been established in the Regulating Act of 1772. That legislation, however, had done little more than create the post of Governor-General with the stipulation that the Crown was to participate in the selection of the appointee. Fox's India Bill of 1783—which won approval in the House of Commons—was far more sweeping. Had it become law, the East India Company would have lost its identity. Its territorial powers would have been stripped away and governing authority in India would have been transferred to a Board appointed by Parliament. The management of commercial operations would also have been transformed. No longer would the Company's business affairs be conducted by directors selected by shareholders. According to Fox's plan, a committee chosen by Parliament from among the owners of the Company's shares would be charged with responsibility for these matters. Fox's Bill died in the House of Lords, but only after Royal intervention had engineered its defeat.

The Company survived this assault, but it soon faced another. Pitt's East India Act of 1784, which was more moderate than the bill which had brought down Fox's government, nevertheless extended the sphere of governmental involvement. A Board of Control (whose members were to be appointed by the Crown) was then instituted to exercise general supervision over the Company's non-commercial activities in India. Though the Company's commercial privileges were not molested, the new formula imparted some of the characteristics of a regulated public utility to the East India Company.

The new regulatory machinery, however, afforded the Company no immunity from public attack. The impeachment trial of Warren Hastings, begun in 1787 to extend over the next seven

---

[2] For a discussion of electoral campaigns for positions within the Company, see C. H. Philips, *The East India Company, 1784–1834* (Bombay, 1961), esp. pp. 3–8.

years, provoked further hostility. To those concerned with the
Company's image, the fact that Hastings was ultimately exoner-
ated mattered little. The damage had already been done—and
sufficiently to cloud prospects for future renewals of the charter.
The Company needed a spokesman who could serve it as Thomas
Mun had done in an earlier age. In particular, its interests called
for persuasive arguments to justify the retention of commercial
monopoly and to demonstrate that linkages between commerce
and sovereignty were socially beneficial. These were the points on
which the fire of the new breed of political economists had been
concentrated.

With the approach of the deadline for renewal of the charter in
1793, a new official position was prepared. It was not articulated
in any single document, nor was it the work of any single hand.
Nevertheless, a coherent defence of the Company was rallied. The
task was eased considerably by reforms which had lately been
accomplished in the East. By this point, the more flagrant abuses
of the early years of Company government in Bengal had been
brought in check and a programme of constructive reform in
administration had been set in motion. Not only were higher
standards of performance expected from Company employees in
the conduct of their official duties; their 'moonlighting' activities
had also been severely restricted. These changes owed much to
Cornwallis who had arrived as Governor-General in 1786. Despite
military defeat at Yorktown, Cornwallis's reputation as an
efficient administrator had not been diminished.

I. THE DEFENCE OF COMMERCIAL MONOPOLY

Part of the case developed in 1793 drew on arguments well-
rooted in the Company's tradition. Central direction of the East
India commerce, it was reasserted, was inescapable in face of the
heavy outlays required to secure the far-flung outposts of the
Eastern trade. Private merchants, acting independently, could
not budget for this essential protection; only a large organization
with monopoly privileges was competent to do so. Moreover, it
was maintained that the visions of a vast untapped potential for
profitable commerce entertained by advocates of free trade were
illusory. The climate of the East and the tastes of its peoples precluded the development of significant markets for British products. The Company had already pushed exports as aggressively

as circumstances would permit—and the fruit of its work should encourage no one who had a respect for facts.[3]

Nor could any national advantage be gained by opening the commerce in Asian goods to all comers. On the contrary, the recommendations of the free traders invited a serious national loss. The East India Company had constructed an intricate commercial network within which the re-export of Indian goods to European markets occupied a strategic place. Not only was this arrangement beneficial to Britain's balance of trade; it also ensured that English textile interests were shielded from competition with finished Indian products. An organization as large and as exposed as the East India Company could not afford to import 'prohibited' goods, whereas the more free-spirited of the private traders were unlikely to be so responsible.[4]

Another practical consideration bore on the question at issue. Roughly half of the gross value of imports by the East India Company was now accounted for by one commodity: tea acquired in China. Even after the reliefs provided by the Commutation Act, tea duties contributed significantly to the national exchequer. Monopoly control over this important traffic ensured that taxes were honourably recorded and faithfully paid. Free trade promised no similar reliability in tax collection.

By 1793 a new ingredient entered the arguments mounted in defence of the *status quo*. In the light of the existence of the Parliamentary Board of Control, it could plausibly be asserted that the East India Company was no longer the institution Smith had condemned. It was now a responsible, publicly regulated body, rather than an objectionable private monopoly. Dundas, President of the Board of Control, drew attention to this point when he observed that 'it had been a favorite topic of late, to

---

[3] For the six seasons 1783–4 to 1788–9, the Company reported a net loss of nearly £38,000 on its exports of woollens to India. Though its export trade in metals showed a profit of nearly £10,000, these returns were insufficient to shift the financial results into the black. (*Second Report of the Select Committee Appointed to Take Into Consideration the Export Trade From Great Britain to the East Indies* (1793), p. 6.)

[4] In this period, re-exports represented about a third of the gross imports brought by the Company from the East. For the years 1789–92, for example, gross imports were in the range of £6 million per annum and re-exports in the range of £2 million. More than half of the value of re-exports was accounted for by calicoes and muslins: i.e. by goods which, in finished form, could not legally be sold in England. See *A Short History of the East India Company and of Their Trade to India and China* (1793), p. 73, signed 'F.R.' and attributed to Francis Russell.

declaim against monopolies, and to confound what was truly a monopoly, with the exclusive privilege of the East-India Company.' Monopoly, in the proper sense of the term, implied that sellers had unchecked power to set prices. Dundas was confident that Members of the Parliament could differentiate that situation from the case of 'an exclusive privilege given by the Legislature to a Company, proceeding upon a capital equal to the magnitude of the concern, and subject to regulation, and to public controul: This distinction being admitted, the Legislature will not be disposed rashly to change a current which is turning the greatest wheel of British commerce, which is giving food to industry and wealth to regulated enterprize, and which is about to become, independently of what we draw from duties and customs, one of the resources of the Nation.'[5]

To these points, spokesmen for the Company needed only to add that a dispassionate appraisal of its behaviour would lead the observer to judge it as socially responsible. If any attributes of private monopoly remained in its structure, they were innocuous. The Company, in fact, was a prime exhibit of the 'good trust'. It did not rig its prices; instead it sold its trade goods at public auction to the highest bidders. Moreover, its profits had been moderate. 'For *four score years past*', one of its champions wrote, 'it will be found that their *dividends*, taken for the average of any reasonable period, have been sometimes *less* than, and *never exceeded the legal rate of interest of money*, computed by a value or a market price of their stock . . .'[6]

In the climate of opinion of the 1790s, caution about the opening of the India trade to all comers had another recommendation. In the light of British experience with colonies in North America, it could be argued with considerable effect that freedom to trade in the East would soon lead to permanent European settlement there. Colonization, in turn, might well disturb the stability of British rule. Dundas put the point as follows:

. . . unrestrained liberty to the Europeans to emigrate to and settle among the Indians, would, in a short time, annihilate the respect made to the British character, and ruin our Indian Empire. Indeed, we have only to advert to

---

[5] *Substance of Mr. Dundas's Speech on India Affairs, April 23, 1793*, p. 28.

[6] *A Short History of the East India Company and of Their Trade to India and China* (London, 1793), p. 27 (italics in the original).

what must be the situation of the settlers and of the natives, we shall at once discover, that this opinion has a solid foundation.[7]

He might also have referred to a fear which then weighed on the minds of many Englishmen. A resident European community in India, even if it did not upset relationships between government and the local peoples, could be expected to demand political autonomy.

The architects of the new defences of the Company in its incarnation as a regulated industry were well aware that their arguments would not completely satisfy a convert to Smith's doctrine. They appealed, however, for the understanding and support of reasonable men acquainted with delicate matters of state. The national interest was best served, it was maintained, when experience, rather than the theoretical speculations of ingenious men, guided practice. The ties with India had a unique history. General rules—even ones which might deservedly win applause in ordinary circumstances—could not usefully be applied to this special case. In the spirit of pragmatic experimentation, however, Dundas offered one modest concession to the free trade lobby: i.e. legislation which would oblige the Company to reserve a limited amount of cargo space for the wares of individual English merchants. By this means, some of the theories of the free traders could be tested, but under conditions which would limit the damage should their expectations be disappointed. The Act of 1793 which extended the charter by two decades not only reaffirmed the Company's exclusive privileges under the supervision of the Board of Control; it also stipulated that 3,000 tons of the Company's shipping space should annually be made available to private traders.

II. THE OFFICIAL RATIONALE FOR THE LINKAGE OF SOVEREIGNTY AND COMMERCE

Smith's critique of the East India Company as a governing authority had rested on the premiss that a contradiction was inherent in a mixture of sovereignty and commerce. No basic improvement in the plight of Bengal could be in sight until these functions had been divorced. That day would be happier still if the Company's commercial monopoly were to be banished. Some Englishmen, though sympathetic to Smith's general intellectual

[7] *Substance of Mr. Dundas's Speech*, p. 25.

position, were nevertheless inclined to back away from his recommendations for India. Part of their hesitation arose from uncertainty about the shape of an alternative government for Bengal. None of the commentators who won a wide audience urged a total evacuation of the British presence from the subcontinent. A political vacuum there would not offer a promising environment for commerce. If responsibilities for government could not safely be abandoned, the question remained: in whose hands should they be placed?

It was not necessary to argue that the East India Company was the ideal instrument for this purpose to conclude that it might still be superior to the more obvious alternatives. The transfer of power directly to the British state was not a persuasively attractive option. The patronage of India could easily overstrain the integrity of the British state. Dundas alluded to this concern when he noted that 'if the Indian patronage should be vested and concentered immediately in the Crown, the weight of it would be too great in the balance of our Government, and might prove dangerous to the spirit of the Constitution.' The existing system might not be perfect but, on balance, he 'preferred a lesser to the greater evil, of placing the administration of the Government and Revenues [of India] in the hands of the State'.[8]

Fears of corruption were not the only worries associated with direct access of the British government to the spoils of India. The claim of the state to a share of India's surplus revenues was also potentially troublesome. How long, it was asked, could the liberties of Englishmen survive if the executive could circumvent Parliamentary constraints on its spending? If the revenues generated from India ultimately fulfilled their initial promise, much of the finance of government would be independent of Parliamentary appropriations. Even Adam Smith (who was no friend of the Company) had been taken to task for promoting the view that the surplus revenues of India should be treated as the property of the British nation, rather than of the East India Company.[9]

These considerations were sufficient to persuade some potential critics that the *status quo* was tolerable as a second-best solution to the problem of governance. They were insufficient, however, to

---

[8] Ibid., p. 14.

[9] See, for example, a pamphlet entitled *A Candid Examination of the Reasons for Depriving the East India Company of Its Charter* (London, 1779) (attributed to Mickle).

demonstrate that trade and governance could successfully be combined by the East India Company. Other arguments were required before this case could be sustained. Within the Company's official family, an attempt was made to generate them in preparation for the 1793 round of debates on renewal of the charter. Their purpose was to show that these two functions had become closely linked in ways that worked to the economic advantage of both India and England.

From England's point of view, it was regarded as self-evident that the innovation of financing the commerce from the Indian tax revenues was in the national interest. No longer was it necessary to withdraw silver from England for this purpose. Now that the working capital of commerce could be acquired locally, the long-standing 'drain' to the East had been checked.

It was less easy to argue convincingly that the new arrangement was advantageous to India. Smith's analysis of the process of economic growth, however, offered categories which seemed to be useful for the task at hand. In his view, productive capacity was enlarged when those who saved extended 'advances' to productive labour. The Company's new role in India could now be portrayed in those terms. As this scheme was described by one of its spokesmen:

The collectors of the revenue advance money to those people [overseers employed by the Company] out of the collection, for the purchase of raw materials, and for supporting the manufacturers and workmen employed. The money has a rapid circulation; it passes instantly from the Manufacturer to the Ryot, or cultivator of the lands, for rice and other food; from thence to the Native Collector of the village for rent, who pays it over to the superior Landlord or Zemindar, through whom it again reaches the Company's Collector. What is paid for the raw material reaches immediately the occupier of the Cotton Grove or Poppy Garden, and is circulated through a like medium to the English Collector. Such being the course of circulation established in all those parts of India, where piece goods, ophium [sic], indigo, or other articles or merchandize, are manufactured and the condition of the Natives employed in them being so abject as to require a regular supply, to keep them from emigrating or starving, it should seem that in either case, of diverting the revenue to any other purpose, or depriving the inhabitants of this means of supporting their families, neither Revenue nor manufactured Goods could be obtained; and if revenue could not be obtained, there must soon be an end to the influence of the British government in Hindustan . . .[10]

---

[10] A Short History of the East India Company and of Their Trade to India and China, pp. 67–8.

This line of argument did not lose sight of the fact that it was in the Company's interest to advance working capital to the farmers and craftsmen who produced goods for export. At the same time, it sought to demonstrate that the people of India had an important stake in a system within which the government performed some of the functions assigned to capitalists in Smith's interpretation of the mechanisms of economic expansion.[11]

Sovereignty, it could thus be maintained, supported the production process within India and improved the terms on which England could conduct the Indian commerce. The arguments invoked to support these conclusions fell short of the analytic standards reached in the Company's briefs in the early seventeenth century. With advocates such as Mun, the Company had been at the cutting edge of intellectual innovation. The official position developed in 1793, by contrast, was pieced together from borrowed materials, not all of which could be easily fused. The attempted demonstration of the system's advantages to England rested primarily on an appeal to unsophisticated bullionist doctrine. The case for the alleged advantages to India, on the other hand, appropriated a fragment of argument employed by the new wave of political economists.

III. A PROJECTED OPERATIONAL STRATEGY

In the struggle for survival in the 1790s, the leadership of the Company was engaged on two fronts. On the one hand, it was under pressure to satsify its critics in Parliament and among the public at large that its organizational arrangements were capable of generating socially desirable (or at least socially innocuous) outcomes. On the other hand, it was imperative to satisfy restive shareholders of the soundness of the organization as a dividend-

---

[11] Much later, the young John Stuart Mill—then a junior member of the East India Company's headquarters staff—defended this mode of operations. Its critics had maintained that the Company distorted normal market processes by asserting preemptive purchase rights to the outputs of producers to whom it had advanced working capital. As Mill wrote in an unsigned article: '... but surely if ... the Company actually advances to the producers the capital with which they carry on production, it is entitled to privileges somewhat greater than those of a simple purchaser; and there is nothing unfair in the transaction, unless it can be shown that, by the abuse of the powers of government, the Company extorts from producers more favourable terms than the private merchants could obtain, for the same equivalent, by the competition of the market.' The critics had not demonstrated that this was the case. See 'Foreign Dependencies: Trade With India', *Parliamentary History and Review* (1826–7), p. 60.

paying enterprise. For the primary purpose of reassuring the latter constituency, the Directors appointed a Select Committee on Accounts which was charged to demonstrate that the amalgamation of commerce with sovereignty made good business sense. The report of this group, which was submitted in February 1793, set out in remarkable detail the linkages within a complex network of transactions—some of which were political and some commercial—and estimated the annual yield in 'surpluses' which could reasonably be expected. The architects of this scheme were careful to note, however, that their projections were predicated on the assumption of a 'peace establishment'.

This formulation of a strategy offers an instructive insight into the prevailing conceptualization of the East India connection. The Company's role, in the first instance, was seen as that of a tax-gatherer and administrative authority in India. Hence, the first step in the planning exercise was the calculation of expected annual revenue surpluses from the territorial administration. The financial results from this part of the Company's activities, expressed in the sterling equivalents of local currencies, were then projected as follows:[12]

	Revenues (£s)	Charges (£s)
Bengal	5 033 000	3 127 000
Madras	1 540 000	1 613 200
Bombay	390 625	552 375
Bencoolen and Prince of Wales Island	—	50 000
Totals	6 963 625	5 342 575
Surplus Revenues	1 621 050	

These calculations did not make allowance for the payment of interest on debts in India—an expenditure amounting to £561,923 —under the heading of 'charges'. Had these outlays been treated as local costs, the adjusted figure for the 'surplus revenue' would be reduced to £1,059,127.

[12] These data and those which follow in the remainder of this section are derived from the Report of the Committee of Accounts, 15 February 1793 as published in the *First, Second, and Third Reports of the Select Committee appointed by the Court of Directors of the East India Company* (1793).

With these funds in hand, the activity of the Company as a trader could begin in earnest. Advances could then be extended to local producers and a regular supply of exportable commodities would thus be assured. Though revenue surpluses from the territorial administration were crucial to the success of the plan, they were not, however, regarded as the sole local source of commercial working capital. Rupee receipts were also expected to be available —in amounts approximating to £300,000 per annum—from the sale of the Company's exports to India. Altogether, some £1,377,000 was visualized as realizable in India for the purchase of the 'investment'.[13]

What dispositions were then to be made of this sum? The scheme mapped in 1793 drew a sharp distinction between two wings of the commerce: one which directed products of India to Europe and one which directed them to China. The major claim on local working capital was for procurement in the former category. An annual appropriation of £250,000, however, was earmarked for the 'China investment'.

India's export trade thus had a dual significance. Her piece goods, raw silk, indigo, saltpetre, and pepper were collected for shipment westward and ultimate sale in European markets.[14] The commodity shipped eastward required separate treatment. From the point of view of the Company, Bengal was prized particularly

[13] The planners prudently set aside £32,000 from the resources available as a reserve in India.

[14] The plan of 1793 itemized the procurement costs and the expected proceeds from sales in Europe as follows:

	Procurement Cost (£s)	Sales Amount (£s)
Bengal piece goods	550 000	1 100 000
Bengal raw silk	178 000	260 000
Indigo	47 300	110 000
Madras piece goods	240 000	585 000
Surat piece goods	50 000	63 300
Pepper	42 000	109 600
Saltpetre	19 000	87 000
Totals	1 126 300	2 314 900

It should be noted that the estimates shown for procurement costs refer only to outlays for the acquisition of trade goods in the East. The difference between sales proceeds and procurement costs is not, therefore, a measure of the Company's profits. Other costs had to be absorbed before goods were disposed of in Europe: among them, provision for freight, insurance, handling charges, and liability for customs duties.

for its capacity to supply opium. The 'China investment' of £250,000 was budgeted exlusively for this commodity.[15]

At this stage of history, India's contribution through opium went only a small part of the way toward financing the full procurement of China goods for export to Europe. The total requirement was estimated at nearly £1,495,000. The balance was to be made up from receipts in China from the sale of British goods (calculated to yield about £600,000 per annum) and by bullion or bills of exchange on London in the amount of about £645,000. Bullion, though no longer a part of the working capital in the commerce with India, still occupied an important place in the China branch of the trade. It followed, however, that the shipment of silver from England to China could be reduced to the extent that Indian goods (particularly opium) could be offered there in its stead. This point did not escape the official mind.

Ultimately, of course, the Company's financial position depended on the proceeds of marketings in Europe. Of the Asian commodities in its offerings, one was of particular importance: tea obtained in China was overwhelmingly its most significant revenue earner.[16] Indeed, much of the value of the East India connection derived from the capacity of Bengal to provide the means to purchase China's tea.

When all these transactions had been tallied, the Committee on Accounts estimated that an annual surplus could be realized in England of more than £1,200,000. This definition of 'surplus' excluded, however, the £400,000 committed to the payment of dividends to shareholders at the rate of eight per cent. Profits before distribution were thus expected to exceed £1,600,000 from gross sales receipts of just under £5,000,000. This result was possible only because the Company was not obliged to pay the full cost of the goods it acquired in the East. A substantial part of

[15] The projections prepared in 1793 included 25,000,000 Court rupees (the equivalent of £250,000) in the revenues of Bengal as receipts from opium; on the expenditure side, 9,750,000 Court rupees (or £97,500) was shown as 'opium allowances and charges'.

[16] Details for the China commerce were projected as follows:

	Procurement Costs (£s)	Sales Amounts (£s)
Tea	1 348 260	2 457 400
China raw silk	137 060	200 000
Nankeens	9 260	16 000
Totals	1 494 580	2 673 400

the financial burden had been shifted to the Indian tax-payer. At the same time, the operation of a government in India committed the Company to some outlays which would not have been required had its activities taken a more conventional form: e.g. expenditures to provide 'stores' for the Indian civil and military establishments and to recruit manpower in England. Even so, the merger of sovereignty with commerce promised profits much in excess of those which would otherwise have been within reach. This outcome, in turn, implied that the Company's ability to contribute to the British exchequer was correspondingly increased—and without compromise to its payment of sizeable returns to shareholders.

IV. PROPERTIES OF THE OFFICIAL BRIEF OF 1793

In immediate practical terms, the Company's brief in 1793 was a success. The arguments contained in it produced a winning case in quarters which mattered most. With the more powerfully-placed critics at least temporarily neutralized, the charter was extended by two decades on terms which were satisfactory to the East India Company. Even so, the strategy of 1793 failed to meet the larger requirements of the day. Mun, in his time, had managed to shape categories which could capture control of the terms of debate. The architects of the Company's position in the late eighteenth century registered no similar accomplishment.

The intellectual challenge presented to the Company's leadership in the early 1790s was, to be sure, a formidable one. A convincing demonstration that the dual roles of the East India Company were beneficial to all parties (Indians and Englishmen alike) may, in fact, have been impossible. Mun had not been expected to show that the people of the East would be significant gainers from the activities of the East India Company. Opinion in his day had required him to argue only that the form in which the trade was conducted was to England's national advantage. By the late eighteenth century—largely owing to the influence of the new political economy—a narrowly nationalistic solution was much less acceptable.

Officials of the Company acknowledged the importance of this new range of concerns. The notion of 'advances' to stimulate production in India had been introduced in an attempt to speak to it. The data provided on the workings of the system did not,

however, support the conclusion that India was a significant
beneficiary from the new scheme. On the contrary, the stark
reality was that India was committed to an export surplus without prospect of compensation. Steuart had recognized this
dimension of the problem and had sought to even the balance by
uplifting India with imaginative economic policies. By 1793 his
contributions had vanished without trace.

But if the strategy of 1793 failed to deal adequately with the
condition of India, it appeared to be able to reassure Englishmen
about the returns they could expect from the system. The
financial disappointments of the early years of territorial governance should now be forgotten. The teething troubles were over.
With the system now stabilized, trade and sovereignty were not
only compatible: a highly profitable commerce with the East
seemed, in fact, to depend on access to the territorial revenues.
With these functions merged, the East India Company—at least
in a period of peace—should be set fair to reward its shareholders
adequately and still have resources to spare for the British state.

This line of reasoning was dominated by the commercial mode
of thought entrenched within the Company. Within this framework, it could be argued that sovereignty reinforced commerce by
generating resources which made trade more profitable. It could
also be argued that commerce reinforced governance—at least to
the extent that it enabled the foreign exchange costs of Company
government to be met. The broader implications of Company
government—and particularly its consequences for the subject
peoples—were, however, largely ignored in this scheme of things.

CHAPTER 7

The Critique of the Official Brief: Lord Lauderdale and the Alleged Incompatibility of Commerce and Sovereignty

As preparations for review of the East India Company's charter (which was again due for renewal in 1813) gathered momentum, it was abundantly clear that the projections prepared in 1793 bore little relation to the Company's actual performance. Surpluses in the territorial account—upon which so much of the strategy for linking trade and governance had hinged—had rarely been realized. On the contrary, the deficits accumulated in the territorial budget between 1792/93 and 1808/09 amounted to nearly £5 million. The Company had again been obliged to borrow in India in order to cover the shortfall in the territorial account and to procure the 'investment'. Over this span of years, its debts in India (most of which were redeemable in London) had swollen by more than £21,700,000.[1]

Meanwhile, the capacity of the Company to honour its obligations in England had failed to keep pace with growth in its commitments. Contrary to expectations in 1793, receipts from the sale of the Company's Asian merchandise had shrunk. Even the private trade authorized by the legislation of 1793 had failed to flourish. In the first decade of this experiment, less than 10 per cent of the shipping space allocated to private English merchants had actually been applied for.[2] The latter result occasioned little surprise within the ranks of the Company, though it was perplexing to the wider public. Once again, the Company appealed to the British government for help. Payments earmarked as the 'participation of the public' in the territorial revenues were deferred and the Company sought fresh funding from the state.

Part of the divergence between expectations and reality could,

---

[1] *Second Report from the Select Committee on the Affairs of the East India Company* (1810), pp. 63–7.

[2] See *Third Report of the Special Committee on Private Trade* (1802).

of course, be attributed to the unforeseen circumstances of war. Napoleon had played havoc with the Company's re-export network on the Continent. Meanwhile, Wellesley's campaigns in India during his tenure of the Governor-Generalship (1798–1805) had stripped all relevance from budget projections which assumed a 'peace establishment'. Between 1793 and 1809, military conquest had more than doubled the area administered by the Company in India. It could be—and was—claimed that fresh revenue resources had thus been acquired. The Company's receipts from its administrative operations in India had, in fact, grown from about £8,200,000 in 1792/93 to more than £15,500,000 in 1808/09.[3] But the growth in expenditure—fed primarily by military charges—had far outstripped these gains.[4]

The financial returns spoke for themselves. Obviously the scheme projected in 1793 had failed to live up to its claims. Deficits, rather than surpluses, had been recorded at each of the crucial steps in the operation. Wars in India and in Europe had, of course, been responsible for much of the disappointment. No analyst could reasonably be faulted for failing to build the impact of such events into his calculations; indeed, those who prepared the projections of 1793 had been quite explicit in stipulating that their estimates referred to outcomes which might be expected during a period of peace. It was still worth asking, however, whether or not British national interests would have been well served even if events had gone according to plan. This, after all, was the crucial test. It could hardly be said that the scheme purporting to link commerce with sovereignty had stressed benefits likely to accrue to India.

In 1809 an arresting reinterpretation of this point emerged from the pen of Lord Lauderdale (1759–1839). Lauderdale's personal involvement with East India questions provided him with a unique perspective from which to appraise the Company and its performance. In 1787 he had served as one of the Parliamentary managers of the impeachment proceedings against Warren Hastings. His zeal in this assignment was not forgotten. When he was nominated—with Fox's sponsorship in 1806—for

[3] *Parliamentary Papers, 1810*, vol. 5, pp. 78–81.

[4] Total 'territorial charges' (including interest on debts) rose from slightly more than £7,000,000 in 1792/93 to more than £15,500,000 in 1808/09. Outlays for military purposes accounted for about 50 per cent of the total charges in 1792/93 and for roughly 47 per cent in 1808/09. (*Parliamentary Papers, 1810*, vol. 5, pp. 78–89.)

the post of Governor-General in India, the Directors of the East India Company successfully blocked his appointment.

When setting out his reasons for producing his pamphlet of 1809, Lauderdale confessed to a sense of shame when he had been called upon to vote in the House of Lords on an appropriation of £1·5 million for the East India Company. His command of the facts pertinent to an intelligent judgement was inadequate. The embarrassment of his position, he added, was heightened by 'a feeling to which he was, perhaps, more sensibly alive, from the recollection that he had been selected, by the partiality of one who is no more, to fill the first situation in the management of the East India Company's affairs'.[5]

I. A REVISED INTERPRETATION OF THE RELATIONSHIP BETWEEN GOVERNANCE AND COMMERCE

Enlargement of the Company's 'estate' in India had generated a fresh paradox. On the one hand, as Lauderdale observed, the public had been led to believe in 'the prosperity and increasing wealth of the Company's possessions . . .'[6] Yet these confident claims did not test well against the evidence. Expansion in the British dominion in the East had not been accompanied by a corresponding expansion in British exports to India. On the contrary, the export traffic had stagnated. As Lauderdale noted: 'That such prosperity, and so great an increase in wealth as was loudly boasted of, should take place, without producing any extension of commercial transactions, appeared to our merchants and manufacturers repugnant to what experience had taught them to regard as the certain consequence of growing opulence . . .'[7]

To students of Smith, there was an obvious explanation for this phenomenon: the persistence of monopoly elements in the trading arrangements necessarily restricted growth in trade. The outcome would have been far different had the commerce been open. Lauderdale, though no apologist for monopoly, regarded this view as much too facile. Indeed, he argued, that 'the regulation of monopoly, nay, even its extinction, could not . . . produce the salutary effect of opening the vent for the produce of our industry, so much desired by our manufacturers.'[8]

---

[5] *An Inquiry into the Practical Merits of the System for the Government of India under the Superintendence of the Board of Controul* (Edinburgh, 1809), p. vi.
[6] Ibid., p. 124.   [7] Ibid., p. 125.   [8] Ibid., p. 133.

If commercial monopoly was not the primary problem, what was the source of the difficulty? In Lauderdale's judgement, the structure of the system controlled by the East India Company precluded the possibility of a beneficial commerce with India. In fact, the system was no longer commercial at all in the normal sense of the term. A revolutionary change in the commerce had occurred, he contended, when the Company added the function of tax collector to that of a merchant. Command over the territorial revenues 'at once furnished means of supplying the British market with Indian produce, independent of all export from Europe, far beyond what the stock of the Company, acting as merchants, could antecedently command . . .'[9]

Spokesmen for the Company could readily agree that access to the territorial revenues had provided local resources for the procurement of the 'investment'. There was thus no quarrel with a finding that the techniques of the commerce had changed. The official view maintained, however, that trade and sovereignty were inseparably linked and that the working capital generated through the Indian tax system necessarily widened the scope for commerce. Lauderdale, on the other hand, insisted that the amalgamation of these functions had foreclosed the possibilities for a normal trade. In his words: 'our intercourse with the East evidently ceased to partake of the nature and character of commerce. There was no exchange of commodities; nothing was given by this country in return for what it annually took away.'[10] And again: 'for a country from which all was taken, and to which nothing was returned, could not partake of those desires originating from the possession of surplus wealth, which could give birth to a demand for foreign commodities.'[11] This indictment gave a new twist to some familiar themes. Whereas the case of the East India Company rested on the proposition that sovereignty advanced commerce, Lauderdale argued that sovereignty had destroyed it.

In this reading of the situation, purchasing power which might otherwise have been allocated by Indians to the acquisition of British exports was sucked up into the tax system and thereafter converted into a form suitable for shipment to Europe. So

[9] *An Inquiry into the Practical Merits of the System for the Government of India under the Superintendence of the Board of Controul* (Edinburgh, 1809), p. 135.
[10] Ibid., p. 137.   [11] Ibid., p. 138.

long as such a state of affairs persisted, Lauderdale held that it
would be idle to expect any substantial demand for foreign goods
to be forthcoming from Indian consumers. The structure of the
system was responsible for the observed outcome, rather than
the climatic or institutional constraints invoked by other commentators to account for the sluggish demand for British goods.
Lauderdale challenged this component of the official view head-
on. The result, he maintained, was 'falsely attributed to the
climate of India, and the religion and the manners of its inhabitants; for there is no country, however opulent, in any climate,
whatever may be the religion and manners of its inhabitants,
that can long continue to have a demand for foreign commodities,
if its surplus wealth, accumulated in the shape of tribute or
savings, by those not permanently resident in the country, is
annually exported.'[12]

A further perplexity could now be resolved. Private British
traders had not rushed to absorb the shipping space allocated to
them by the legislation of 1793 with goods for sale in the East.
But while space on the outward voyages went unfilled, demand
for tonnage to convey Indian goods to Europe could not be
satisfied. Serious consideration was given to the use of Indian-
built ships to enlarge the traffic from East to West.[13] This
asymmetry was a puzzle to some of the enthusiasts for a more
open trade, but it was no mystery to Lauderdale. No other outcome should reasonably have been expected. The Company's use
of the territorial revenues of India as commercial capital necessarily restricted the demand for imports and augmented the
supply of exports. What needed to be explained was how this
truth had been obscured. Lauderdale advanced the following
suggestions: 'By a strange perversion of reasoning, . . . the extent
of the Company's investment, a sure barometer for ascertaining
its success in impoverishing India, was held out as the measure
by which the wealth and prosperity of our settlements was to be
estimated; and pompous descriptions of the flourishing state of
our possessions, grounded on documents from which in reason
we ought to have inferred the progress of calamity, dazzled and
delighted the multitude, who, always disposed to give credit to a

[12] Ibid., p. 159.
[13] Discussion of this possibility was prompted by rising fears of shortage in England
of timbers suitable for ship construction. Despite this concern, the Company did not
act on proposals that it encourage shipbuilding in India.

result that flatters their hopes, never thought of disputing the truth of reasoning they would have been sorry to see refuted.'[14] The East India Company was thus charged with practising deceit on an audience which was eager to be deceived.

II. RAMIFICATIONS OF THE OFFICIAL STRATEGY FOR THE BRITISH ECONOMY

To Lauderdale, it was virtually self-evident that the system organized by the East India Company had an 'obvious tendency . . . to inflict irretrievable ruin' on India.[15] But it also had serious implications for the British economy. Concern was not confined to the prospects for British exports to India. The problem was both broader and more serious. In Lauderdale's diagnosis, the intercourse between India and England—'with the exception of the necessaries or luxuries which the Company's servants may require'—was 'as at present managed, a trade of pure remittance . . .'[16] Its main purpose was to transfer funds from local Indian currencies into sterling. So long as this objective remained paramount, normal commercial considerations of profit and loss were largely matters of indifference. As Lauderdale described the situation: 'it was the amount of the tribute that could be collected, and of the fortunes the Company's servants wished to remit, and no consideration of the state of our European markets, that decided the quantity of exports from India . . .'[17]

The system, as Lauderdale saw it, was thus constructed primarily as an international transfer mechanism, rather than as a trading network. The Company needed to acquire sterling to cover the 'home charges' (in particular, payments of dividends and interest on debt held in England). In addition, sterling was required to settle the bills on London which had been issued to its creditors in India (many of whom were Company servants who wished to repatriate fortunes acquired abroad). The main function of trade was to acquire the sterling needed for these purposes. While the Company naturally preferred to dispose of goods procured through its 'investment' in India and China goods at higher prices rather than lower ones, the price itself was

[14] *An Inquiry into the Practical Merits of the System for the Government of India under the Superintendence of the Board of Controul* (Edinburgh, 1809), pp. 140–1.
[15] Ibid., p. 139.   [16] Ibid., p. 163.   [17] Ibid., p. 137.

less important than the form in which sales proceeds could be
realized. Normal considerations of profit and loss were thus secon-
dary to considerations of international finance. Lauderdale concluded from his inspection of the system that no one should be surprised when the Company reported losses on commercial account.
Its very structure made such an outcome virtually inevitable.

But this was not the end of the story. An international trading
network organized to facilitate financial transfers was a mixed
blessing to the country receiving the tribute. Indeed a buoyant
remittance trade and growth in home manufacturing in rival
commodity lines were fundamentally 'incompatible'.[18] Those
primarily concerned with commodity trade for the purpose of
transferring funds internationally could readily undercut their
competitors. When pressed for funds in Europe, the Company
could be expected to resort to a strategy of 'dumping'.

Lauderdale's approach to the consequences for England of the
Indian tribute system bears a striking parallel to an analysis of a
similar problem offered more than a century later. Keynes's
treatment of reparations payments by Germany, called for by
the Versailles Treaty, is an argument of the same genre. Like
Lauderdale, he feared the impact of unrequited transfers on
levels of income and employment in the recipient country. The
mechanisms through which dislocation would be transmitted to
the home economy were not, however, discussed in the same
terms. Keynes's analysis focused primarily on the adjustments
in foreign exchange rates which would be required to permit a
country to absorb the import surplus necessary to effect the
transfer.[19] This aspect of the matter did not enter directly into
Lauderdale's treatment of the transfer problem. His attention
was directed instead to the confrontation between home products
and Indian-made goods which could be sold below their cost in
the English market. In the world Lauderdale observed, the
sterling–rupee exchange rate was effectively pegged by the Company's practice in selling its bills for rupees on the understanding
that they would be redeemed in stipulated sums in sterling. The
burden of adjustment to the transfer mechanism thus fell directly
on the prices of goods without the intermediation of changes in
foreign exchange rates.

[18] Ibid., p. 173.
[19] See Keynes, *The Economic Consequences of the Peace* (London, 1919).

BETI—F

III. THE IMPLICATIONS FOR ECONOMIC POLICY

Indictments of the East India trade on the grounds that it was detrimental to producer interests in England had, of course, been heard before. In the seventeenth century, the weavers had insisted passionately that trade with the East was 'inconsistent' with the growth of manufacturing at home. The remedies they sought called for a prohibition of further imports of finished Indian textiles into the home market.

Lauderale had absorbed too much *laissez-faire* doctrine for this solution to be attractive. In his pamphlet of 1809, he quoted approvingly from the bold statement of free trade produced by the author of *Considerations upon the East-India Trade* in 1701.[20] Moreover, he was well aware that an important change in England's economic structure had transpired since the days when protectionist polemics had first flourished. By the early nineteenth century, mechanized manufacture of cotton textiles in England had come of age. The product of Lancashire had been developed to the point that it could be offered to the English consumer at prices below the costs of textiles supplied from India. He noted that 'to those who have attended to the great improvement of our cotton manufactures, and marked the preference, that taste in pattern, as well as diminution of price, has secured to them, it must be a matter of doubt, whether if, by economic arrangement abroad, the Company should again acquire a surplus revenue, it can be remitted in India goods, even if conveyed in India built ships, without great loss.'[21] So long as the Company was prepared to accept heavy commercial losses to facilitate remittances, a threat to the prosperity of English industry remained. Dumping of Indian textiles, however, was not in the long-term interests of any of the parties involved.

The outcome, in Lauderdale's judgement, would be much happier if a fundamental reorientation of the trading pattern between East and West could be accomplished. A basic incompatibility would remain, he asserted, 'unless the industry of India is diverted into some new channel, in which it may be instrumental in producing such raw materials as our climate cannot furnish, and thus aid and assist the prosperity of our

[20] *An Inquiry into the Practical Merits of the System for the Government of India under the Superintendence of the Board of Controul (Edinburgh, 1809)*, pp. 169–70.
[21] Ibid., p. 170.

manufactures, which must otherwise suffer from the rivalship of
a remittance trade; always ruinous to those, the produce of
whose industry enters into competition with it, because its extent
is neither bounded by the demand for the goods it conveys, nor
by the loss it occasions to the adventurers on whose account it is
conducted.'[22] In short, the times required a new international
division of labour. India's primary role should be redefined as
one of supplying raw materials for British industry. Raw cotton
was an obvious candidate for this assignment.[23]

Change in this direction could dispose of one of the problems
arising from the merger of commerce with governance. But a
difficulty remained. So long as the Company drained it of purchasing power, India could not be expected to offer a lively
market for British exports. In his *Inquiry* of 1809, Lauderdale
stopped short of recommending that the British involvement in
the governance of India be terminated. The idea, however, had
crossed his mind. In his private correspondence at that time, he
deplored the restrictions imposed by the Company on permanent
European settlement in India. Without a body of colonists who
could be trusted with the 'defence of your dominions', he was
'convinced that you had much better relinquish the possession'.[24]
Otherwise the human costs of maintaining a governing role were
unacceptable.[25] His public comments, however, were more
cautious—and directed primarily to those modifications in the
commodity composition of the trade which could minimize the
contradictions between commerce and sovereignty.

IV. LAUDERDALE'S MESSAGE AND ITS AUDIENCE

Lauderdale's analysis of the trade and payments pattern had
added a dimension to the discussion of Indian economic problems.

[22] Ibid., pp. 173–4.

[23] Though shipments of raw cotton from India had expanded considerably in the
late eighteenth century, the Southern states of America were the predominant suppliers of Britain's textile mills. This source of supply, however, was vulnerable to
international frictions. Those which erupted into the War of 1812 were already visible
in 1809.

[24] Letter of Lauderdale to Grey, 2 January 1809. I am indebted to Professor Bernard
Corry for this information.

[25] Lauderdale calculated that 5,000 Europeans (one-fifth of whom died every year)
were engaged in military activities in India and added: 'It is not to be borne that there
should exist such an expenditure of human life for such a purpose ...' (Letter of
Lauderdale to Grey, 2 January 1809.)

One of its clear implications was that sovereignty was destructive to commerce. Not only was India being bled; the future prosperity of some sectors of British industry was also in jeopardy. Regulation of the East India Company by a Parliamentary Board of Control could not address the fundamental problem. The system was intellectually as well as financially bankrupt.

This was heterodox doctrine indeed. Yet it passed virtually without notice. In a notable departure from its usual treatment of hostile tracts, the East India Company did not bother to sponsor a rebuttal. Only one significant journal of the day took note of Lauderdale's pamphlet. The reviewer, however, missed the central point. No comment was offered on his diagnosis of a 'remittance trade'; instead, the reviewer rehearsed the familiar arguments invoked to explain the failure of trade with the East to expand dramatically.[26]

Why should Lauderdale's argument have been so largely ignored? In his case, part of the answer must lie in his general reputation for irascibility. As the *Edinburgh Review* alluded to the assessment of contemporaries: 'With all his industry . . . and all his talents, his adversaries have sometimes imputed to Lord Lauderdale a degree of rashness and violence, which would make him an unsafe guide in questions of great political importance; and even his friends have acknowledged, that his zeal has sometimes been at least a match for his discretion, and that the views which his sagacity has opened, have sometimes taken a little colouring from his prejudices or his passions.'[27]

Lauderdale was undoubtedly a passionate polemicist who won more enemies than friends. It is not difficult to understand why some of his contemporaries had little faith in his judgement. There were reasonable grounds on which to question his personal stability; he was known to have defended his honour on the duelling field (Benedict Arnold was an opponent in 1791 in an engagement from which both emerged unscathed). Nor was his record on public issues one which could reliably inspire confidence

[26] In connection with the lack of demand for English exports, for example, the reviewer observed: 'To lament that they have no taste for objects which afford us great gratification, is to lament that they are Hindus. But really, whilst the climate continues what it is, and whilst their domestic habits remain unaltered, the sale of broadcloth and hardware must unavoidably be extremely limited.' ('Lord Lauderdale on Indian Affairs', *Edinburgh Review* (January 1810), p. 267.)

[27] Ibid., p. 256.

in his intellectual integrity. In the 1780s and 1790s, he champ-
ioned radical causes and was a founder of 'The Friends of the
People'. In later life, he had become a vigorous opponent of the
reform bills which would widen the franchise.

Yet these factors were insufficient to account for the lack of
impact of Lauderdale's message. Perhaps more important was
the new orthodoxy among critics of the Company. The terms of
debate had been captured by Adam Smith. Those who relied on
his teaching were persuaded that persistence of commercial
monopoly was the fundamental problem. All that was needed to
bring prosperity to the Indian commerce was freedom of trade
and freedom of entry to India for European settlers. Those whose
views were moulded by this conviction had little patience with
doctrines which did not regard monopoly as the basic source of
difficulties.

While Lauderdale's critique left little mark on the thought of
his time, other factors pressed the trade relationship between
Britain and India in a direction suggested by part of his analysis.
The calls of British textile interests to convert India into a
supplier of raw materials (especially raw cotton) became more
insistent with rising uncertainties about the dependability of the
American South as a cotton supplier. While the burdens of
adjustment on Britain as a recipient of remittances could thus
be relieved, those on India as the supplier would remain. This
was a far cry from an earlier approach to the reconciliation of
conflicts between sovereignty and trade through policy intervention. In the doctrine Steuart had enunciated in 1772, the task
should be addressed through policies which held the interests of
subject peoples to be paramount.

CHAPTER 8

New Premisses for an Official Model of Governance: the Early Career of James Mill

THE case presented by the Company in 1793 had attempted to demonstrate the interdependence of commerce and governance. The subsequent flow of events—much more than the arguments of the critics—had destroyed the credibility of the propositions which had then been advanced. The Company was deep in deficits on both its political and commercial accounts. Meanwhile the lobbies against the Company's monopoly had gained new recruits. The case for excluding private English traders from the Eastern commerce had lost some of its persuasive power now that American merchants (no longer subject to British jurisdiction) competed freely and successfully with the Company in that sphere of operations. At the same time, a reversal of roles was underway at home. The textile manufacturers of England—who as recently as the late 1780s had supported strict controls over the East India commerce—had begun to shift their position. With a self-confidence supplied by power-driven looms, English textile producers joined the classical economists in championing the cause of free trade in the debates preceding the renewal of the charter in 1813.

The problem of the Indian commerce could apparently be solved by terminating the East India Company's monopoly, but the problem of governance remained. What rationale could be offered for government supplied by a private company which, despite the creation of a Parliamentary Board of Control, still had considerable scope for discretionary action? New arguments were needed—and they were to be supplied by one of the most vigorous critics of the Company's commercial monopoly.

The major contributor to this stream of thought about Indian problems was a man whose upbringing would seem to have made him an unlikely candidate for this assignment. The boyhood of James Mill (1773–1836) in the modest household of a Scottish shoemaker certainly afforded him no opportunity to develop an interest in Indian affairs. Nor were his studies at Edinburgh

University, which he attended through the sponsorship of a local aristocrat for whom he was later to name his eldest son, likely to have inclined him in that direction. As a student, he pursued a classical curriculum as a candidate for the clergy. He left the University of Edinburgh in 1797 with a qualification to preach, but his career as a minister was short-lived. Five years later, he abandoned his calling and set off for London. Later he was to acknowledge that his sceptical turn of mind had led him to disqualify himself from the career originally charted for him.[1]

Mill sought to support himself as a freelance journalist and was soon appointed to the editorship of two small journals. In this capacity he contributed reviews and commentaries on public issues. In 1806, however, he identified a subject—the study of British India—which was to engage much of his energy for the remainder of his life. He then embarked upon a history with the expectation that he could complete it in three years. In fact, this programme absorbed the next twelve. Though he contributed numerous essays on Indian subjects to the reviews during this span of time, his financial circumstances were still severely strained. More than once during the preparation of the massive *History of British India*, Mill was obliged to rely on his friends to sustain himself and his family. Jeremy Bentham—whom Mill met in 1808—came to his aid at a crucial stage by providing housing at a subsidized rental and Francis Place proved to be a reliable source of loans.[2]

What, it may be asked, had the study of India to recommend it to the attention of a young man with uncertain prospects, but with a radical turn of mind? In part, Mill's engagement with this issue reflected a genuine intellectual curiosity about a part of the world which was imperfectly understood. But it was not simply an urge to fill gaps in the stock of knowledge which inspired this enterprise. Mill had already been caught up in the movements of philosophical radicalism and Benthamite utilitarianism and had acquired a confidence—which bordered on arrogance—that these doctrines could yield a scientific design for improvement in the human condition. One did not, of course,

[1] See Mill's letter to Ricardo of 3 December 1817 as printed in *The Works and Correspondence of David Ricardo*, ed. P. Sraffa (Cambridge, 1952), vol. 7, pp. 212–13.

[2] For details on Mill's life, see Alexander Bain, *James Mill: a Biography* (London, 1882), and the introductory essay by Donald Winch in *James Mill: Selected Economic Writings*, ed. Winch, (London, 1966).

need to look to India to find important social problems which could be illuminated by the new scientific method. Ample material was available closer to home. The atmosphere of the Napoleonic Wars did not, however, offer a hospitable climate for anti-establishment views. The East India Company, on the other hand, was a safe target. It was closely enough tied to the establishment to be eligible for a radical critique, and it also had enough long-standing enemies at home to insure immunity for the critic.[3]

It was against this intellectual backdrop that Mill set out to produce a 'judging history'. He did so without any first-hand acquaintance with India or any knowledge of its languages. Indeed, he proclaimed that his innocence of direct experience of conditions in India was a recommendation for his task. His judgements would be spared the distortions 'excited by those impulses, called partial impressions'.[4] He added that 'a man who is duly qualified may obtain more knowledge of India, in one year, in his closet in England, than he could obtain during the course of the longest life, by the use of his eyes and his ears in India.'[5] The essential qualification for the historian of British India was 'a most profound knowledge of the laws of human nature', of the 'principles of human society', and a comprehension of the 'practical play of machinery of government'.[6] These insights could be acquired only in Europe.[7]

I. THE CONDITION OF INDIAN SOCIETY AND ITS IMPLICATIONS FOR GOVERNANCE

The greater part of the first volume of Mill's *History of British India* was devoted to a massive assault on what he regarded to be the 'rude' and decadent state of Hindu civilization. His criticisms were harsh and unstinting, but he held them to be therapeutic. Europeans, for far too long, had been bemused by a myth of an opulent culture and a rich civilization in India. As a result, much intellectual energy had been wasted in a misguided search for an explanation of India's decline.

From Mill's perspective, such inquiries had pursued a false

[3] On this point, see Duncan Forbes, 'James Mill and India', *The Cambridge Journal* (October 1951).

[4] James Mill, *The History of British India* (London, 1817), vol. 1, p. xv.

[5] Ibid., vol. 1, p. xv.   [6] Ibid., vol. 1, p. xix.

[7] As Mill put it: 'It will not, I presume, admit of much dispute, that the habits which are subservient to the successful exploration of evidence are more likely to be acquired in Europe, than in India.' (Ibid., vol. 1, p. xiv.)

question. Hindu society at its peak had managed to rise only a short distance above the level of barbarism. It was thus unnecessary to speculate about the causes of deterioration and decay. The reality was quite different: Indian economic life had been a prolonged chapter, centuries in length, of uninterrupted stagnation. Banishment of European misperceptions was a matter of high practical as well as intellectual importance. In Mill's words: 'If the mistake in regard to Hindu society, committed by the British nation, and the British government, be very great; if they have conceived the Hindus to be a people of high civilization, while they have in reality made but a few of the earliest steps in the progress of high civilization, it is impossible that in many of the measures pursued for the government of that people, the mark aimed at should not have been wrong.'[8]

Wherever he turned his eye, Mill found Hindu society to be wanting. He was prepared to accept that India had enjoyed great advantages in soil and climate and that at some point in time her people had been less depressed than the barbarians of Europe. He was willing to allow that 'perhaps they acquired the first rude form of national polity at fully as early a period as any portion of the race.'[9] But Hindu society and its institutions seemed thereafter to have been frozen. He concluded that 'from the stationary condition in which their institutions first, and then their manners and character, have a tendency to fix them, it is no unreasonable supposition that they have presented a very uniform appearance from the visit of the Greeks to that of the English.'[10] On virtually all counts, the system had failed to rise above a mean and degrading level. Its government was based on an 'uncontrollable sway of superstition' and in the system of laws the 'most essential and obvious distinctions are neglected and confounded'.[11]

Even activities in which India excelled were regarded by Mill as evidence of an inferior form of social organization. He was little impressed, for example, by the high skill of the Hindus in weaving. The development of this craft, he maintained, flowed easily from a resource endowment capable of producing the world's finest cotton. Nor was it remarkable that the Hindu should find weaving congenial. This craft, he observed, was a sedentary occupation and 'thus in harmony with his predominant

8 Ibid., vol. 1, p. 429.
10 Ibid., vol. 1, p. 101.
9 Ibid., vol. 1, p. 104.
11 Ibid., vol. 1, p. 131.

inclination'; moreover, the skill called for little bodily exertion, 'of which he is always exceedingly sparing, and the finer the production, the more slender the force which he is called upon to apply'.[12] Mill also rejected the claim that the invention of the game of chess by Hindus was evidence of a high civilization. On the contrary, 'the invention of ingenious games', Mill maintained, 'is a feat most commonly displayed by nations in their rude condition. It is prior to the birth of industry, that men have the strongest need for games, to relieve them from the pain of idleness . . .'[13] His over-all judgement was that 'the progress of knowledge, and the force of observation, demonstrated the actual state of the Hindus as little removed from that of half-civilized nations.'[14]

This reading of traditional Hindu society gave a different twist to a long-standing problem. If Mill's account were to be accepted as accurate, why then had so many European intellectuals been deluded? Mill suggested that several factors had contributed to this massive misunderstanding. Much of the blame fell on the shoulders of European writers of the 'Orientalist' school who were the amateur anthropologists of that day. Mill indicted them for gullibility in crediting the reports of the Brahmins of an earlier golden age. Their legends, Mill asserted, testified not to the existence of a high civilization at an earlier moment in time, but rather to the reverse. 'All rude nations', he wrote, 'have pretensions to high antiquity.'[15] The tales which Europeans had so readily absorbed were, in fact, 'the offspring of a wild and ungoverned imagination' which bore 'the strongest marks of a rude and credulous people, whom the marvellous delights . . .'[16] There were, he added, no historical records to document such claims.[17]

Mill suspected also that the image of Indian glory which had so forcefully impressed itself on European minds was, in part, a by-product of exaggerated tales of the riches appropriated by early conquerors, dating back to the first Mohammedan ones. These reports, he asserted, concealed the fundamental truth: 'a state of poverty and wretchedness, as far as the great body of

[12] James Mill, *The History of British India* (London, 1817) vol. 1, p. 342.
[13] Ibid., vol. 1, p. 360.   [14] Ibid., vol. 1, p. 436.
[15] Ibid., vol. 1, p. 91.   [16] Ibid., vol. 1, p. 98.
[17] Mill's principal target for these criticisms was the 'Orientalist' tradition promoted by Sir William Jones who had pioneered Sanskrit studies and founded the Bengal Asiatic Society. For background on this tradition, see S. N. Mukherjee, *Sir William Jones: a Study in Eighteenth-Century British Attitudes to India* (Cambridge, 1968).

people are concerned . . .'[18] Precious metals may have been pro-
fusely displayed, but this was evidence, not of wealth, but of a
scarcity which could gratify an authoritarian monarch. Misjudgements of the reality had also been encouraged by the East
India Company and its officials. Mill held that the 'most pernicious perhaps' of Clive's errors had been 'the belief which he
created, that India overflowed with riches'.[19]

No less serious was a distorted view of India which had been
constructed by Europeans to serve European intellectual needs.
For some, Mill maintained, a laudatory view of past Indian
achievements conveniently buttressed charges of insensitivity
and rapacity on the part of the East India Company. Others,
however, had embraced certain Indian claims as weapons against
the Catholic establishment in Europe. Voltaire's praise of Hindu
achievements in astronomy, for example, was 'actuated by an
abhorrence of the evils which [he] saw attached to Catholicism'.[20]
In the context of French anti-clericalism in the eighteenth century, Hindu astronomy was opportune as a challenge to Old
Testament chronology. All of these interpretations, in Mill's
view, had proceeded from a false premiss.

II. THE ACCOUNT OF STAGNATION IN THE INDIAN ECONOMY

Within this interpretative framework, the economic stagnation
of traditional India was no mystery. The behaviour of the East
India Company may have aggravated a distressing situation, but
it could not be held responsible for the basic difficulties. The
problem was rooted in the deficiencies of traditional society.

Indeed, in the light of the crudeness of Hindu civilization, the
intervention of outsiders was not necessarily unfortunate. The
Mohammedan conquerors had brought distinct advance in social
and economic structure to the Indian sub-continent. Muslim
culture, though well below the European in Mill's hierarchy of
civilizations, was still superior to that of the Hindus. The Muslim
tradition was exempt from a caste system which Mill regarded as
'that institution which stands a more effectual barrier against
the good of human nature than any other institution which the
workings of caprice and of selfishness have ever produced'.[21] In

---

[18] Ibid., vol. 1, p. 463.   [19] Ibid., vol. 2, p. 260.   [20] Ibid., vol. 1, p. 395.
[21] Ibid., vol. 1, p. 628.

addition, Muslim government and administration had generally been organized around reasonably rational principles.

Even so, day-to-day economic life in the Indian sub-continent was still predominantly Hindu. From such a weak base, little significant economic achievement could have been expected. Mill described its basic industry—agriculture—as follows: 'Nothing exceeds the rudeness and inefficiency of the Hindu implements of agriculture.'[22] He added: 'The most irrational practice that ever found existence in the agriculture of any nation is general in India . . .'[23] The only agricultural improvement of note was in irrigation and most of that work had been organized by Muslim rulers.

The disappointing level of economic performance in the Indian sub-continent could not, Mill insisted, be explained by deficiencies in the resource base. Nature had indeed endowed the area comfortably. Yet 'even in the richest parts of India', he maintained, 'one half of the soil [had] never been under cultivation.'[24]

How could such inexcusable waste be explained? Much of the blame could be assigned to the misgovernment of pre-British India. Hindu rulers, in particular, were seen as recognizing only one restraint on their revenue demands: 'the non-existence of anything further to take'.[24] As a result, 'cultivators were left a bare compensation, often not so much as a bare compensation, for the labour and cost of cultivation: they got the benefit of their labour; all the benefit of the land went to the King.'[26]

Such a system erected formidable barriers to economic improvement. It suppressed extension in the cultivated area, kept down the size of the population, and blunted incentives to productive work. It was not surprising that the individual cultivator lacked economic motivation for he was in 'subjection to a rigid government under which the fruits of labour were never secure'.[27]

Mill was not opposed to the taxation of agricultural income. The preponderant weight of agriculture in the economic life of the sub-continent would oblige any government to draw heavily on this sector for revenue. His criticism was instead addressed to arrangements in which the sovereign claimed not a stipulated sum but a proportion of the total output. Adam Smith, it will be

[22] James Mill, The History of British India (London, 1817) vol. 1, p. 346.
[23] Ibid., vol. 1, p. 348.   [24] Ibid., vol. 1, p. 191.   [25] Ibid., vol. 1, p. 191.
[26] Ibid., vol. 1, p. 186.   [27] Ibid., vol. 1, p. 314.

recalled, had applauded the traditional scheme (as he understood it) for its capacity to build a community of interest between the ruler and the ruled. Mill, on the other hand, attacked it on the grounds that the amount of the tax obligation was uncertain, that a host of tax-collectors was required, and that opportunities for corruption were maximized. He further noted that a tax system based on a proportion of the gross product produced unequal burdens: the cultivator of poor-quality land would bear its weight much more heavily than would the cultivator of superior soils. But these were not the only unfortunate consequences of a crop-share system of taxation. Mill maintained that it would also tend to increase agricultural prices because 'whatever is the amount of tax raised from the poorest of the cultivated land, the price must be sufficient to afford that tax over and above the expense of cultivation'.[28] Owners of the best soil would thus be enriched at the expense of the rest of the community.

At this stage in the discussion, Mill did not mention explicitly the concept of differential rent recently formulated by Ricardo and by Malthus. This analytic innovation was being offered to the world at about the time Mill's *History* went to press. His treatment of the inadequacies of the proportional tax on agricultural production reflected, however, an understanding of its significance. His friendship with Ricardo (a relationship in which Mill acted as an editor of Ricardo's work) had given him an early exposure to the theory of differential rent. The influence of this doctrine was latent in the structure of Mill's discussion of Indian agriculture, though its full significance was to emerge only later.

Mill's reading of India's past produced a sharp shift in thought about the tasks of the present and future. The main responsibility for the miserable state of Indian economic life fell squarely on indigenous society and its institutions. The blame could not be transferred to foreigners. On the contrary, India might well look to the example of foreigners for its economic salvation.

III. THE PROBLEM OF COMMERCIAL MONOPOLY

Though Mill tracked the roots of India's misery to circumstances which antedated British contact with the sub-continent, there was little hope for basic improvement so long as the

[28] Ibid., vol. 1, p. 196.

Company's commercial monopoly remained. His treatment of this aspect of the problem followed the path already charted by Smith. Freedom of trade, he maintained, would stimulate growth in England's export commerce. It was not remarkable that 'the careless ignorance of a chartered Company' should have failed to adapt export lines to 'the taste and accommodation of the people of Asia'. On the other hand, 'it would, indeed, be a matter of astonishment, if the acuteness and ardour of private adventurers should not find means of producing commodities to the taste of every people in the world who have enough to give for them.'[29]

Free entry into the trade would harness India's productive potential more effectively and would stimulate healthy expansion in her exports. By contrast with monopoly which shielded the inefficient and unimaginative, unrestricted markets were creative instruments for change which benefited all participants. Fears that India might suffer if not sheltered from the power-driven textile industry of England were groundless. An open competition in the commerce would yield a happy outcome. As Mill put it, 'the productive powers of the soil and trade of India are not limited to one sort of fabric; and fifty new articles, we doubt not, could be produced, were the vivifying powers of individual enterprise, and of augmenting capital, to be allowed their free operation . . . The fact is . . . that, under the cheap freight, the expedition and economy of private trade, all the more valuable productions of the soil—not to speak of the arts actual or possible of India—might be brought to Europe with a profit.'[30] Nor was confidence in this conclusion shaken by the failure of private British traders to use fully the space allocated to them on the Company's ships by the legislation of 1793. Mill maintained that this experiment had proved only that the East India Company's freight charges had been excessive and that its sailing schedules were too unreliable.

The most serious shortcoming of the East India monopoly, however, hinged precisely on a point which directors of the Company had insisted was crucial to the maintenance of sovereignty. It had been a long-standing practice of the Company to block permanent European settlement in India and, indeed, to deter even the temporary residence of Englishmen who were not

[29] 'East Indian Monopoly', *Edinburgh Review* (November 1812), p. 476.
[30] Ibid., p. 475.

officially associated with the Company. The rationale offered for this policy rested primarily on political arguments. Freedom of European settlement in India would, it was asserted, open the doors to an unscrupulous rabble who would exploit the native population mercilessly and shatter the allegedly high repute of the small but select European community in India. Not only would seeds of dissension be sowed among the local peoples; it was also to be expected that a sizeable settler population would soon imitate Americans by demanding governing power in their own right. This line of argument reflected, of course, the aristocratic bias of the first generation of rulers of British India. In this period, emigration to North America provided an outlet for the restless energies of one class of Englishman. A career in India provided a similar outlet for quite a different class.

At this stage in his career, Mill had no patience with this doctrine. He insisted that the larger the European population in India, the better conditions would be for all—and not least for the native peoples. 'The pace of civilization', he wrote, 'would be quickened beyond all example. The arts, the knowledge, and the manners of Europe would be brought to their doors, and forced by an irresistible moral pressure on their acceptance. The happiness of the human race would be thus prodigiously augmented . . .'[31] But the civilizing influence of European colonists would not be possible on any scale 'so long as the Company trade themselves', for 'it must be their interest to discourage all other traders . . . This is an evil of great magnitude. We see no remedy for it, but one; and that is, that the Company should altogether cease to be traders, and content themselves with the revenues. This would every way be a great improvement.'[32] In short, the Company should not only lose its commercial monopoly, but should close out its trading activities completely. The energies of its officials could then be concentrated on the business of government. No longer distracted by 'the details of a multifarious trade, they would govern better . . .'[33]

IV. TRADE, TRIBUTE, AND GOVERNANCE

Mill's remedy for the evils of commercial monopoly called for a sharp separation of trade from governance and for the total

[31] 'Bruce's Report on the East-India Negotiation', *Monthly Review* (1813), p. 30.
[32] 'East Indian Monopoly', *Edinburgh Review* (November 1812), p. 490.
[33] Ibid., p. 491

transfer of commerce to private hands. Was such a division of functions likely to be feasible? The authors of the briefs for the Company, it will be recalled, had argued that trade and sovereignty had become inseparably linked. Mill dismissed this position as sheer nonsense. The East India Company had been able to promote it only because 'so little is known about the government, and so credulous are the mass of full-grown children in the nation, that the Company may assert anything which they please about the government of India, and will find a ready belief'.[34] Trade, after all, had been successfully conducted before a territorial revenue had been available to finance the 'investment'. In any event, the recent history of the Company had demonstrated that there were no surplus revenues for this purpose. The capital required for the trade could be provided much more satisfactorily by private individuals.[35]

But a question remained. If the East India Company were henceforth to specialize in governance, would not a remittance problem persist? Even if the working capital for commerce were no longer to be drawn from the territorial revenues, the Indian economy would remain under pressure to finance remittances. Much of the cost of government supplied from abroad required settlement in sterling. At least one of the features of a structure which Lauderdale had diagnosed as 'ruinous' would be intact. Part of proceeds of the Indian revenue system would still need to be converted into forms suitable for settling the 'home charges' in England (especially for the servicing of debt, for emoluments to officials, and for the procurement of government stores). Even if government no longer paid for trade, were not transfers still necessary to pay for government?

Mill did not address directly this aspect of Lauderdale's critique.[36] He chose instead to regard the remittance of a 'surplus revenue' from India as an altogether spurious issue. In 1813 he dealt with the matter as follows: 'Now, on the score of surplus revenue,—of any share of the taxes levied on the people of India being ever brought to this country,— if our minds could even

---

[34] 'Bruce's Report on the East-India Negotiation', *Monthly Review* (1813), p. 24.

[35] 'East India Monopoly', *Edinburgh Review* (November 1811), esp. pp. 234–7.

[36] It is clear, however, that he was familiar with Lauderdale's *Inquiry* of 1809. In one of his reviews, Mill cited the Lauderdale essay as the source of a point of fact, though he did not comment on its analytic content. (See 'Affairs of India', *Edinburgh* (April 1810), p. 133.)

reconcile themselves to the justice of it, our experience tells us
that nothing of the sort has ever yet happened; and all that we
know of human affairs combines to assure us, and with a force
of which few assurances can boast, that no such event will ever
come to pass. Neither we nor our posterity shall ever see any
share in the revenues of India brought to this country.'[37]

Mill's confidence in his conclusion rested, in the first instance, on
observation of the Company's mounting deficits since its acquisition of a territorial dominion. Nor—despite the continuing optimism of officials—could he conceive that any fundamental break
from this pattern could occur in the future. Mill asserted that 'the
causes which have prevented any surplus-revenue exist in the
nature of circumstances, which it is not in the power of the Company to alter; and if they were to govern India till the final consum-
mation of all things, they would never have any surplus revenue.'[38]

When he later returned to this theme, he was even more outspoken. It was, he insisted, 'a moral impossibility, that a colony
should ever benefit the mother country, by yielding it a permanent tribute'.[39] Governments everywhere could be expected
to spend all of the revenues they acquired. 'If', Mill asked,
'government of the mother country is sure to spend up to the
resources of the country; and if a still stronger necessity operates
upon the government of the colony to produce this effect, how
can it possibly afford any tribute?'[40] He was aware that an illusion
persisted that 'some how or other, a tribute, or what is equivalent
to a tribute, does come from the East Indies.' But, he contended:
'Never did an opinion exist, more completely without evidence,
contrary to evidence, evidence notorious, and well known to the
persons themselves, by whom the belief is entertained. India,
instead of yielding a tribute to England, has never yielded enough
for the expence of its own government.'[41]

Tribute—and the threat to the conduct of a normal commerce
which Lauderdale insisted that it implied—could thus be excluded from further consideration. Mill did not claim that the
task of governing India could be performed by Englishmen
without some payments in sterling. The issue, however, had been

[37] 'Bruce's Report on The East-India Negotiation', *Monthly Review* (1813), p. 35.
[38] Ibid., p. 26.
[39] The article 'Colony' in the *Encyclopaedia Britannica* (1826), p. 18.
[40] Ibid., p. 18.   [41] Ibid., p. 17.

redefined. These transactions should be regarded as regular purchases of invisible imports. They represented remuneration for services rendered, not unrequited remittances.

V. AN OUTLINE OF THE TASKS AND STRUCTURE OF A GOVERN- MENT FOR INDIA

Mill's indictments of traditional misrule in India and of the commercial monopoly of the East India Company had been harsh and incisive. But his diagnoses also suggested some remedies. The debased condition of the mass of the population in India cried out for uplift. If the fetters of commercial monopoly could be stripped away, the civilizing influence of Englishmen could be harnessed to the general benefit of humanity. Britain had a 'great trust' to discharge.

Though Mill acknowledged that the acquisition of territorial sovereignty by the East India Company may have been 'improvident', it did not follow that the British involvement in India should be terminated. As early as 1810, he took a position against 'abandoning of the people to themselves' and expressed an earnest hope 'for the sake of the natives, that it will not be found necessary to leave them to their own direction'.[42]

How then should a government appropriate to India's condition be structured? Mill contended that two general principles should guide the search for a sound solution. The first began from a recognition of a situational reality: 'that no government for India can be a good government, but a government upon the spot'.[43] It was quite unrealistic to expect intelligent decisions on day-to-day matters of governance to be made by men removed by 'half the circumference of the globe' from the scene of the action. The second general principle was enunciated as follows: 'that no government can be a good government, but that which has an interest, and a paramount interest, in the prosperity of the countries to be governed'.[44]

In principle, these conditions could readily be satisfied if governing authority were placed in the hands of the Indian peoples themselves. For Mill this approach was unthinkable. He dismissed it emphatically when he wrote: 'Is a legislative

[42] 'Affairs of India', *Edinburgh Review* (April 1810), p. 154.
[43] Ibid., p. 155.   [44] Ibid

assembly to be convoked in India? Certainly not. The stage of
civilization, and the moral and political situation in which the
people of India are placed, render the establishment of legislative
assemblies impracticable. They would be productive of nothing
but confusion . . . A simple form of arbitrary government, tem-
pered by European honour and European intelligence, is the only
form which is now fit for Hindustan.'[45]

The maintenance of a British connection did not, of course,
necessarily imply that governance should continue as the responsibility of the East India Company. For several decades many of
its critics had proposed that the government of India should be
transferred to the British state. Mill found no merit in this
suggestion. His position on this matter reflected his deep distrust
of the unreformed parliamentary institution. Parliament, he held,
was a corrupt and unrepresentative body. To place at its disposal
the considerable patronage of India would not only be detrimental to the people of India, it would also tend to weaken the
standards of British public life. Moreover, the type of government
called for in India could not function when subject to 'the
fluctuations of party politics' in Britain.[46] Continuity and expertise were needed in the management of Indian affairs. A
system at the mercy of domestic partisanship would lack the
essential continuity and stability.

As early as 1810 Mill had produced a sketch of an optimal
governing structure for India. Though his design was couched in
rather tentative language, its direction was still clear: 'Instead of
sending out a Governor-General, to be recalled in a few years,
why should we not constitute one of our Royal family Emperor
of Hindustan, with hereditary succession? The sovereign would
then be surrounded by Britons; and the spirit of Britons would
animate and direct his government: Europeans of all descriptions
would be invited to settle in his country, and to identify their
interests with those of the nation. The productive powers of
European industry, under the protecting hand of a British
government on the spot, would soon give new life and new riches
to the state: and the commercial enterprise of Britons would find
a field of boundless extent, every year presenting a more vast
and precious produce, from which to cull for the commercial
aggrandizement of their country.'[47]

[45] Ibid.   [46] 'Malcolm on India', *Edinburgh Review* (July 1812), p. 54.

VI. THE INTERIM SOLUTION TO THE PROBLEM OF GOVERNANCE

The terms of the renewal of the East India Company's Charter in 1813 went at least part of the way toward translating James Mill's objectives into reality. The life of the East India Company was extended for a further twenty years, but its monopoly over the English commerce with India (though not with China) was terminated. Thereafter, the central preoccupation of the Company was with the government of British India. While it could continue to conduct a commerce on its own account, the functions of trader and sovereign in the Indian domain had effectively been divorced.

But another change had transpired which, though subtler, had perhaps a more lasting significance. Largely owing to the work of James Mill, the raw materials for an official rationale for the Company's governance of India had been supplied. The case presented by the Company in 1793 had clearly disintegrated. With its functions now more specialized, the Company needed an intellectual justification—and, if possible, a strategy—for its new primary role. Mill's theory of historical progress, in which the world's cultures were ranked by levels of their achievement, cast an aura of scientific truth on the claim of British superiority and of Indian (and, most particularly, Hindu) inferiority. At the same time, the utilitarian strand of Mill's thought suggested a programme of action. British intervention to enlighten and uplift the backward peoples of the East was elevated to the status of a moral imperative.

With the legislation renewing the Charter in 1813, the debates of the preceding four decades on the relationships between commerce and sovereignty achieved a tentative equilibrium. A new orthodoxy—moulded more by intellectual currents in Europe than by perceptions of the realities of India—had taken command. In less self-confident days Indian affairs had touched the European mind as a supplier of challenging questions. With the ascendency of a new orthodoxy, India was intellectually interesting to the extent that it could be supplied with answers.

47 'Affairs of India', *Edinburgh Review* (April 1810), p. 156.

PART III

Problems of Economic Policy and Administration: 1813–1853

THE parliamentary disposition of the East India problem in 1813 had been a victory for the Company's critics. After assaults which had been conducted for more than two centuries, the Company's exclusive privileges in the trade with India were at last surrendered. The triumph of the free traders was not, however, complete: the monopoly position of the Company in the English trade with China remained intact.

Though redefinition in its jurisdiction had been resisted by the Company before the fact, its opposition to the change of 1813 had not been intense. Only the China wing of the commerce was regarded as a significant source of gain.[1] So long as the territorial revenues of India remained at the disposal of the Company, its overseas commerce could be opened to all comers without great sacrifice. Despite the fact that the Company's position as a sovereign had not generated the outcomes sought in 1793, hope had not been abandoned that the territorial revenues could finance the 'investment', particularly with China.

Even so, a major structural adjustment in the functions of the East India Company had been accomplished. Though the Company was not debarred from commercial activities, its primary role was now the governance of British India. With this step toward specialization, the attention of economic thinkers tended to shift to questions of economic policy and administration. In some quarters, uneasiness lingered about the wisdom of an arrangement that tolerated such a concentration of political power which (though technically under the jurisdiction of a

---

[1] The Company had often reported losses from its export trade to India. Differential results from the Indian and the Chinese wings of the commerce were to continue after the Company's monopoly position in the Indian trade had been terminated. Returns for the period 1820/21 to 1828/29, for example, revealed that the commercial account with India resulted in losses of more than £2,100,000 while the Company's China trade yielded a gain in excess of £9,250,000. (*Parliamentary Papers*, *1831–32*, vol. 10, pt. 1, pp. 42–5.)

Parliamentary Board of Control) was still effectively in private hands. The bulk of articulate British opinion, however, was prepared to accept the solution of 1813 as reasonably workable—or at least as superior to the more obvious alternatives. With commercial monopoly divorced from sovereignty, Britain's connection with India no longer seemed so sinister.

India now presented a fresh challenge to analytic ingenuity. What conceptual categories were appropriate to an enlightened strategy of goverance? What goals should be identified and how best might they be reached? After 1813 it was plain to all that the intellectual framework inherited from the Company's commercial tradition was inapplicable. But what should replace it? James Mill's critique of Indian civilization had supplied arguments to justify continued British intervention in the subcontinent. His early work, however, had been less than specific about the programmes to which it should be committed.

Before these questions were formally debated, officials responsible for day-to-day decisions in the field sensed the need for a conceptual system to guide their interpretation of the realities confronting them. Responsibilities of governance imposed insistent demands and called for judgements with sweeping implications. How, for example, should the tax system be organized? What priorities should be assigned in the allocation of public expenditures? What monetary arrangements could satisfy the dual requirements of convenience in revenue collection and of stimulation to economic expansion? The answers provided by practical men to these questions were frequently innocent of intellectual influences. Nevertheless, they were usually alert to the usefulness of theoretical arguments in providing a rationale for their actions.

In the early decades of the nineteenth century, interest in a fresh strategy was also aroused at the East India Company's headquarters. Both the disappointments of the past and the restructuring of the operational context in the present underscored the importance of new approaches. At the same time, it was increasingly appreciated that the best-conceived plans for India would have little significance unless backed by a competent cadre of administrators. Further questions thus came to the surface. What intellectual equipment should be supplied to the future rulers of British India? How best could it be transmitted?

And how should candidates for these high responsibilities be recruited and selected?

The British political economists who addressed these issues in the first half of the nineteenth century did not speak with one voice on any of them. They shared, however, a basic presupposition: that the British connection should advance the well-being of the Indian people. This attitude contrasted markedly with the one which had been dominant earlier. It was now an article of faith that improvement in the Indian economy should be promoted. Otherwise, the British position in the East would not survive, nor would it deserve to. None would deny that abuses had occurred in the past. But that chapter had been closed. The task of the new era was to make the interests of Britain and India genuinely compatible.

The expressed desire of the administrators of British India to improve the condition of the local peoples was not, of course, purely altruistic. All Englishmen were acutely aware that the weight of numbers was heavily against them. Even by mid-century, only about 50,000 British nationals were resident in India, the overwhelming majority of whom were there in official capacities.[2] The native population in the areas under direct British jurisdiction was estimated at nearly 100 million in 1852 and that of the tributary Native States at more than 52 million.[3]

Other considerations also commended measures to stimulate growth in the Indian economy. Even from the narrowest point of view, the interests of the Company's government were closely linked to economic expansion. The capacity to obtain revenues was dependent on the size of the local tax base. Similarly, the servicing of the Indian debt called for growth in the country's

[2] In 1852 the numbers of European residents in British India 'who were not in the service of the Queen or the East India Company' was recorded as 5,729 males and 4,277 females (exclusive of the wives and families of civil and military servants). No significant settlement of non-official British subjects had occurred in the preceding two decades. The numbers resident in the interior (and 'engaged in agricultural or manufacturing pursuits, including indigo and sugar planters, farmers, landed proprietors, cotton agents, etc.') did not exceed 317. (*Parliamentary Papers, 1852*, vol. 10, p. 339.) In 1805, British-born subjects in Hindustan numbered 31,000, more than two-thirds of whom were in the army. (See J. R. McCulloch, *Dictionary of Commerce* (1859), p. 564.)

[3] *Parliamentary Papers, 1852*, vol. 10, p. 339. The area of British India was then calculated at nearly 678,000 square miles and that of the Native States at more than 690,000 square miles.

export sector. Those who sought to fill the market space opened by the legislation of 1813 were more sensitive to another aspect of the matter. In their view, the prospects for British exporters would obviously be brightened when Indian incomes were rising.

The intellectual challenge of India was now one of devising policies to engineer economic development. One of the earlier constraints on growth—the Company's monopoly of the Indian trade—had been removed. The attention of the model-builders of a new age was focused on the fulfilment of latent, but un-realized, opportunities.

CHAPTER 9

The Formulation of the Rent Doctrine: Malthus and the Haileybury Tradition

AT some turning points in its affairs, the East India Company had found within its ranks the talents the times required. At other moments, its internal resources were less adequate. By the early 1800s, it was widely acknowledged (though with varying degrees of conviction) that fresh skills were needed. The mode then chosen to supply them was to bring the Company into sustained contact with practitioners of the new political economy. Indirectly, this association was to serve as a catalyst to an analytic innovation which directed official thinking on economic policy down a novel path.

I. THE FOUNDATION OF THE EAST-INDIA COLLEGE AT HAILEYBURY

Even before the Company's primary role had been formally redefined in 1813, its personnel requirements had begun to change. In 1800 Governor-General Wellesley had diagnosed the problem and sought to remedy it by establishing a college in Calcutta to train newly arrived cadets. As he then observed, 'the great body of the civil servants in Bengal is not at present sufficiently qualified to discharge the duties of the several arduous stations in the administration of this empire; and . . . it is peculiarly deficient in the judicial, fiscal, financial, and political branches of the government . . .'[1]

News of the foundation of this institution (known as Fort William College) was not warmly received by the Court of Directors in London. On more than one occasion, Wellesley's attitude of independence from his headquarters had provoked displeasure at home. His educational scheme provided an opportunity to rein him in. The senior leadership of the Company concluded that the programme contemplated for Fort William

---

[1] Memorandum by Wellesley (as quoted by Malthus in *A Letter to the Rt. Hon. Lord Grenville Occasioned by Some Observations of His Lordship on the East India Company's Establishment for the Education of Their Civil Servants* (London, 1813), p. 9.

College was likely 'to involve an indefinite expense, to embrace far too wide a field, and to contemplate the acquirement of various branches of knowledge, the study of which, it was conceived, might be prosecuted with far better prospect of success at home'.[2] In 1804—without great enthusiasm—the Directors authorized the establishment of an East-India College at Haileybury, Hertfordshire, to replace Wellesley's unauthorized project.

The curriculum of the new institution (which was to accept young men of ages seventeen and eighteen) was designed as a mixture of standard academic subjects and 'Oriental' ones. Students were expected to acquaint themselves with Indian history and to gain some exposure to an Asian language. The new discipline of political economy was also assigned a prominent place in the programme of studies. The man chosen to present it to the future class of guardians was the Revd. T. R. Malthus who was thus to become the first of the new wave of economic thinkers to obtain a full-time position under the auspices of the East India Company. Before this appointment Malthus had been known primarily for his writings on population. Though the scope of his interests had already begun to broaden, his major work on economic issues was produced during his tenure of the chair of History and Political Economy at Haileybury.

As a charter member of the East-India College's faculty, Malthus was to be an able spokesman for the institution. The existence of the college, he maintained, belied 'one of the great objections urged by Adam Smith against the government of an exclusive Company': i.e. that its proper concerns as a sovereign would be submerged by its trading interests. 'In the establishment of the East-India college', he insisted, 'the feelings of the sovereign conspicuously predominated . . .'[3]

Serious tensions were none the less inherent in the structure of the East-India College. Whereas members of the academic staff aspired to rigorous intellectual standards for the institution, the Company's Directors were reluctant to accept the costs they would entail. Appointments in the Company's service formed an important part of the patronage of senior members of the East

[2] *Memorials of Old Haileybury College*, ed. Frederick Charles Danvers (Westminster, 1894), p. 13.

[3] T. R. Malthus, *Statements respecting the East-India College with an Appeal to Facts in Refutation of the Charges Lately Brought Against It in the Court of Proprietors* (London, 1817), p. 31.

India Company.[4] Under the new arrangements, confirmation of these appointments was now contingent upon completion of four terms at Haileybury. The Directors did not welcome the possibility that their judgements on personnel matters might be overruled. For this reason, the East-India College was explicitly not empowered to expel an errant cadet. Haileybury soon became known as a hot-bed of student insurrection and insubordination. Sydney Smith, the editor of the *Edinburgh Review*, touched a sensitive nerve when he advised a friend who had been invited to fill the chair of law at Haileybury to decline unless he was assured of 'pebble money' (i.e. an annual pension in the event of his being 'disabled by the pelting of the students'.[5] Malthus lobbied hard for the autonomy of the College and enlisted the support of his friend Ricardo, a member of the East India Company's Court of Proprietors.[6]

Its reputation for unruliness and laxity in academic standards was not the only threat to the survival of the East-India College. Wellesley's scheme still had some supporters. In their view, preparation for a career in the Company's overseas service could best be made in India at a strengthened Fort William College. Malthus attacked this proposal on the ground that he could not 'readily conceive a more inauspicious situation for the commencement of new and difficult studies, than that of a young man on his first arrival in India, surrounded by natives devoted to his will, discouraged from application by the enfeebling effects of the climate; and beset by every temptation and novelty, which can attract his imagination, and divert his attention from serious pursuits'.[7]

II. THE INDIAN LAND REVENUE SYSTEM AS A PROBLEM FOR ECONOMIC ANALYSIS

The founders of Haileybury expected the science of political economy to be able to speak to at least one obvious practical

[4] By 1809 it was reported that 'writerships' (the most junior appointments) to Bengal had been sold for £3,500. (See *Report From the Committee Appointed to Inquire Into the Existence of Any Abuses in the Disposal of the Patronage of the East India Company*, 23 March 1809, pp. 4–5.)

[5] As cited in *The Works and Correspondence of David Ricardo*, ed. P. Sraffa, vol. 7, p. 251.

[6] See, for example, ibid., vol. 7, esp. pp. 119 and 130–8. Ricardo was sympathetic to Malthus's appeal for enlarged powers for the College's academic staff. In correspondence with Trower in 1816, he lamented the 'disgraceful disturbances at the College' which had interfered with Malthus's leisure. (Ibid., vol. 7, p. 26.)

[7] Malthus, *A Letter to the Rt. Hon. Lord Grenville Occasioned By some Observations*

issue: the administration of the land revenue system of British
India. There was no doubt that any government in that part of
the world would need to rely heavily on the taxation of land. But
how should the land tax be designed? Among officials in the field,
two divergent approaches had emerged. Practice in Bengal had
been shaped by one of them while policy throughout much of
Madras had been guided by the other. It was already apparent
that these two procedures had quite different administrative
requirements. The broader economic implications of these respective systems, however, were far from being fully understood.

In Bengal the objective of Cornwallis's 'Permanent Settlement'
of 1793 had been to produce a stable class of large landowners
(known as zemindars) who would be held responsible for the
annual payment of stipulated sums to the state. By treating the
zemindars as intermediaries in the revenue system, the land tax
could be collected at mimimal cost. The government, in turn,
rewarded the *zemindars* by issuing to them titles to large blocks
of land and by committing itself to freeze the tax claim in perpetuity (hence the 'permanence' of the Permanent Settlement).
Though the terms on which the government could deal with the
zemindars were thus fixed, the terms on which the *zemindars* as
landlords could deal with their tenants were unregulated. It was,
of course, expected that landowners would behave responsibly.[8]
The architects of the system had faith that a class of large landowners in India would acquire the attributes of socially concerned
paternalism to be found among landed aristocrats in England.

The approach adopted in Bengal in the 1790s reflected the
best thinking of the times on the vexed question of land taxation.
The system was uncomplicated and administratively straightforward. The government was required to deal directly only with
a manageable number of large landowners and was spared the
detailed work of collecting small sums from a mass of cultivators.
At the same time, impressive authority could be mustered to
bolster the conviction that codified private rights in landed
property—when combined with strict limits on taxation—would
create an environment favourable to economic growth. Adam

---

*of His Lordship on the East India Company's Establishment for the Education of Their
Civil Servants* (London, 1813), p. 29.

[8] For an excellent discussion of the issues involved in the alternate approaches to
the taxation of land, see Eric Stokes, *The English Utilitarians and India* (Oxford,
1959).

Smith, who had argued that uncertainties about taxation invited abuses of state power and could easily frustrate healthy expansion in the private sector, was invoked in support of the Bengal strategy.[9] This line of reasoning had a further impressive recommendation in the political climate of the late eighteenth century. To Englishmen horrified by the excesses of the French Revolution, it seemed self-evident that a high priority should be assigned to stability in the social order. A landed class in Bengal with its rights in property legally secured appeared to offer good social insurance.

In Madras, on the other hand, a different set of procedures was being developed. Official thinking there attached prime importance to the protection of the small man. As in Bengal, the creation of codified titles to land was regarded as necessary for social and economic uplift. But doctrine diverged on the persons to whom such titles should be assigned. The Madras strategy sought to create a regime of small freeholders. Land titles were thus to be held by the peasant cultivators (or *ryots*). This scheme obliged the state in its capacity as a tax-gatherer to deal directly with a large number of small farmers. Administratively expensive though this operation might be, its advocates—most notably Sir Thomas Munro who later rose to the Governorship of the Madras Presidency—insisted that it was well worth the cost. No other system could so effectively ensure that the special circumstances of individual peasants were adequately taken into account in the assessment of taxes and none appeared to be better designed for the purpose of building a community of self-reliant peasant proprietors. Munro was personally sympathetic to a ceiling on tax claims, though he avoided an official commitment to a 'permanent settlement'. The longer-term needs of the state could not be fully anticipated. The manoeuverability of future governments should not be compromised, he maintained, by formal restrictions on their revenue-raising capacity.

In the early 1800s, controversies over the respective merits of the *zemindari* revenue system in Bengal and of the *ryotwari* system in Madras turned primarily on points of political and social philosophy. Serious debate over the economic issues was to

[9] One of the architects of the Permanent Settlement cited Smith approvingly on these points. See *Remarks on the Ryotwari and Morcurrery Systems*, an undated pamphlet attributed to Thomas Law.

come later. When that stage in the discussion arrived, Hailey-bury was to play an important part in shaping the categories of discourse.

III. THE THEORY OF DIFFERENTIAL RENT

Malthus's position at the East-India College obliged him to become familiar with the problems of land taxation in India. When he published a small pamphlet on rent in 1815, he acknow-ledged the stimulus it had provided to his thinking: 'The follow-ing Tract contains the substance of some notes on Rent, which, with others on different subjects relating to political economy, I have collected in the course of my professional duties at the East India College.'[10] Though his involvement with Indian problems had no doubt helped to direct his attention to the subject of land rent, his comments in this publication dealt primarily with the sharp increases in corn prices and in land rents which had occurred in England during the Napoleonic wars.

The results of Malthus's reflections—along with those of Ricardo and West who simultaneously puzzled over similar phenomena—led to a fundamental rethinking of the mechanisms governing the distribution of incomes. The doctrine inherited from Smith had distinguished between three shares of income: a wage share paid to a labouring class; a profit share which arose from the ownership of 'stock' (and which in Britain would accrue to a capitalist class); and a rent share appropriated by the owners of land. Smith had pressed the analysis of rent to two conclusions: that this share of income did not enter into the costs of production (and thus played no part in the determination of prices); and that the rent received by landowners was a residual income share, arrived at after total costs had been deducted from total agricultural receipts. The further insights contributed by Malthus, Ricardo, and West rested on a demon-stration that rent originated in the natural fertility of the soil and that rents as a proportion of the national income could be expected to swell with growth in the economy and in the size of the population.

Reduced to its essentials, the reasoning supporting this analytic

---

[10] Malthus, *An Inquiry Into The Nature and Progress of Rent* (London, 1815), Preface.

innovation rested on the proposition that land suited to cultivation was limited in quantity and quite uneven in quality. In most
societies, it was presupposed that land of high fertility would be
the first to be cultivated. As population grew (and, with it,
demand for the products of the land), acreages of lower fertility
would be broken by the plough. Such an extension in the cultivated area would be worthwhile, however, only after the prices
of agricultural products had increased. Otherwise, those who
worked inferior soils would be unable to meet their costs of production. Under the new scale of prices, receipts from the marginal
lands would be just sufficient to reward labour and capital inputs
at normal rates—but would leave no surplus as rent. Meanwhile,
the owners of superior acreages would find that their circumstances had improved without effort on their part. Whereas the
prices at which they could sell their outputs had increased, their
costs has not risen correspondingly. The resulting increment in
their net receipts was a rental income; i.e. a windfall attributable
to the differential fertility of the soil. Rent could thus be identified as the 'net product' of the land. Its share of the gross product
of any particular farm would depend on the qualities with which
it had been endowed by nature.

In a growing economy, the mechanisms governing the formation of rent could be expected to produce a substantial redistribution of income between various groups within society. Growth in
the demand for agricultural products would tend to swell the
income of landowners. The relative position of other groups in
the community, on the other hand, would suffer. Wage earners
would face higher food costs. If their real wages—which were
assumed to be low already—were not to deteriorate, increases in
money wages would be required. An easing of the burden on the
working class, however, would be at the expense of the capitalist's
profits.

With these insights, the behaviour of land rents in England
during the Napoleonic Wars became much easier to comprehend.
Demand for home-produced foodstuffs had swollen enormously
during these years. With a sharp upward trend in agricultural
prices, lands of inferior quality had indeed been drawn into
cultivation. This process had brought substantial windfall gains
to the owners of superior soils. A redistribution of the national
income in favour of landowners had thus occurred. Landlords,

however, had not been rewarded for any additional effort. Instead they had appropriated an unearned gift of nature.

If this conceptual formulation proved to be helpful in interpreting recent events in England, it was also useful as a key to understanding the economic environment of India. It could now be argued that a substantial part of India's misery stemmed from the failure of its traditional rulers to understand correctly the phenomenon of rent. James Mill had hinted at this conclusion in his *History of British India*, basing his argument at the time on the version of the differential rent doctrine contained in the manuscripts of Ricardo's *Principles of Political Economy and Taxation*. Malthus, however, was the first to argue that there was a systematic connection between the phenomenon of rent and the economic ills of India.

IV. THE DIFFERENTIAL RENT DOCTRINE AND THE RE-INTERPRETATION OF ECONOMIC BACKWARD-NESS IN TRADITIONAL INDIA

Though Malthus's students at Haileybury were exposed to his application of the rent theory to India's problems at an earlier date, his views were made available to a wider audience with the publication of his *Principles of Political Economy* in 1820. India's backwardness, as Malthus then saw it, derived primarily from the fact that traditional Indian sovereigns had abused their power by creating 'a premature monopoly of land'. They had been able to do so by establishing claims to ownership of the soil. They had appropriated, however, an 'excessive' share of its fruits: in Malthus's judgement, the traditional sovereign was likely to 'demand all that was not necessary to allow of a moderate increase in cultivators'.[11] These claims by the sovereign bore no relation to the differential rent (or the net product of the soil). Instead, traditional practice—in which a proportion of the gross product of the land was transferred to the state—produced major distortions in the economy. It meant, Malthus argued, that 'only the most fertile lands of the country could be cultivated . . .'[12]

The problem of arrested development in the Indian economy— with which many late eighteenth-century men had grappled— could now be given a coherent analytic explanation. A misguided

[11] Malthus, *Principles of Political Economy* (London, 1820), p. 156.   [12] Ibid.

tax strategy applied by traditional Indian rulers had been the villain of the piece. As a result, market forces could not assert themselves. Stimuli for economic growth, which in the natural course of things should have arisen in an environment so richly endowed, had been stifled.

But if the agricultural sector had been penalized by improper taxation, could not labour and capital 'quit the land'? In Malthus's view, the circumstances of India foreclosed such a line of adjustment. 'It should be recollected', he wrote, 'that the actual cultivators of the soil in these countries are generally in a very low and degraded condition; that very little capital is employed by them, and scarcely any which they can remove and employ in any other business . . .'[13] The Indian agriculturalist was so drained of resources that he had no effective mobility. For most practical purposes, he was tied to the land and obliged to accept an unfortunate fate.

But this was not the end of the difficulties. A tax system based on the gross (rather than the net) product of the land necessarily encroached on the legitimate shares of wages and profits. Such distortions from the natural pattern of income distribution tended, in turn, to frustrate normal expansion in the economy at large. An overtaxed and impoverished agrarian population could not be a flourishing source of demand for the outputs of other sectors. Aggregate production had thus been suppressed and employment opportunities off the land severely restricted. India had indeed been trapped in a vicious circle of poverty. Not only had a 'premature monopoly rent' starved the working agriculturalist of resources; it had also created a climate hostile to capital accumulation in other sectors. Monopoly, as Smith had argued, was indeed responsible for much of the outcome. But the monopoly of an alien company was no longer the target for criticism. Instead it was the abuse by traditional rulers of a monopoly power over land which had produced this unhappy state of affairs.

With the theory of differential rent at his disposal, Malthus could offer a solution to a problem which had perplexed his predecessors. The stagnation of pre-British India was now persuasively interpretable in economic terms. Though the cultural condition of the people (to which James Mill had attached such importance in his *History*) made a contribution to the total

13 Ibid., p. 158.

explanation, the main burden fell on the unfortunate distortions in the economic structure which flowed from taxation of the gross (rather than the net) agricultural product.

An understanding of the handicaps thus imposed on the economy also made India's demographic problems more comprehensible. With its production pattern unnecessarily weakened, India was especially vulnerable to natural disaster. Positive checks on population growth were not unusual occurrences. As Malthus read Indian history, '. . . every failure in the crops from unfavourable seasons would be felt most severely; and India, as might be expected, has in all ages been subject to the most dreadful famines.'[14] Much of the harshness of this outcome (which would be felt with particular force by the lower castes in Hindu society) could have been avoided had not the tax system impeded expansion in the cultivated area.

While the misguided policies of traditional rulers had aggravated India's difficulties, it was also true that population growth had damaged prospects for economic improvement. In Malthus's view, the dominant cultural pattern had tended to encourage early and universal marriage, the 'natural consequence' of which 'was, that the lower classes of people were reduced to extreme poverty, and were compelled to adopt the most frugal and scanty mode of subsistence'.[15] At the same time, he maintained that forms of social stratification unique to Hindu society promoted some exercise of a preventive check to excessive population growth. The institution of castes—however unfortunate its consequences for occupational mobility—at least had something to commend it in this respect. Malthus maintained that the 'division of the people into classes, and the continuance of the same profession in the same family, would be the means of pointing out to each individual, in a clear and distinct manner, his future prospects respecting a livelihood; and from the gains of his father he would be easily enabled to judge whether he could support a family by the same employment.'[16]

[14] Malthus, *An Essay on the Principle of Population* (5th edn., London, 1817), p. 278.
[15] Ibid., pp. 277–8.
[16] Ibid., pp. 273–4.

V. THE BROADER SIGNIFICANCE OF DIFFERENTIAL RENT

Malthus's view of the subject of land rents opened new vistas. Not only had a satisfactory solution to a long-standing intellectual problem seemingly been reached: the form of that solution also suggested a course for administrative action. Now that the fundamental cause of economic stagnation in pre-British India had been identified, it was possible to think constructively about appropriate remedies.

Malthus himself did not probe deeply into the implications of the rent doctrine for specific policy decisions in British India. Sorting out the relative merits of the *zemindari* and the *ryotwari* systems (or, for that matter, evaluating other possible modes for the collection of land revenue) was a task for others. He was content to equip his Haileybury students with the tools needed to ask the right questions. Once in the field, it would be their job to find the practical answers.

While the theory of differential rent spoke most directly to concerns about the taxation of land, its influence on strategies of economic policy was far more pervasive. If misperceptions about the phenomenon of rent accounted for the economic failure of pre-British India, then surely a correct perception offered a key to economic success for the subcontinent under British guidance. The rent doctrine thus became the crucial ingredient of a more general approach to economic development.

Malthus was the first to link differential rent theory with Indian problems and to transmit it to India's future 'guardians'. The same insight reached the headquarters of the East India Company via another route. In the formulation of rent theory, Malthus and Ricardo had shared the honours. It was primarily through Ricardo's influence on James Mill that the doctrine was appropriated to build a new official model for economic policy in India.

CHAPTER 10

An Official Model of Economic Policy: James Mill as an East India Executive

JAMES MILL had emerged from the dozen years devoted to the preparation of his *History* with firm convictions about the condition of India. Traditional society was hopelessly debased and corrupt. The image so long entertained by European intellectuals had been totally incorrect. A golden age of achievement in the sub-continent had never, in fact, existed.

The facts, as Mill saw them, were ugly—but they were not immutable. In the phase of his career which began in 1819, Mill sought to change them. At that point, he joined the headquarters staff of the East India Company as an Assistant Examiner of the India Correspondence. His functions there were not accurately described by his title. In more modern parlance, the concerns of the Examiner's office were those of an economic planning staff for British India.

Had such a position been offered to Mill before 1813 (i.e. before the Company's monopoly of the commerce with India had been surrendered), he could hardly have accepted without serious compromise in fundamental principles. The legislation of 1813, however, had purged the Company of its most objectionable feature. Under the new dispensation, an association with it meant opportunity to apply the Western intelligence to the task of uplifting the miserable and the deprived. Practitioners of the science of political economy could speak to their condition and, in Mill's judgement, they had an obligation to do so. If one sought to increase the sum of human happiness, there could be no more productive allocation of intellectual energies.

Mill was obviously an eager candidate for this assignment. In February 1818 he wrote to a friend: 'It is fit also I should mention to you (though at present it is a secret which is to be kept very close) that there are some friends of mine among the East India Directors, who have views in my favour of considerable importance in the East India house. The possibilities of success, they

reckon, are strong . . .'[1] Writing to the same correspondent in
April 1819, Mill solicited his support with the East India directors,
adding that 'several of the Directors are my declared friends, and
a good deal of application of considerable weight has been made
to others of them. The reputation of my book, too, I am told is
even a strong recommendation.'[2] For its part, the Committee
appointed by the Directors to screen candidates for positions in
the Examiners' department reported on Mill's qualifications as
follows: 'This gentleman's character is before the public as the
author of a *History of India* and from the research displayed in
the course of that work, as also from private testimony, the
Committee have every reason to believe that his talents will
prove beneficial to the Company's interest.'[3]

When his appointment was confirmed, Mill embraced his new
duties with enthusiasm. As he then described his functions: 'It
is the very essence of the internal government of 60 millions of
people with which I have to deal; and as you know that the
government of India is carried on by correspondence; and that I
am the only man whose business it is, or who has the time, to
make himself master of the facts scattered in the most voluminous
correspondence, on which a just decision must rest, you will conceive to what an extent the real decision on matters belonging to
my department rests with the man who is in my situation.'[4]
Mill's assessment of the challenge of his assignment was conveyed
equally vividly in the arguments he invoked in a futile attempt
to persuade Ricardo to become a candidate for a Directorship in
the East India Company. He pleaded to his friend in 1820: 'It
would put you in a situation in which your means of doing
good to your fellow creatures would be prodigious; it would increase your dignity and importance in a very high degree; and
the occupation which it would afford would add to your

[1] Letter from James Mill to Dr. Thomson, 22 February 1818, quoted in Alexander
Bain, *James Mill: A Biography* (London, 1882), p. 167.
[2] Ibid., p. 184. Among Mill's most active sponsors was Joseph Hume (1777–1855),
with whom he had maintained a close personal friendship since schooldays in Scotland.
Hume had acquired a considerable fortune in India as an army surgeon and paymaster.
Upon his return to England, he had entered Parliament in 1812. Ricardo and Francis
Place were also among his supporters.
[3] As quoted by William Foster, *The East India House: Its History and Associations*
(London, 1924), p. 196.
[4] James Mill to Dumont, 13 December 1819, in the *Works and Correspondence of
David Ricardo*, ed. Sraffa, vol. 8, p. 40.

happiness ... On your own account, therefore, on account of the millions of creatures over whose happiness and misery you would be invested with so much power, on account of your family to whose dignity and advantage it would redound in so many ways, and on my account, whose welfare I am sure is a matter of no small importance to you, I hope you will give the subject not only a most serious but a favourable consideration.'[5]

Mill's delight with his new task was shared by his closest friends. As Ricardo reported to McCulloch: 'You have probably heard that Mr. Mill has got a highly respectable situation in the East India House. Considering the opinions which he has so freely given of the Government of India this appointment reflects great credit on the Directors.'[6] Jeremy Bentham joined in the general rejoicing. It was later in life, however, that Bentham observed: 'Mill will be the living executive—I shall be the dead legislative of British India.'[7]

I. THE SCIENTIFIC TAX IN THE STRATEGY FOR INDIAN UPLIFT

The central problem facing the man responsible for the 'very essence' of the internal government of British India was one of devising policies to elevate the masses of the population. Mill brought to this task a reasonably clear set of goals. In the first instance, the economy should be structured to foster economic growth. As a utilitarian liberal, he also attached importance to a satisfactory distribution of income. Aggregate economic expan-

---

[5] Mill to Ricardo, 23 September 1820, in the *Works and Correspondence of David Ricardo*, ed., Sraffa vol. 8, pp. 251–2.

[6] Ricardo to McCulloch, 22 June 1819, ibid., vol. 8, p. 40.

[7] *The Works of Jeremy Bentham*, ed. J. Bowring (London, 1843), vol. 10, p. 490. It is worth noting in passing that the zest for work displayed by Mill was not shared by all his associates. One of his colleagues in the Examiner's Office was the novelist Thomas Love Peacock who sustained the links between the Company's headquarters and the world of the arts which had been established by John Hoole (a poet and translator of Italian poets who had been an auditor and senior official of the Company from 1770 to 1785) and Charles Lamb (who served in the Accounts Department from 1792 to 1826). Peacock put his view of a typical day at East India House into verse:

> From ten to eleven, ate a breakfast for seven:
> From eleven till noon, to begin was too soon;
> From twelve to one, asked 'What's to be done?'
> From one to two, found nothing to do;
> From two to three, began to foresee
> That from three to four would be a damned bore.

(As quoted by Elwen W. Campbell, *Thomas Love Peacock* (London, 1953), p. 74.) I am indebted to William Diebold for bringing this citation to my attention.

sion would ultimately be self-defeating unless the masses shared in its fruits. But success could not be measured solely by improvement in material standards. No less important was cultural change which would liberate the bulk of the population from the chains of superstition. Mill did not expect Hindu civilization to be transformed rapidly, but he was convinced that economic improvement would hasten the process.

How were these goals to be achieved? To Mill, the theory of differential rent provided insights crucial to the formulation of sound economic strategy for India. In particular, it offered the design for a 'scientific' tax: i.e. one which insured an elastic revenue base but which did not distort costs of production. So long as the revenue demand was confined within that portion of the social product attributable to the differential fertility of the soil, wages and profits would approach their natural level. Meanwhile, the state—by drawing off the rental share—would acquire the resources it needed to promote public improvement. Mill confidently assured the Parliamentary Committee in 1831 of the relevance of the theory to India: 'I conceive . . . that the peculiarity of India, in deriving a large proportion of its revenue from the land, is a very great advantage. Nine-tenths probably of the revenue of the government in India is derived from the rent of land, never appropriated to individuals, and always considered to be the property of government; and to me that appears to be one of the most fortunate circumstances that can occur in any country; because in consequence of this the wants of the state are supplied really and truly without taxation. As far as this source goes, the people of the country remain untaxed. The wants of government are supplied without any drain either upon the produce of any man's labour, or the produce of any man's capital.'[8] This theme was to be a persistent one in Mill's approach to economic policy in India. At one point, he drew on it to proclaim that if taxation 'were limited to the rent merely, and the collection were not carried beyond the limits of a moderate rent; if that could be obtained, and I am not aware of any impossibility of attaining it, then I should say that the revenue system in India is the best in the world.'[9]

---

[8] Mill, Minutes of Evidence Before the Select Committee on the Affairs of the East India Company, 2 August 1831, *Parliamentary Papers, 1831*, vol. 5, p. 292.

[9] James Mill, Testimony of 11 August 1831, ibid., p. 336.

In principle, the strategy for a scientific tax should have been as applicable to Britain as to India. Why should Mill's home country be denied the benefits of the best revenue system in the world? The answer was straightforward. Political reality in England blocked the application of the theory there. At least until the franchise could be considerably widened and the formidable weight of the large landowning interests correspondingly reduced, serious consideration of a tax system based on the principle of differential rent was not worthwhile.[10] All that one could reasonably hope for were reforms which would arrest growth in the rental share of income—such as the repeal of the Corn Laws which sheltered a high-cost domestic agriculture and enriched landowners. India, on the other hand, offered much greater freedom of manoeuvre. Programmes of economic reform confronted no major political constraints. The blessings of the latest scientific thinking could be conferred there. The attractiveness of India as a laboratory for Western social scientists considerably antedates the Ford Foundation.

II. THE TAX SYSTEM: FROM THEORY TO PRACTICE

While the executive in British India had no local Parliament to deal with, the full achievement of the ideal system still faced major obstacles. The most serious was Cornwallis's Permanent Settlement in Bengal. From Mill's point of view, this arrangement had been totally misconceived. The first error, in his judgement, lay in the very permanence of the system. Those equipped with the insights of the rent theory could now identify the enormity of the mistake. With growth in population and in the demand for foodstuffs over time, the rental share of income would necessarily rise. As the process unfolded, the unearned gains accruing to the owners of superior soils ought properly to be appropriated by the state. Cornwallis's unfortunate decision precluded this result. Private landowners would be the exclusive beneficiaries of the windfall.

But this was not the only difficulty. The assumption that the *zemindari* would develop an attitude of sympathetic concern toward the tenantry has been far wide of the mark. Mill credited the architects of the Permanent Settlement with the 'best of all

[10] As an ideal, Mill held that nationalization of the land in Britain would be a highly desirable step. See Mill's comment on this matter in his *Elements of Political Economy*.

possible motives'. They had expected the *zemindari* to behave as English landlords and to develop a paternal interest in the welfare of their tenants. 'Unhappily', he observed, 'that last expectation has been found to be very far from corresponding with the facts; they little understood the nature of the men with whom they were transacting.'[11]

In fact, Mill maintained, the Permanent Settlement had left the cultivating *ryot* completely at the mercy of the *zemindar*. The cultivators had been exposed to victimization and exploitation without legal means of redress. The exacting demands imposed on the tenantry had, in turn, inhibited agricultural progress. Mill had no doubt 'that what is collected by the *zemindar* from the *ryots* is a full rent; there is reason to apprehend that it is more.'[12]

Though much damage had been done by the mistakes of 1793, there was still some prospect for improvement. The government could not, of course, disavow the solemn undertaking it had given to freeze the revenue claims on the *zemindari*. Mill's respect for legality ruled out such action. The state could intervene, however, when *zemindary* estates were offered for sale. Mill proposed that the government should then be the pre-emptive buyer of such lands. As a landlord in its own right, government could then deal directly with individual cultivators and could apply the teachings of the rent doctrine. This procedure might entail some sacrifice in land revenues, at least in the returns net of costs of collection. Should this be the case, Mill insisted that a government faced with a choice between maximizing its receipts and promoting the 'happiness of the people' should always prefer the latter course.[13]

In Madras the situation was much more satisfactory. Munro had already laid the foundation for a proper revenue administration by dealing, not through intermediaries, but directly with the *ryots* themselves. The full translation of the rent formula for taxation into practice, however, required identification of differentials in the natural fertility of the soil. Some plots of land would yield no rent and would thus be entirely exempt from taxation. But those which generated surpluses above the normal

---

[11] Testimony of 2 August 1831, *Parliamentary Papers, 1831*, vol. 5, p. 293.
[12] Testimony of 4 August 1831, *Parliamentary Papers, 1831*, vol. 5, p. 309.
[13] Ibid., p. 310.

costs of production could be expected to vary in their tax-paying
capacity. Mill recognized that it was not an easy task to measure
the portion of the agricultural product attributable to the
endowment of nature. As a matter of procedure, he proposed that
officials 'estimate as accurately as can be what such and such
lands would yield under such and such a cultivation, and what is
the cost of that cultivation'.[14] Though calculations of this sort
were necessarily fallible, mistakes—when they became visible—
could readily be corrected. Revenue officers on the spot were
encouraged to be flexible. 'The best mode of approximating to
correctness', he advised, 'will probably be an attentive observation of the effect of any particular amount collected; whether
the payment is made with difficulty or with ease; to watch care-
fully till evidence is obtained, that what is exacted of the *ryot*,
is only a moderate exaction.'[15] Mill's counsel to administrators in
the field was that 'in all doubtful cases . . . the error, if any, be
on the safe side, by taking less than the rent rather than more.'[16]
Tax claims which went beyond the bounds of the rent could only
magnify misery. 'When too high an assessment is operated for a
few years, or even for one year', Mill noted, 'the condition of the
country is permanently injured, because the *ryots* dispose of
their bullocks, and various other means of carrying on the
cultivation, to pay the demand upon them for that one year; so
that in the succeeding years the cultivation declines, and the
revenue along with it.'[17] In its own interest (as well as the
interests of cultivators), government should ensure that tax
claims did not impinge on the normal returns to labour and
capital.

While the broad guidelines for an ideal tax system could be
set out with reasonable simplicity, perfection in practice could
not be expected overnight. The 'fine tuning' sought by Mill
called for administrative talents which were not readily available.
Improved performance would be the product of time. On this
point, he observed: 'We have none but very imperfect instruments to employ; with the total absence of a moral feeling in
the country to aid us, it is not shameful to be dishonest in a
public trust; no discredit attaches to a man in such a situation
for robbing either his fellow subjects or the government; and if

[14] Testimony of 11 August 1831, *Parliamentary Papers*, 1831, vol. 5, p. 329.
[15] Ibid., p. 335.   [16] Testimony of 9 August 1831, ibid., p. 323.   [17] Ibid., p. 322.

he does not avail himself of his advantages to make himself rich by any means, he is rather reckoned to have behaved unskilfully than to have behaved honourably. When we consider . . . how imperfectly any one European with an imperfect knowledge of the natives, their language and circumstances, and with a large extent of country to attend to, can watch over the numerous individuals that he employs, it will be easily understood that the difficulty is exceedingly great of limiting the exaction upon the *ryot* to the rent . . .'[18]

Recognition of these problems did not shake Mill's confidence in the wisdom and validity of his recommendations. Nor did he despair of ultimate improvement in the intellectual and moral condition of the people. As this occurred, standards of revenue administration would come closer to the ideal. At that point, he insisted, 'I have no doubt that means will be found of limiting the demand upon the *ryot* to a moderate rent, and then I conceive that the prosperity of that country will be as fully secured as it can be.'[19]

III. THE THEORY OF PUBLIC EXPENDITURE

The creation of an ideal tax system—central though it was—formed only one component of Mill's model of development for India. The other side of the coin was a strategy for public expenditure. Mill was unambiguous in his priorities. His programme attached primary importance to sound administration and to the provision of law and order. The use of public funds for investment in physical or human capital had far less significance.

Within Mill's perspective, 'good government' for India was the indispensable pre-condition for economic improvement. By this he meant assurance of security to person and property by an administrative and judicial system which was non-arbitrary and non-corrupt. Most of the ills of traditional India could be traced to the 'subjection of the population to a rigid government under which the fruits of labour were never secure'.[20] Correction of this intolerable situation was the overriding imperative of British administration. If this mission could be successfully accomplished, healthy progress would follow as a matter of course. 'Elevation', he told the Parliamentary Committee in 1831, 'is the natural

18 Testimony of 11 August 1831, ibid., pp. 334–5. 19 Ibid., p. 335.
20 Mill, *History of British India*, vol. 2, p. 314.

state of a man who has nothing to fear; and the best riches are the effects of man's own industry; effects which never fail when the protection is good.'[21] Expenditure on good government would thus pay handsome dividends in stimulating economic dynamism in India.

Mill's faith in the capacity of good government to stimulate growth and his thinking on the land revenue question were part of a single package. The theory of differential rent offered more than a design for optimal revenue collection. It also set clear limits to the tax demands of government. Taxation in excess of the true rent would impinge on costs of production and thus frustrate the accumulation of capital. Moreover, it would be patently unjust. Traditional Indian rulers—who had based their levies on a share of the gross product of the land—had failed to appreciate these points. This lapse went a long way toward explaining the backwardness of the Indian economy. Nor would British administrators satisfy the requirements of justice if they allowed other forms of taxation to be substituted for the scientific tax on rent. As Mill put it, 'if the Government were to give it up, . . . it must bestow the rent in gift upon certain individuals, and make up for the want of it by taxing others; it would be a plan to enrich a portion of the people by impoverishing the rest.'[22]

Though good government was indispensable to the improvement of India, Mill saw little prospect that Indians themselves would soon be able to provide it. Only the unchallenged integrity of Europeans would be equal to the job. He did not wish to be understood as recommending a permanent colour bar. On this point he commented as follows: 'I would have no exclusion; wherever a fit native appears, he should be considered a proper candidate for employment . . .' He further recognized that there might be impressive budgetary reasons for substituting Indian administrators for highly paid Europeans. Even so, his over-all judgement was that 'the great object with me is to obtain the fittest instruments, native or not. The mere employment of natives in itself does not appear to me to be a matter of so much importance as it does to some other persons, whose opinions

[21] Testimony of 25 August 1831, *Parliamentary Papers, 1831*, vol. 5, p. 396.
[22] Mill, 'Observations on the Land Revenue of India', *Parliamentary Papers, 1831–32*, vol. 11, Appendix 7, p. 48.

nevertheless I highly respect. It appears to me ten thousand times more important, with respect to the good of the population in general, that the business of the Government should be well done, than that it should be done by any particular class of persons.'[23]

This did not imply that the Englishmen currently engaged in administrative assignments under the East India Company were necessarily the ablest to be found. On the contrary, Mill held that both the recruitment to and training for the service were imperfect. He was particularly critical of the East-India College at Haileybury.[24] Candidates for the Indian Civil Service should be selected by competitive examination (rather than through the patronage system of the Directors of the East India Company). The quality of Indian administration would be further improved by recruiting men from the universities and by scrapping the requirement that they attend Haileybury before posting to the East.[25]

There was an obvious alternate solution to the staffing problems of the government of India: the training of Indians to serve in official capacities. Mill saw serious risks in such a course. He stated his position as follows: 'The idea generally entertained is, that you would elevate the people of India by giving them a greater share in their own government; but I think that to encourage any people in a train of believing that the grand source of elevation is in being an *employé* of government, is anything but desirable. The right thing, in my opinion, is to teach people to look for their elevation to their own resources, their industry and economy. Let the means of accumulation be afforded to our Indian subjects; let them grow rich as cultivators, merchants, manufacturers; and not accustom themselves to look

[23] Testimony of 21 February 1832, ibid., vol. 9, p. 56.

[24] With respect to the training offered there, he observed: 'I conceive that there is very little done in the way of study, except by a small number of the best disposed of the pupils, who would study anywhere; and that the tendency which is inseparable from assemblages of young men to run into dissolute courses, operates there to a deplorable extent.' Testimony of 21 February 1832, ibid., p. 54.

[25] Mill's views on these matters were largely adopted—though not in his own lifetime. Legislation in 1854 terminated the privileges of Directors of the Company to nominate candidates for the Indian administration. The committee reporting on these matters (which included in its membership T. B. Macaulay and Benjamin Jowett, the Master of Balliol College, Oxford) recommended that candidates for the Indian Civil Service be selected by competitive examination. With the new era of 'competition wallahs', Haileybury's existence as the East-India College was terminated in 1858.

for wealth and dignity to successful intriguing for places under government; the benefit from which, whatever it may be, can never extend beyond a very insignificant portion of the whole population.'[26] Thus, in Mill's view, India would be best served— at least for the time being—if Britain remained the monopoly supplier of administrative services. Good government, when imported, might be expensive, but its costs were more than repaid through its unique contributions to the moral and material advancement of the people.

Within this perspective, the commitment of the East India Company to good governance should be regarded as an investment in the social infrastructure of India and it clearly took precedence in the allocation of public resources. Mill fully recognized that there were other worthwhile outlays of public funds. Educational improvement, for example, was among them. 'On every account', he maintained, 'I consider the improvement of the natives in education as an object of paramount importance; and that it ought to be forwarded by every possible means.'[27] But he warned that it would be unrealistic to expect rapid results. India was too vast and the number of Englishmen in direct contact with the population too small. In his opinion, 'the progress of education among them, so as to produce any very perceptible effect, will be exceedingly slow.'[28]

IV. THE ROLE OF GOVERNMENT: THE AGENDA AND THE NON-AGENDA

Mill's perspective on the longer-term prospects of the Indian economy and on the role appropriate for the state in promoting economic expansion was in the mould of classical thinking on the proper division between the private and public sectors. The state was responsible for creating an institutional framework favourable to economic expansion and it was especially qualified to supply certain of the required supporting services. Though government should open space for private initiative, it was not its job to channel public funds to the private sector or to accumulate capital on its own account. Primary responsibility for accumulation should be in private hands. Though the govern-

---

[26] Testimony of 25 August 1831, *Parliamentary Papers, 1831*, vol. 5, p. 396.
[27] Testimony of 21 February 1832, *Parliamentary Papers, 1831–32*, vol. 9, p. 55.
[28] Ibid.

ment's role was vital, it was also limited. As Mill put it: 'it is through the *ryots*, and by giving a proper protection to their property and to themselves in the exercise of their industry, and through that mainly, that the improvement of India must take place.'[29] The creation of the ideal climate for economic advance depended heavily on the implementation of the scientific tax. Building the tax base around the rent share of income was, after all, a step toward perfection of the market. Distortions in costs and in prices which would be generated by alternate modes of taxation could thereby be avoided. Factors of production could then be allocated more rationally with results which would more closely approximate the natural equilibrium.

But was a free market—even when buttressed by security to person and property—likely to be sufficient to stimulate economic expansion in India? The growth theory worked out by the classical economists in England, it will be recalled, had placed heavy reliance on the accumulation of capital by members of a capitalist class. In the India of the early nineteenth century, such a class was virtually non-existent. Men with high incomes could be found (particularly among the *zemindari* of Bengal), but they could not be relied upon to behave as productive investors. In Mill's view, the *zemindari* were 'notoriously not accumulators'; as a group, they were 'habitually and even proverbially improvident and spendthrift'.[30] In this respect, their behaviour was similar to that of the larger landowners in England whose unproductive expenditures had attracted so much hostility from the classical economists. Mill asserted that he knew 'no country in which the class of men whose income is derived from rent can be considered as accumulators; they are men who spend their incomes, with a very moderate portion of exceptions.'[31]

Just as Mill followed the classical tradition in expecting little saving to be forthcoming from members of the working class in England, so also did he think it unreasonable to expect Indian peasants to be significant contributors to the national pool of saving. Even if the state was moderate in its exactions, peasant incomes would still be low. Over the course of time, the environ-

[29] Testimony of 4 August 1831, *Parliamentary Papers, 1831*, vol. 5, p. 309.
[30] Testimony of 9 August 1831, Ibid., p. 313.
[31] Ibid., p. 314. In the case of the *zemindari*, Mill added a qualification. Some accumulation, he believed, might be forthcoming from those who had purchased estates but who lived in Calcutta. (See ibid., p. 313.)

ment created by British administration and by British example would change this situation for the better. Nevertheless, the propensities to improvidence rooted in traditional patterns were stubbornly persistent. As Mill lamented: 'notwithstanding the simplicity of their habits, they found means very easily of spending what comes into their hands, for they run to immense expenses at marriages, and at the births of children, in religious obsequies, and in feeding Brahmins, which is their great delight.'[32]

If Indians themselves could not be relied upon to generate saving at the rates desirable for the promotion of economic growth, much of the task of capital formation could be assigned to foreigners. Mill was not unsympathetic to this solution. Not only would foreign investment remedy at least part of the problem arising from local capital deficiency; it would also provide external benefits by exposing Indians to European industry and organization. His enthusiasm, however, was not unrestrained. Officers of the East India Company had long questioned the wisdom of unrestricted European settlement in India. Some of these reservations were removed following the loss of the Company's monopoly in the trade with India: there was no longer a privileged commercial position to protect. Nevertheless, doubts on political grounds remained. An open door to English settlers might, over the longer run, disturb the stability of the Company's government. Mill did not anticipate that the community of Englishmen permanently resident in India would ever be large. A country already abundantly supplied with low-wage labour would never be a magnet for unskilled Englishmen. Nor was it likely that those equipped with the skills India needed would be attracted there in substantial numbers. The discomfort of the climate was a major deterrent to massive settlement. While he was persuaded that India had much to gain from the diffusion of European influence, Mill opposed governmental actions which would create special incentives for European settlement. Government, for example, should not yield to the requests of Europeans that they be placed under the jurisdiction of a separate court system and thus afforded immunity from Indian judges. The law, Mill maintained, was indivisible. The paramount concern of the judicial system in India should be the protection of the rights of natives, not those of foreigners.

[32] Testimony of 9 August 1831, *Parliamentary Papers, 1831*, vol. 5, p. 316.

One other approach to India's capital deficiency was conceivable: the use of the resources of government to perform the functions required of a capitalist class in a growing economy. Eager though he was for the Indian government to assume the role of a landlord as a rent recipient, Mill shrank from recommending that the state become the economy's major investor. His thinking was too much in the mould of classical liberalism for this possibility to be seriously entertained.

V. THE MODEL AND THE 'FACTS'

Mill's confidence in the ultimate success of his strategy for the uplift of British India was complete. His conviction was not shared by all observers of the Indian scene. By 1831—when he had risen to the position of Head Examiner of the India Correspondence—questions had begun to surface about the applicability of his model of development to the economic environment of India. At a number of points, the presuppositions of his analysis seemed to be at odds with observable realities.

To some members of the Parliamentary Select Committee investigating East India affairs in 1831–2, trends in the land revenues during the preceding two decades raised puzzling problems. At least at first inspection, the fiscal returns did not validate claims to the superiority of a tax system based on the rental share of agricultural income. In Bengal (where the allegedly mistaken 'Permanent Settlement' with the *zemindari* had guided the land revenue arrangements), receipts from the taxation of land had increased. In Madras, on the other hand, the fiscal yield of the land revenue had shrunk, despite major reliance on a mode of assessment supposedly adjusted to the differential fertility of individual plots. This finding did not seem to testify to a clear association between the scientific tax and agricultural prosperity. Nor was other evidence supplied by the behaviour of the revenue returns reassuring on this matter. Government receipts from all sources had grown markedly in Bengal, while they had shrunk in Madras.

These results did not shake Mill's faith in the general strategy. Even if the authenticity of these findings were admitted, they would 'afford no ground whatever for the inference that the *zemindary* system is preferable to the *ryotwar* . . . It does not by any means follow, because the *zemindary* system was contemporary with prosperity in the one case, the detailed and temporary settlement, with the want of prosperity in the other cases, that they were respectively the causes of these opposite results.'[33] The correct interpretation of the evidence, Mill insisted, was that the natural endowments of Bengal were superior to those of Madras. In face of the advantages Bengal enjoyed in fertility, in regular irrigation, and in access to navigable waterways, the most notable feature of the fiscal results was the modesty of growth in Bengal's revenues. 'The small amount of comparative financial prosperity' there offered 'one of the strongest proofs which can be adduced, that it is under some very pernicious system of management'.[34] Disappointments in Madras, on the other hand, could largely be explained by the accidents of the seasons and, in some cases, by deliberate reductions in tax demands on cultivators when evidence of erroneous assessments had come to light. The *zemindar* in Bengal had the resources to tide him over short-term distresses; he could discharge his tax obligations even when his income dropped. Regularity in payments from the *zemindari* was to be expected because 'if they are not men of property, they are almost always men of credit, and are able to borrow the money required.'[35] The small men in Madras were not so fortunately situated. They needed protection and in forms which were expensive. Prosperity for the *ryots* could be assured only when the government was at pains to confine taxation within the limits of the net rent. This required detailed and sensitive administration which meant, in turn, that the costs of assessment and revenue collection were necessarily high. In Madras, a substantial divergence between the gross land revenues and the net land revenues (i.e. gross receipts less the expenses of tax administration) would always be large. This outcome, however, was not a weakness of the system but a reflection of its basic strength.[36] In short, the 'facts' produced by the critics

[33] Testimony of 23 August 1831, *Parliamentary Papers, 1831*, vol. 5, p. 376.
[34] Ibid., p. 381.   [35] Ibid., p. 378.
[36] Mill offered the following explanation for the increase in costs of collecting land revenue in the *ryotwari* areas: 'I believe that a great proportion of this increase has arisen from a growing conviction, that the establishments were unequal to all the duties they had to perform. To afford that protection to the *ryots*, which cannot be afforded without accurate inquiry into the circumstances of each, and the state of his land, and without minute supervision of the different agents employed in that difficult work, an increase of agency was necessary.' (Testimony of 25 August 1831, *Parliamentary Papers, 1831*, vol. 5, p. 386.)

supported a conclusion quite the reverse of the one they had suspected.

On the expenditure side of the public accounts, Mill's ideal scheme also diverged from the reality. Outlays for military purposes claimed the largest single share of the government's resources. In the first decade of the century, military and naval spending accounted for more than half of the total; even in the relative calm of the 1830s, the military budget usually absorbed more than a third of public expenditures.[37] British India, in fact, supported one of the largest standing armies in the world, surpassed in size only by the formations of the Russian Czar.[38]

Mill was of the opinion that no country was enriched by the maintenance of armies. Nevertheless, he accepted this expenditure allocation as a necessity, albeit a regretable one. It might have been tempting to conclude that a military capability of such magnitude invited adventurism. Mill gave a much less menacing construction to the armed forces of British India. Most of the actions to which the Company's armies had been committed, he maintained, had been initiated by native rulers or by unruly native factions.[39] He acknowledged that not all engagements could be so described. Nevertheless, the force at the disposal of the Company's government made an essential contribution to peacekeeping. Indeed such was Mill's belief in the civilizing effect of the British presence that he would not have been dismayed to see the Native States (with whose rulers treaties had been negotiated) taken over directly by the Company. He had no doubt that the welfare of their populations would be greatly enhanced by British administration. While a change in their status would benefit the local peoples, Mill counselled against such intervention. The storm of protest it would predictably touch off in England would be distracting and unedifying.[40]

Even though Mill was satisfied that heavy military spending

[37] *Parliamentary Papers, 1810,* vol. 5, pp. 78–89; *Parliamentary Papers, 1852,* vol. 10, pp. 278–79.

[38] In 1852, regular troop strength within British India was about 290,000 men, supplemented by about 32,000 under the command of British officers in the Native States.

[39] As he phrased this point: 'All our wars cannot perhaps be, with propriety, considered wars of necessity; but most of those by which the territories we possess have been obtained ... have been, I think, of necessity, and not of choice.' (Testimony of 16 February 1832, *Parliamentary Papers, 1831–32,* vol. 14, p. 7.)

[40] See ibid., p. 10.

was justified, the fact remained that outlays under this head drained resources which might otherwise have been available for programmes with more immediate bearing on the improvement of the economy. In the light of the importance attached to good government, heavy and increasing expenditures on the civil and judicial administrations were to be expected and should be welcomed. Indian budgets were under strain to meet these prior claims on public funding. The fiscal resources available for other worthwhile purposes were scant. The Charter Renewal Act of 1813 had directed the government to allocate the first lakh of rupees (100,000 rupees or about £10,000) from the surplus revenues to native education; further appropriations under this heading, however, were minuscule. The sums allocated to public works were also insignificant.[41]

Another set of 'facts' had potentially more serious implications for the pattern and pace of change in the Indian economy. Mill's insistence on the indispensability of good government—combined with his view that India's needs could be satisfied only by expatriate administrators—necessarily imposed claims on the foreign exchange earned by India. The transfers involved in the 'home charges' (i.e. payments in England on behalf of the government of India) amounted to about £2 million per year in the late 1820s.[42] In the nature of the case, the settlement of these charges in foreign exchange committed India to the pursuit of a sizeable export surplus. In Mill's reading of matters, these transfers should not be confused with a 'tribute'. On the contrary, they represented payments for essential invisible imports. Long before he had any official association with the East India Company, Mill had expressed himself unambiguously on this subject; his later experiences merely reinforced his earlier position. No tribute was paid by India. Indeed he maintained that it was inconceivable that India should ever have a 'surplus revenue' to remit.

Mill's interpretation of the matter of tribute was not, however,

[41] By 1830 the performance of the government on infrastructure capital projects could be quickly itemized: a few dozens of miles of roadways and the beginnings of irrigation works on the Ganges Canal.

[42] J. R. McCulloch, *Dictionary of Commerce* (1832), p. 512. The 'home charges' included payments to cover the costs of the headquarters in London, remittances and pensions for civil and military servants, dividends to East India Company stockholders, procurement of government stores (including considerable outlays for military equipment), and the servicing of the East India debt.

unanimously applauded within the senior ranks of the East India
Company. Its directors, after all, were at pains to assure shareholders that their money was in sound hands and that—despite
continuing deficits—dividends paid on the Company's stock
would ultimately improve. One of the directors, Henry St.
George Tucker, estimated in 1824 that the Company had every
prospect of realizing a surplus of about £2,000,000 per year
'during a period of peace' from its activities in India. At the same
time, he maintained that the Company should deliberately
forgo maximization of its profits. Even if it were 'in our option
to extend the annual tribute to four millions', he wrote, 'I should
not hesitate to say that considerations of policy, of justice and
humanity, would all alike concur to condemn the unmeasured
exaction.'[43] Should surpluses of such magnitude arise, they
should be returned to the local people through tax reliefs or
through increased expenditures on services for their welfare.[44]
Though Mill continued to rule out the possibility of a tribute
from India, he also excluded from consideration a detailed
inspection of the impact on the Indian economy of its payments
in sterling to settle the 'home charges'.

At yet another point there was a potential discrepancy between
a reality of Indian economic life and the vision Mill had projected from its future. The East India Company itself did not
always live by the competitive rules which its planners commended to the local peoples. Though the Company was no longer
a monopolist in the trade between India and Europe, its government maintained a monopoly position in the trade of Bengal
opium (the bulk of which was destined for China) and in the
manufacture and distribution of salt within India. Mill did not
attempt to defend these practices in principle. In the case of

---

[43] Henry St. George Tucker, *A Review of the Financial Situation of the East-India
Company in 1824* (London, 1825), p. 47.

[44] There is more than a touch of irony in the circumstances which prompted the
preparation of Tucker's pamphlet. The document was designed as a rebuttal to views
advanced by the French economist, Jean-Baptiste Say. In a tract published in English
in 1824, Say had concluded that the Indian connection offered no possibilities for
Britain to realize a tribute and that British India was a charge on the mother country
of at least £2,000,000 per year. Say's *Historical Essay on the Rise, Progress, and
Probable Results of the British Dominion in India* drew heavily on James Mill's early
writings on the question of tribute. In the history of economic ideas, Say is far better
known for the 'law of markets' (i.e. that 'supply creates its own demand') which he and
James Mill had formulated independently.

opium, he maintained that the effect of the government's bilateral monopoly was to swell the state's revenues at the expense of foreigners.[45] There is some kinship between his position on this matter and one advanced more recently to justify state marketing boards to handle major export crops in less-developed countries. A public monopoly, it was alleged both then and now, provides an efficient and convenient instrument for collecting much needed revenues. Mill, nevertheless, was not totally at ease with this departure from *laissez-faire*. The prevailing organization of the opium trade was intellectually more acceptable when buttressed by a further argument. He maintained that free trade in the procurement of opium in Bengal (as opposed to the monopsony pattern of purchasing developed by the East India Company) would not benefit those most in need of assistance, i.e. the cultivating *ryots*. Even if competition in the trade were to bid up opium prices, the gains would immediately be siphoned off by the *zemindari*.

VI. GENERAL PROPERTIES OF MILL'S APPROACH

James Mill's model imposed analytical intelligibility on an otherwise highly diffuse subject. With its aid, priorities for action could be clearly identified. Once the general target of economic uplift for the masses had been stipulated, the steps appropriate for governmental policy could be set out with reasonable precision. Obstacles to the speedy implementation of the programme were to be expected. Yet, with persistence and dedication on the part of the administration, there were rational grounds for confidence in the ultimate success of the strategy. Nor was there any doubt about the persuasive power of this doctrine. Indians who had been exposed to the new learning found it compelling. Ram Mohun Roy, for example, reassured sceptics in England of the wisdom of Mill's programme.[46] Later, when a limited number of institutions for higher education were opened to Indians, the doctrine became a standard part of the curricu-

[45] The magnitudes involved were not inconsiderable. By 1835 opium contributed more than £1,250,000 to the gross revenues (a figure which approached 7 per cent of gross government receipts). The absolute sum had risen more than threefold by 1850 and its percentage of total public receipts had more than doubled. (*Parliamentary Papers, 1852*, vol. 10, pp. 276–9.)

[46] See the Communication between Ram Mohun Roy and the Board of Control Relative to the Revenue and Judicial Systems of India, *Parliamentary Papers, 1831*, vol. 5.

lum. That it was absorbed was apparent in the sample examination papers submitted in evidence to parliamentary committees.[47]

At the same time, two properties of Mill's model attracted critical attention from contemporaries. The first concerned the general role assigned to the state. Though Mill sought a regime which offered uninhibited scope for private initiative, the process of creating it in India necessarily implied a high degree of state intervention. Traditional society had erected immense barriers to the natural interplay of market forces. The mission of British administration was to remove them. Through the implementation of the scientific tax, the market would be perfected. Simultaneously, the state would be assured of the revenues required to ensure security to person and property and to guarantee incorruptibility in the administrative and judicial systems. The resulting structure, in turn, would activate unused potential in the private sector. Before these gains could be realized, however, the hand of the state would necessarily be very visible. The planner's success, of course, was ultimately to be measured by the achievements of the private sector. Nevertheless, the mere activity of economic planning—even when directed to the opening of new market space—was suspect in many influential circles in England. The strand of classical teaching which argued that governmental intervention in the economy was at best unproductive (and, more often than not, socially malevolent) had done its work well.

A second—and more subtle—attribute of Mill's approach to planning was also subject to criticism. His framework of thought began from the premiss that the civilization of India was radically different from (and indeed inferior to) that of Western Europe. The organizing categories of economic analysis, on the other hand, were alleged to have universal applicability. Trans-

---

[47] The General Assembly's Institution at Calcutta, which opened a 'higher or collegiate department' in 1841, reported at length on the progress of students in the early 1850s. The answers of its students to questions on political economy would have warmed the heart of James Mill. Rent, for example, was discussed as follows in a student paper: 'Rent *is not* in the *least affected* by price. For it originates with the degree of fertility of some land as *superior* to the fertility of other lands, and is regulated *entirely* by the relation of the degree of fertility of other lands, superior or inferior . . .' (Statement of the Progress and Success of the General Assembly's (now, Free Church) Institution at Calcutta, Appendix G, *Parliamentary Papers, 1852–53*, vol. 32, p. 431; emphases in the original).

ferring the concept of differential rent from one setting to another thus presented no difficulties. As a statement of a general truth, the rent doctrine appeared not to be bounded by space or time. Confidence that the usefulness of theoretical propositions transcends differences in economic and cultural environments is by no means unique to any moment in history. There is, for example, a kinship in analytic attitude (though not in analytic substance) between Mill and some of the formulators of independent India's initial development plans. Both employed conceptual schemes devised against the backdrop of alien modes of economic organization in their attempts to reshape the Indian economy. Both, moreover, proceeded from the conviction that they had adopted the correct procedure. Claims to certainty, none the less, tend to invite questions—particularly from commentators more disposed to observe the richness of institutional variety associated with the economic process.

CHAPTER 11

An Unofficial Model for India: J. R. McCulloch and the *Laissez-Faire* Strand of Ricardianism

THE intellectual roots of James Mill's economic strategy for India were to be found in Ricardian analysis. His reading of Ricardo, however, did not exhaust the interpretative possibilities. With but a slight shift in emphasis, the same theoretical system was capable of inspiring rather different recommendations for India.

The most able spokesman for an alternate version of the Ricardian message was James Ramsey McCulloch (1789–1864), a Scotsman who regarded his credentials as an anointed disciple of Ricardo as being nearly as well established as those claimed by James Mill.[1] McCulloch was a tireless propagator of the master's teaching in nineteenth-century England. His role then was not dissimilar to the one played by Professor Alvin Hansen a century later when he carried the message of the Keynesian revolution to an American audience. Neither of these men would have claimed high originality for his own writings. Each in his time was a highly effective transmitter of significant intellectual innovation.[2]

McCulloch wrote prolifically and the bulk of his output was

---

[1] Beginning with the first edition of Ricardo's *Principles*, McCulloch had taken on the task of replying to critical notices of Ricardo's work. In 1824 McCulloch was designated as the initial incumbent of the Ricardo Lectureship on Political Economy. Mill had conceived this plan as an 'appropriate testimony of respect for his [Ricardo's] memory'. When writing to McCulloch only a few days after Ricardo's death, Mill observed: '. . . you and I are his two and only two genuine disciples, his memory must be a bond of connection between us. In your friendship I look for compensation for the loss of his.' (Mill to McCulloch, 19 September 1823, *The Works and Correspondence of David Ricardo*, ed. Sraffa, vol. 9, pp. 391–2.)

[2] As testimony to McCulloch's prominence, it may be noted that his contemporaries had little difficulty in identifying him as the model for the character 'Mr. MacQuedy' in Thomas Love Peacock's novel *Crotchet Castle*. Peacock depicted MacQuedy as a dogmatic and totally humourless expositor of the new science of political economy. For a modern appreciation of McCulloch, see D. P. O'Brien, *J. R. McCulloch: a Study in Classical Economics* (London, 1970).

directed to the general reader. He contributed regularly to such periodicals as the *Edinburgh Review* and the *Scotsman* and compiled three series of reference works (*The Commercial Dictionary*, *The Geographical Dictionary*, and *The Statistical Account of the British Empire*), each of which went through multiple editions. In addition, his activities included the authorship of a *Principles of Political Economy*, the preparation of an edited collection of tracts produced in the seventeenth and eighteenth centuries, and the production of a volume of commentary on *The Literature of Political Economy*. All of this material was given a faithful Ricardian gloss.

The economic problems of India were only peripherally within McCulloch's field of vision. Over the course of a lengthy career, however, he took a position on most points of controversy touching Indian affairs. All of his writing was informed by two fundamental premisses: that monopoly in any of its manifestations should be rooted out and that direct governmental intervention in economic affairs should be avoided. With respect to the English wing of the Indian trade, the views of McCulloch and James Mill tended to converge. Both favoured freedom of entry into the commerce and both opposed commercial regulations by government. They clashed, however, in their views on policies appropriate in India. Mill approached this part of the problem from the perspective of the official planner. McCulloch, on the other hand, spoke from outside the establishment to an audience of outsiders. Many of his listeners—particularly within the British mercantile and industrial communities—were convinced that they too had a stake in the economic strategies applied in British India. The version of the Ricardian message they heard differed significantly from the one promoted within the East India Company's headquarters.

I. MARKET-LED GROWTH AND ITS APPARENT VALIDATION

To an advocate of *laissez-faire* Ricardianism, the 'facts' which emerged in the years immediately following the opening of English trade with India told an impressive tale. Commercial freedom had been associated with a dramatic expansion of British exports to India. Within a decade and a half, they had risen in aggregate value by nearly two and a half times: from less than £1·9 million in 1814 to nearly £4·5 million in 1828. The effort of private merchants, formerly excluded from the Indian commerce, had been entirely responsible for this result. Over this span of years, the trade conducted by the East India Company had shrunk considerably.[3]

These outcomes seemed more than sufficient to confirm faith in the creative power of free markets. If further substantiation were needed, it could be found in the dramatic transformation which had occurred in the commodity composition of Britain's trade with India. By 1827 about one third of the aggregate value of British exports to India was accounted for by cotton textiles from the mills of Lancashire. In the days when the East India Company controlled the trade, such shipments had been insignificant. The new regime of commercial freedom had been less than a decade and a half old when exports to Indian markets reached 13 million yards of printed cotton goods and more than 32 million yards of plain cotton manufactures.[4] Within a remarkably short span of time, the historic roles of the two countries in international commerce had been reversed. India, which had so long been a major exporter of cotton goods, had now become a significant importer. Meanwhile, English textile producers had achieved pre-eminence in world markets.[5]

These developments appeared to expose an error which had long been promoted by the East India monopoly. For two centuries, its spokesmen had argued that India could not offer a substantial market for English goods. Now, McCulloch insisted, it should be obvious to all that Indian tastes were in fact quite pliable. 'It is difficult to suppose', he observed, 'that the directors

[3] J. R. McCulloch, *Dictionary of Commerce* (London, 1832), p. 504.

[4] Ibid., p. 502.

[5] Even in the later years of the eighteenth century, English textile interests had insisted on a reaffirmation of prohibitions against finished cotton goods in British markets. A pamphleteer in 1788 noted that the volume of 'muslins, callicoes and nankeens' sold at the East India House had recently increased markedly. This trend had set in at a time 'when the great augmentation of the powers of machinery had enabled the British artists to double their Manufacture'. Meanwhile, there had been 'a rapid reduction in the prices of India goods, in consequence of the system of the Company to press forward their merchandize, without any regard to the original cost; thereby annihilating those laws of competition which brings every article to its natural level. And hence arises the distress of which the British Manufactures complain.' (*Observations Relative to the Resources of the East India Company for Productive Remittance; and the National Loss occasioned by the Importation of the same Species of Cotton Goods which can be Manufactured in Great Britain* (1788), p. 9.) It was recommended that the problem should be resolved by reorienting the East India trade to the supply of raw materials. This theme was elaborated more fully by Lauderdale in 1809; see Chapter 7.

of the East India Company should not have been early aware of
the fallacy of the opinions as to the fixedness of Indian habits.
So far, however, as we know, they have not, in this instance,
evidenced any acquaintance with the discoveries of their servants.'[6] But while the evidence now available was adequate to
banish permanently such 'elasticity pessimism', McCulloch
warned that false doctrine lived on. By the early 1830s, he saw the
same fictions being invoked to defend the Company's monopoly
of the trade with China. He charged that 'the more skilful or
cunning of the Company's advocates . . . contend that the existence of the monopoly is indispensable to the existence of the
trade; that the Chinese are a peculiar people, whose habits and
modes of thinking and acting are quite different from those of
other nations; that the East India Company have luckily found
out the secret of managing them; but that private traders would
infallibly get embroiled; and that were the experiment of opening
the trade once made, the inevitable consequence would be, that
we should, in a very short time, be driven from the Chinese
markets . . .'[7]

From a British point of view, post-1814 developments in the
export trade with India were indeed impressive. The lobbyists
for free trade could perhaps be excused for boasting a bit. For
his part, McCulloch wondered 'whether, in the whole history of
commerce, another equally striking example can be produced of
the powerful influence of competition in opening new and almost
boundless fields for the successful prosecution of commercial
enterprise'.[8] The conditions had seemed to approximate to those
of a controlled experiment and the results had fully lived up to
expectations.

But what had been the impact of these changes on India? The
output of its textile craftsmen could no longer compete with the
product of England's power-driven looms in markets at home or
abroad.[9] Some Englishmen read this side of the story with alarm.

[6] J. R. McCulloch, *Dictionary of Commerce* (1832), p. 501. Much the same argument
was developed in his article entitled 'Institution of Castes—Indian Society', *Edinburgh
Review* (September 1828).

[7] McCulloch, 'East India Company—China Question', *Edinburgh Review* (January
1831), p. 292.   [8] *Dictionary of Commerce* (1832), p. 502.

[9] According to C. Vakil, S. Bose, and P. Deolalkar, exports of cotton goods from
India fell from 90 lakhs of rupees to 1·3 lakhs between 1819 and 1829 and imports rose
during the same period from 16 lakhs to 52 lakhs; as cited by S. B. Saul, *Studies in
British Overseas Trade, 1870–1914* (Liverpool, 1960), p. 14.

Charles Grant, chairman of the East India Company, detected symptoms of distress in the early 1820s and protested the injustice of arrangements which denied protections to India's craftsmen but which tolerated them for British manufacturers.[10] By the late 1820s, Bentinck—a Governor-General well tutored in utilitarian teaching—asserted that 'the effect which European skill and industry have produced against the prosperity of India' gave urgency to programmes of uplift and reform.[11] A decade later, officials of the Company in the East were reporting the nearly complete destruction of India's cotton textile production.[12]

McCulloch had no doubt that free trade had called for adjustments in India's production pattern. The alarmists, however, had failed to understand the problem properly. When reviewing the situation in 1842, he estimated that 'cotton fabrics of the value of about 20,000,000 l. a year are made by the population of British India, or of the value of 34,000,000 l. including the tributary states.'[13]

By contrast, manufactured cotton goods imported from Britain amounted to only about £2 million in value in 1842 and the figure was still below £4 million in 1851.[14] These calculations suggested that India's textile crafts were far from extinct. It was acknowledged that one group of craftsmen—the producers of the finest luxury textiles of Dacca—had virtually disappeared. Their fate, however, was unrelated to imports from Britain. It reflected instead the demise of the traditional courts upon which they had depended for patronage. The market for this line of out-

[10] George D. Bearce, *British Attitudes Towards India, 1784–1858* (London, 1961), esp. pp. 56–60.

[11] 'Minute of the Governor-General, 30 May 1829' (as reported by Mangles, 'Wrongs and Claims of Indian Commerce', *Edinburgh Review* (January 1841), p. 358). In December 1827 (shortly before his departure for India), Bentinck was entertained at Grote's house where he received 'the pure milk of the Benthamite word'. On that occasion, he remarked (apparently to James Mill): 'I am going to British India, but I shall not be Governor-General. It is you that will be Governor-General.' (Stokes, *The English Utilitarians and India*, p. 51.)

[12] These reports are reviewed in Mangles, loc. cit.

[13] McCulloch, *Geographical Dictionary* (London, 1842), vol. 2, p. 26. The 1851 edition reproduced the same numbers, but substituted the expression 'used to be made' for 'are made'. (*Geographical Dictionary* (London, 1851), vol. 2, p. 26.)

[14] *Geographical Dictionary* (1842), vol. 2, p. 26; (1851), vol. 2, p. 26. T. Ellison in *The Cotton Trade of Great Britain* (London, 1886) has estimated that imported cotton textiles accounted for 4 per cent of India's consumption in 1832 and for 35 per cent in 1857; as cited by Saul, op. cit., p. 14.

puts, McCulloch maintained, had evaporated 'before a yard of British muslin or calico found its way to India'.[15]

In McCulloch's vision of the benevolence of *laissez-faire*, concerns for the plight of traditional craftsmen were misplaced. The magnitudes of imported textiles were not overwhelming. Even if the volume of imports had been much greater, 'the circumstance would be an advantage, not an injury, to India; for they would not be imported were they not cheaper, and, consequently, more easily attainable than their own by the great bulk of the population.'[16] For the community as a whole, any losses sustained by individual producers would be overcompensated by gains to consumers. There could be no doubt that McCulloch's position was authentically Ricardian. The master himself had addressed this issue in 1823. As Ricardo then put it: 'If we send cotton goods to India, they must be paid for. Our cotton goods were purchased with other manufactures; new branches of trade were thus struck out, and both countries were ultimately benefited.'[17]

II. FREE MARKETS AND ECONOMIC EXPANSION: UNFINISHED BUSINESS IN ENGLAND

As McCulloch saw matters, free entry into the trade between India and England afforded by the legislation of 1813 had produced healthy change for all concerned. Yet a substantial gap persisted between the potential performance of the Indian economy and its actual achievement. Despite new stimuli for improvement, the condition of the bulk of the population remained wretched. Not only was this situation unfortunate for the people of India; it also threatened prospects for sustained growth in British exports to India.

How was this disappointing side of the story to be understood? The outcome could not be explained by deficiencies in India's resources. 'No country in the world', McCulloch declared, 'has greater capacities of production than India.'[18] Responsibility should be assigned to the persistence of impediments to the free play of market forces.

[15] *Geographical Dictionary* (1851), vol. 1, p. 669.

[16] *Geographical Dictionary* (1842), vol. 2, p. 26.

[17] Ricardo, Speech to the General Court of the East India Company, 19 March 1823, *Works and Correspondence of David Ricardo*, ed. Sraffa, vol. 5, p. 482.

[18] McCulloch, *Reasons for the Establishment of a New Bank in India with Answers to Objections Against It* (London, 1836), p. 28.

At least part of the difficulty could be traced to pernicious policies in Britain. In consequence, India's export prospects were unfortunately constrained. In this context, McCulloch did not mention the treatment accorded to Indian textiles in British markets. He directed attention instead to discriminatory duties applied to some of her primary commodities, particularly to sugar. In the 1820s East India sugar bore an import duty eight shillings per cwt. higher than that imposed on West Indian sugar. In McCulloch's opinion, this was an outrageous injustice. It meant that one group of British subjects had been favoured over another. But that was not all: the beneficiaries of British customs regulations in this instance were slave-owners in the West Indies. To continue to penalize the sugar growers of India, McCulloch maintained, would be 'to refuse to avail ourselves of such obvious and effectual means of increasing the commercial prosperity of the empire, and of adding to the public wealth, for the sake of granting an unjust protection to the cultivators of the inferior soils in the West India islands, would be a degree of folly and infatuation unparalleled in the history of the world.'[19] McCulloch and Ricardo spoke with one voice on this matter. Appealing for a free trade in sugar before the East India Company's General Court of Proprietors, Ricardo declared that he would not alter his position even 'if he thought that the East-Indies or the West-Indies would be severed from this country within a month . . .'[20]

In this diagnosis, the British government had before it a golden opportunity to spur fuller utilization of India's productive potential. Commercial freedom would necessarily promote advances in income and output. Before the most objectionable discriminatory duties on India's primary commodities were removed in the mid-1830s, this conclusion was more a matter of faith than of fact. The growth in the total volume of trade in the 1840s seemed to demonstrate that confidence had been well placed. In 1847 McCulloch asserted that 'each rapid extension of the demand for British cottons and other goods in India, is principally ascribed to the increased imports of sugar, coffee, and other Indian

---

[19] McCulloch, 'East and West India Sugar', *Edinburgh Review* (February 1823), p. 222.

[20] Ricardo, Speech to the General Court of the East India Company, 19 March 1823, *Works and Correspondence of David Ricardo*, ed. Sraffa, vol. 5, p. 481.

articles.'[21] The adoption of more enlightened commercial policies in England had thus brought gains to all.

III. THE GOVERNMENT OF BRITISH INDIA AS AN OBSTACLE TO ECONOMIC IMPROVEMENT

Though policies in England had retarded India's growth, the economic consequences of intervention by the government of British India were far more serious. While McCulloch found errors aplenty in the practices of the East India Company, his sharpest invective was reserved for its misguided approach to the land revenue system. James Mill, he charged, had drawn the wrong lessons from Ricardian teaching. The massive governmental interference called for by his approach to land revenues was dangerous. 'It seems', wrote McCulloch in 1827, 'as if there were some strange fatality attending the government of India; and that the greatest talents and the best intentions should, when applied to legislate for that country, produce only the most pernicious projects.'[22]

McCulloch did not challenge the analytic soundness of the theory of differential rent. He maintained, however, that those who derived from it guidelines for taxation in India had overlooked a central truth: the population was poor and already heavily overtaxed. The ambitious designs of the tax reformers had claimed resources which should properly have been left in private hands. As early as 1827, McCulloch called for reforms which would transform the cultivating tenantry into peasant proprietors—or, failing that, would make land available to them at moderate rates on long leases. It was essential that the *ryots* should have access to land '*at such a reduced rent as they may be able to pay without difficulty*'.[23] If such reforms could be implemented, 'industry would revive, and the peasantry would become attached to Government. But so long as we compel the *ryots* to cultivate land that is over assessed—so long, in short, as we compel them to raise the crops, not for their own advantage, but for the exclusive advantage of Government and the host of harpies it is obliged to employ, so long will the scourge of universal poverty continue to afflict the country; so long will the benevolent intentions of the Company be frustrated; and their

---

[21] McCulloch, *Dictionary of Commerce* (1847), p. 557.

[22] McCulloch, 'Revenue and Commerce of India', *Edinburgh Review* (March 1827), p. 354.   [23] Ibid., p. 358 (italics in the original).

Government be looked upon as the prolific source of Indian degradation and misery.'[24]

On this issue, two strands of Ricardian doctrine clashed head-on. Mill's vision of the scientific tax could not be reconciled with McCulloch's commitment to non-interventionist market solutions. Neither camp wavered in its convictions. McCulloch, who outlived the East India Company's government, offered the following judgement in 1859: 'We regret we are not able to say that the British government has made any material deductions from this enormous assessment. Its oppressiveness, and the impossibility of assessing it on anything like a fair and sound principle, has done far more than anything else to prevent our ascendancy in India, and the comparative good order and tranquillity we have introduced, from having the beneficial effects that might have been anticipated.'[25]

The moral of McCulloch's tale was that the government of India had acted on a distorted interpretation of the Ricardian model. Massive state intervention in the land revenue system had been buttressed by the argument that taxation directed to the rental share of income would perfect the market by being neutral in its effects on costs. In fact, its claims on the purchasing power of a poverty-ridden populace had stifled the normal development of markets. Englishmen as well as Indians had been the losers. By 1859 McCulloch concluded that 'there is but little ground to think that the legitimate trade we carry on with India is greater than it would have been had it continued subject to its native rulers . . .'[26]

Though the land revenue system was the main villain, India's problems were further complicated by the government's behaviour as a monopolist in the salt and opium markets. From McCulloch's perspective, monopoly in any of its manifestations was likely to be malevolent. The government's position as the single seller of salt imposed an oppressive burden on the mass of the population. 'Few things', he wrote in 1832, 'would do more

[24] Ibid., p. 358.

[25] McCulloch, *Dictionary of Commerce* (1859), p. 565. In 1851 he had been no less stinging in his indictment: 'The organisation and maintenance of the existing *ryotwar* system is, in truth, the most discreditable fact connected with the history of British India.' (McCulloch, *Geographical Dictionary* (1851), vol. 2, p. 23.)

[26] McCulloch, *Dictionary of Commerce* (1859), p. 565. In a footnote he added: 'we say *legitimate*, for a considerable portion of our trade with India is carried on upon account of the British troops serving in the Peninsula.'

to promote the improvement of India, than the total abolition of this monopoly. An open trade in salt, with moderate duties, would, there can be no doubt, be productive of the greatest advantage to the public, and of a large increase of revenue to the government.'[27] His position on the opium monopoly, however, was more cautious. It was no less true that a monopoly mode of organization interfered with the 'industry of the inhabitants' and denied them income which was rightfully their due. But the nature of this product made governmental control less objectionable. Though the individual cultivator was disadvantaged by the sub-market procurement prices set by the government, the total set of circumstances seemed to justify a departure from *laissez-faire*. India's opium output was exported in its entirety to China where it was disposed of at inflated monopoly prices. Late in life, McCulloch stated his position as follows: '. . . though it be nowise incumbent on the government of India to look beyond the interests of their own subjects, yet, as opium when taken in excess is highly injurious, it is obvious that in raising its price to the point at which it will yield the maximum amount of revenue, they do that which is best for the well-being of the Chinese, as well as for the wants of the Indian Treasury.'[28]

Though McCulloch was ultimately prepared to make some compromise in his commitment to full-blooded *laissez-faire* in the case of the procurement and distribution of opium, he was unrelenting in his criticism of other governmental impediments to the free play of markets. The lingering resistance of the East India Company's government to permanent European settlement in the sub-continent was especially objectionable. He took it to be self-evident that capital in massive quantities was required if the productive potential of the country was to be harnessed. Though the controls which the East India Company could exercise over foreign investors had been severely reduced in the Charter Renewal Act of 1833, the government had not actively encouraged private capital inflows. Europeans still

[27] McCulloch, *Dictionary of Commerce* (1832), p. 510.

[28] McCulloch, Note XX to his third edition of Adam Smith, *The Wealth of Nations* (Edinburgh, 1863), p. 577. A similar rationalization was offered in an anonymous pamphlet published in 1858 under the title *How We Tax India*. The author maintained that, under a regime of free trade, 'the drug would be supplied vastly cheaper to the Chinese—and mark you, to the Hindoos also; its cultivation would be increased; more Chinese, and many more Hindoos would be poisoned . . .' (p. 9).

encountered difficulties in purchasing land and the court system, in the view of many, was too preoccupied with the protection of native rights to reassure foreign investors anxious about the security of their position. McCulloch was aware that the government itself had taken some steps to broaden and diversify India's export base. Consultants from the United States had been brought to India in the 1820s to provide technical guidance on cotton production and processing. The government had also launched experiments with tea and coffee in the 1830s.[29] But these initiatives, welcome though they were, had been too little and too late. India's capacity to earn foreign exchange was still excessively dependent on traditional commodities for which the longer-term prospects on world markets were not particularly bright. By 1834–5, about four-fifths of India's export earnings were accounted for by six items: indigo, raw silk, piece goods (which, though declining in significance, still accounted for about 7 per cent of the total), sugar, raw cotton (most of which was shipped to China), and opium (all of which was destined for China).[30] It was much later before tea was to figure significantly in India's export pattern—and, when it did so, the result reflected the discovery of an indigenous leaf in Assam rather than success for the government's attempts to adapt Chinese varieties to Indian conditions. Meanwhile, there was an unsatisfied demand in Britain for commodities which were within India's capabilities. Cotton headed the list. The importance attached to it was magnified in the late 1840s and 1850s by rising fears that turmoil in the United States might interrupt supplies from the American South.

In McCulloch's judgement, proper adjustments in India's export pattern could readily be achieved if European capital and enterprise enjoyed unhampered freedom. Moreover, resident European skills in India would confer significant external benefits on the local population. At this point, the views of McCulloch and James Mill converged: '. . . the increase and diffusion of the English population, and their permanent settlement in the country, are at once the most likely means of spreading a know-

[29] Daniel H. Buchanan, *The Beginnings of Capitalistic Enterprise in India* (New York, 1934), esp. chap. IV.

[30] See K. N. Chaudhuri, *The Economic Development of India Under the East India Company, 1814–1858* (Cambridge, 1971), p. 26.

ledge of our arts and sciences, and of widening and strengthening the foundations of our ascendance . . . Nor will it, I conceive, be doubted that the diffusion of useful knowledge, and its application to the arts and business of life, must be comparatively tardy, unless we add to precept the example of Europeans, mingling familiarly with the natives in the course of their profession, and practically demonstrating, by daily recurring evidence, the nature and value of principles we desire to inculcate, and of the plans we seek to have adopted.'[31] These heirs of Ricardo differed, however, in their appraisals of the type of hospitality the government of India should accord to foreigners. Mill, eager though he was to promote economic improvement for the Indian peoples, sought to avoid a legally sanctioned dualism in the economic structure and was always solicitous of the welfare of the small man. For McCulloch, on the other hand, a free market should be allowed to take its own course. If unimpeded market forces produced a structure in which India's export economy was dominated by European-owned plantations, who then—he might ask—could claim that any other outcome would be superior?

IV. AN ALTERNATE APPROACH TO PERFECTING THE MARKET

McCulloch placed his main bets on private initiative. Most activities of governments were suspect—and particularly those of a government with a heritage linked with a chartered monopoly. At the same time, it was clear that India did not offer a climate ideal for the full flowering of free markets. Some restructuring was in order. The official model developed by James Mill was not, however, the answer. The heavy-handed interventionism it required was distasteful and its consequences in practice had been unfortunate. Institutional innovation in a different form was called for.

McCulloch spurned Mill's fiscal prescriptions and recommended instead that priority be assigned to providing India with a modern set of financial institutions. If equipped with well-managed banking institutions, the country's economic growth could be accelerated and a 'powerful stimulus' could be given to 'all sorts of industry'.[32] Savings which had formerly been

---

[31] McCulloch, *Dictionary of Commerce* (1859), p. 563.
[32] McCulloch, *Reasons for the Establishment of a New Bank in India with Answers to Objections Against It*, p. 7.

hoarded could thereafter be mobilized for worthwhile investment. Properly structured financial institutions would offer 'to the Hindoo merchants and cultivators the means, of which they have hitherto been destitute, of profitably and safely investing their surplus or spare funds'.[33] McCulloch's confidence in the efficacy of his recommendations was virtually complete. 'It is all but certain', he wrote, 'that, in no long time it would bring forth and vivify millions of capital that now lie dormant in the earth, or in secret hiding places; while, by increasing the advantages of accumulation, and making savings available as well for immediate profit as for future resource, it would, at one and the same time, add new strength to the spirit of industry, and to the cumulative principle.'[34]

An opportunity to spur the fuller utilization of the country's potential was thus readily at hand. Should it be missed, the savings behaviour of much of the population would be locked into the traditional mould. He asserted that 'the habit of wearing rings, bracelets, brooches, hair-pins and such like personal ornaments of gold and silver, but generally the latter, is universal in India, and cannot fail to occasion a very large expenditure.'[35] India could ill afford to import precious metals to the value of £4 million sterling per annum (the sums McCulloch estimated were required to offset the wastage through loss, wear, and tear in a metallic monetary circulation).[36]

Financial modernization through a sound note-issuing bank also promised other advantages. Through the issue of properly secured banknotes, requirements of bullion could be reduced.[37] Similarly, the dispersal of branch banks throughout the country would facilitate national economic integration. The multiplicity of local currencies could more readily be phased out and the ease

[33] Ibid., p. 18.   [34] Ibid., p. 19.

[35] McCulloch, *Dictionary of Commerce* (1859), p. 561.

[36] Ibid., p. 560. The annual losses of precious metals seemed, however, to make one otherwise puzzling phenomenon more explicable: 'the vast sums lost in consequence of this practice, is the chief cause why prices do not seem to have risen materially in the East, or the precious metals to have become more abundant, notwithstanding the vast quantities that used to be sent thither.' (McCulloch, *Reasons for the Establishment of a New Bank in India with Answers to the Objections Against It*, p. 17.)

[37] This was not the only economy which might be effected. As late as the 1850s, the commander-in-chief of military forces in British India estimated that some 30,000 troops were required to ensure the safe transport of 'treasure' throughout the country. See S. Ambirijan, 'Economic Ideas and Indian Economic Policies in the 19th Century', University of Manchester Ph.D. thesis, 1964, chap. III.

and efficiency with which monetized transactions could be conducted would be enhanced. Reforms along the lines McCulloch proposed would widen the scope for market activities.

McCulloch's views on these matters were most fully articulated in a pamphlet published anonymously in 1836 in which he solicited support for the formation of a Bank of India to be chartered by the Crown and sanctioned by the East India Company. Though the organization would perform some of the functions of a central bank for India, much of its orientation would be toward international transactions. In the mid-1830s the European trading community sensed acutely the need for improved financial facilities. Most of the major 'Agency Houses' which provided financial services to European traders had closed during the commercial slump of the early 1830s.[38]

McCulloch's perspective on monetary institutions for India was heavily influenced by the importance he attached to the role of foreign trade and investment in the process of economic growth, but it was also bounded by the constraints of classical orthodoxy. Banks were creative in the sense that they improved the allocation of resources and narrowed the gap between actual and potential output. But, in the context of the international economy, imaginative monetary schemes also had their limits. Enlargements in the domestic money supply were necessarily tied to the availability of internationally acceptable reserves. Should monetary expansion be excessive, price adjustments would be adverse to the balance of trade. There was no room in McCulloch's account for Steuart's scepticism of 1772 about the applicability of the quantity theory to predominantly agrarian economies. Nor did the local flavour of Steuart's report on Bengal penetrate McCulloch's writings. Whereas Steuart perceived that an integrated monetary system in India would require the assimilation of the traditional *shroffs* into modern financial institutions, McCulloch assumed that his monetary scheme would eliminate them.

V. THE AUDIENCE FOR THE MESSAGE

Not all of McCulloch's analysis of Indian problems found its way into practice. His proposition for a new bank did not. Even

[38] K. N. Chaudhuri, *Economic Development of India*, esp. pp. 18–25. John Crawfurd, *A Sketch of the Commercial Resources and Monetary and Mercantile System of British*

so, much of his doctrine was heard by receptive ears. Though he was not alone in propagating the *laissez-faire* strand of Ricardian teaching, he could take comfort in the submissions of business groups to Parliamentary Committees concerned with Indian affairs.

The Select Committee on the Indian Territories in 1852–3, for example, was flooded with petitions from Manchester, Birmingham, Liverpool, and Bristol. Each of them demonstrated that the fundamental teaching had been absorbed. Policies pursued by the East India Company's government, these groups protested, urgently required correction. The tax system had drained the purchasing power of the Indian peasantry. As the Liverpool East India and China Association put it: '. . . your petitioners consider that the land tax or rent paid by the cultivators of the soil is excessive; that it is injurious to the commercial and agricultural interests of that country, and highly detrimental to the moral and physical condition of the people.'[38]

No less iniquitous was the monopoly pricing of salt. Petitioners from Manchester affirmed a feeling 'of great interest in the future well-being of India' and deeply deplored 'the existence of a law which all but deprives the working classes in that country of one of the most essential articles of life, namely, salt'. It was added that 'if salt manufactured in England could be imported into India upon the same terms as other imports, a sufficient quantity could be sent to meet the wants of that country, pure in quality, certain and sufficient in supply, and at a comparatively small cost.'[40]

But if the government of British India had been misguided in its decisions on techniques for raising revenue, its policies in the allocation of public expenditures were equally reprehensible. Funds had been misallocated in the prosecution of military campaigns. Despite the propaganda of the East India Company's administration, confidence in the fair-mindedness of the judicial system was lacking. In the view of the petitioners at least,

---

India, with suggestions for their improvement, by means of Banking Establishments (1837; reprinted by Chaudhuri), argued in support of the banking scheme discussed by McCulloch.

[39] The Humble Petition of the Liverpool East India and China Association, *Parliamentary Papers, 1852–53*, vol. 28, p. 238.

[40] The Humble Petition of the Merchants, Manufacturers, Tradesmen, and Others of the City of Manchester, *Parliamentary Papers, 1852–53*, vol. 28, p. 252.

security for persons and property in India had not yet been assured. The government had also been negligent in its provisions for public works. The transport system of India was scandalously underdeveloped. To the petitioners of 1852–3, an instruction to the government of India that it allocate 10 per cent of its revenues to improvement in the transport and communications system seemed essential.[41]

There was an affinity between these views and the teachings McCulloch promoted. The enemy was governmental obstruction to commerce. The objective was maximization of market space. An optimal division of labour—with benefits to all—could then emerge. India would be a more attractive market for British manufacturers when money incomes were rising there. Moreover, it seemed to be ordained that India's income would be maximized when its producers specialized in primary commodities for export. This was indeed the imperialism of free trade.

VI. PROPERTIES OF THE UNOFFICIAL MODEL

McCulloch's version of the Ricardian message for India was straightforward. Freedom of commerce—both in domestic markets and in international ones—was the formula for economic uplift. Policies should be guided by this truth, not only in India, but also in England.

The unofficial Ricardian model for India differed from the official one primarily on the points selected for emphasis. To James Mill, the rent doctrine provided the analytic insight most crucial to India's condition. McCulloch, while accepting its theoretical soundness, rejected its practical implications. When applied to India, Mill's fiscal scheme diverted too much purchasing power from the private sector and thus frustrated the healthy development of markets.

41 These calls were directed to improvement in the inland transport system of India, particularly as it affected access of the interior to the major ports. It is worth noting in passing that another improvement in the sea links between Britain and India had been considered and rejected. Some two decades earlier, Thomas Love Peacock in his capacity as an official in the Examiner's Office of the East India Company had reported: 'If a ship canal were in existence from Suez to the Mediterranean, the trade between India and England might be carried on through that channel . . . but it would give an advantage to Marseilles and all the French ports of the Mediterranean.' (*Parliamentary Papers, 1831–32*, vol. 10, pt. ii, p. 495.)

Despite these differences, the official and unofficial models shared a central presupposition. Though it was well understood that the economic structures of India and England were fundamentally dissimilar, both readings of Ricardo assumed implicitly that the same conceptual apparatus could embrace them both. No significant theoretical adaptations were required before one prescribed remedies for India's plight. Differences in the reality did not challenge the adequacy of the master model. The task instead was to reshape reality. It was also characteristic of this line of reasoning that changes in the observed world, as they occurred, tended to reinforce confidence in the premisses with which one began.

CHAPTER 12

Richard Jones and the Conceptual Challenge to Ricardian Orthodoxies

AMONG British economic analysts in the first half of the nine-teenth century, only one significant thinker directly challenged the conceptual adequacy of Ricardian reasoning to Indian con-ditions. Richard Jones (1790–1855) addressed himself to this task as Malthus's successor in the chair of Political Economy at Haileybury. Though an insider in the sense that he was on the pay-roll of the East India Company, Jones was very much out-side the mainstream of fashionable intellectual currents. He did identify himself with the new political economy to the extent of asking the classical question: i.e. what were the inter-relation-ships between the distribution of income and economic growth? In his search for the answers, however, he immediately parted company with most of his contemporaries on points of method.

Jones's major published work, *An Essay on the Distribution of Wealth and on the Sources of Taxation* which appeared in 1831, was written while he was a curate at a parish in Kent. At the time of publication, this treatise was announced as the first instalment of a multi-volume work on income distribution. The projected sequels never appeared. Volume One—dealing with the subject of rent—was sufficient, however, to qualify him for an appointment to the chair in Political Economy at King's College, London. This shift to an academic career placed him at an institution newly established by the Church of England as a counterweight to the secular religion preached nearby at the Benthamite foundation—University College, London.[1] In 1835 Jones transferred his base: this time to accept an invitation from the East-India College where he was to teach until shortly before his death.

---

[1] There can be no doubt that Bentham sought immortality for his influence at University College. He left instructions in his will that his body should be pickled and positioned in a posture 'as if engaged in thought'. In this form, he would always be available to attend meetings of the academic staff.

I. JONES'S INTELLECTUAL POSTURE

One central premiss underlay Jones's work: that abstract propositions on matters of political economy were suspect. What mattered—and what deserved to be studied—were the central facts of economic life. Once they had been mastered, significant empirical generalizations might then be possible. Conclusions reached purely by deductive reasoning, on the other hand, were not admissible. Statements about the 'laws' of political economy, for example, were dangerously misleading unless grounded in experience. Jones put his fundamental position as follows:

> It wants no great deal of logical acuteness to perceive that in political econ-
> omy, maxims which profess to be universal can only be founded on the most
> comprehensive views of society. The principles which determine the position
> and progress, and govern the conduct, of large bodies of the human race,
> placed under different circumstances, can be learnt only by an appeal to
> experience. He must, indeed, be a shallow reasoner, who by mere efforts of
> consciousness, by consulting his own views, feelings and motives, and the nar-
> row sphere of his personal observations, and reasoning *a priori*, from them
> expects that he shall be able to anticipate the conduct, progress and fortunes
> of large bodies of men, differing from himself in moral or physical temperament,
> and influenced by differences, varying in extent and variously combined in
> climate, soil, religion, education and government.[2]

When measured against these criteria, orthodox Ricardianism could readily be judged to be deficient. Jones indicted its practitioners for having 'quitted too soon the duty of dwelling long and humbly among things . . .' Instead they had presumptuously taken up 'the more fascinating employment of laying down those maxims of imposing generality, which seemed to elevate the enquirer at once into the legislator of his subject, and gift him, as if by some sudden manifestation of intellectual power, with an instant command over its remotest details'.[3] Correct analytic statements about the economic process were not, in principle, beyond reach. Valid general propositions could follow—but could never precede—detailed studies of the specific circumstances of particular societies. Jones set exacting standards for the student of economic affairs. They could be met only with diligence, patience, and the intellectual toughness to resist premature conclusions.

In Jones's view, the Ricardian approach to rent was a prime

---

[2] Richard Jones, *An Essay on the Distribution of Wealth and on the Sources of Taxation* (Cambridge, 1831), p. xv.   [3] Ibid., p. xxiii.

example of an offence against proper procedure. The hard problems had been evaded. As Jones saw matters: '. . . the greater part of the nations of the earth are still in that state which is properly called agricultural; that is, in which the bulk of their population depends wholly on agriculture for subsistence: . . . in this state of society, the relations between proprietors of the soil and its occupiers determine the details of the condition of the majority of the people, and the spirit and forms of their political institutions.'[4] Precisely because the subject was of such importance, it deserved to be investigated with special care. Universal statements—such as the proposition that the rental share of income derived from the scarcity of land and from diversity in its quality—should be avoided. The phenomenon of rent could be understood only when attention was paid to the variations in agricultural systems and in agricultural practices to be found throughout the world.

Understandably, those who held political economy to be a science organized around universal laws regarded Jones's methodological strictures as an invitation to analytic chaos. When charged with looseness and imprecision in his thinking, he was unrepentant. 'To begin, or indeed to end, an enquiry into the nature of any subject . . . by a definition', he maintained, 'is to shew how little we know how to set about our task—how little of the inductive spirit is within us.'[5] As he further asserted: 'It is obvious that, in inquiring into the principles and laws relating to things as they exist in the world, words may be used to indicate the subjects of research but not to supersede them.'[6]

If the Ricardian definition of rent offered no help, what alternative was available? Jones proposed that the matter be studied in an operational context: i.e. rent should be regarded as the share of income claimed by the proprietor of the soil. The interesting problem was to establish how that claim was exercised in different social and cultural situations.

II. A CRITIQUE OF THE APPLICATION OF DIFFERENTIAL RENT THEORY TO INDIA

James Mill's approach to taxation in India was a conscious exercise in applied Ricardianism. From Jones's perspective, it

[4] Jones, *Essay on the Distribution of Wealth*, p. xxv.

[5] *Literary Remains, Consisting of Lectures and Tracts on Political Economy, of the late Rev. Richard Jones*, ed. William Whewell (London, 1859), p. 598.

[6] Ibid., p. 600.

was a misapplication: only those blind to the realities of the wider world could fail to be alert to the limitations of the doctrine. 'Mr. Ricardo', Jones charged, 'overlooking altogether the peasant tenantry, which occupy ninety-nine hundredths of the globe, had persuaded himself that the existence of a gradation of soils of different fertility was the only cause, why rents ever existed at all.'[7] Rent, as Jones saw it, had quite different origins. It had usually begun with 'the appropriation of the soil, at a time when the bulk of the people must cultivate it on such terms as they can obtain, or starve . . . A necessity which then, compels them to pay a rent . . . is wholly independent of any difference in the quality of the ground they occupy, and would not be removed were the soils all equalised.'[8] This interpretation has much in common with the attitude Marx expressed when attacking the classical economists as victims of a 'Physiocratic illusion' when they insisted that rent grew out of the soil, rather than out of society.[9]

While outspoken in his denunciation of Ricardian rent in agrarian societies, Jones accepted that Ricardian analysis might apply reasonably well to contemporary England. Unique institutional circumstances there brought the categories of the model into their own. But this was a special case—one which Jones described as that of 'farmers' rent'. The conditions required to give meaning to this variation on the larger theme prevailed in England because individual property rights in land, combined with well-established markets for both the outputs and the inputs of agriculture, had been developed. From a global perspective, these circumstances were much more the exception than the rule. Most of the world's cultivation was conducted by peasants, and the institutional contexts within which they worked were far from uniform. Jones identified a number of distinct forms of 'peasant rents': among them, those of the cottier, the *metayer*, and the *ryot*. His work at Haileybury obliged him to concentrate much of his attention on cases of the latter type and to analyse their relationship to the Anglo-Indian revenue systems.

[7] Jones, *Essay on the Distribution of Wealth*, pp. 205–6. By analogy with Professor Stigler's characterization of Ricardo's approach to value as a '93 per cent theory', one might depict Jones as charging Ricardo with a 'one per cent theory of rent'. (See George J. Stigler, 'Ricardo and the 93 Per Cent Theory of Value', *American Economic Review*, vol. 48 (1958).) [8] Ibid., p. 11.

[9] Jones, in fact, was among the highly select group of 'bourgeois' economists whose works were treated charitably by Marx.

In this phase of his work, Jones sought to demonstrate that the Ricardian doctrine had been mistakenly appropriated in India and with unfortunate consequences. 'Some', he observed, 'have considered rents in every form and position of society, as furnishing a fund peculiarly suitable to be applied by governments for the common weal.' It was tempting, he acknowledged, to regard rent 'as the boon of nature, whose gifts ought not to be confined to any particular class, but to be equally shared by all'. The temptation, however, should be resisted. The doctrine, Jones maintained, was 'so false and so pernicious that some pains must not be grudged to refute it'.[10]

As far as Indian affairs were concerned, there could be no mistaking James Mill as Jones's primary target. The official notion of rent, he asserted, was adequate 'only in a country of capitalists, whose capital is endowed with mobility, such as England. It is not so in a country whose capital is immobile, like Ireland. Nor is it so in a country where no classes of capitalists are found, as India.'[11] Put bluntly, India lacked the institutional supports to identify the Ricardian rent.

One could, of course, still speak about rent in the sense of the share of output landlords could claim. But the factors controlling the size of that claim were not the same in England and in India. In England, the flow of market forces tended to establish income shares which, apart from the case of the small owner-operator, could be broadly identified with the classical concepts of distributive shares: wages, profits, and rents. For most practical purposes, it was reasonable to assume that the rent actually paid and the portion of output identifiable as the Ricardian rent would tend to coincide. But there was no basis for confidence that the outcome would be similar in a peasant economy. In Indian agriculture, conducted primarily for subsistence purposes with unpaid family labour, the income shares written about in classical theory could not be readily distinguished. Only a total physical product was visible. No market criteria were available to decompose real output into shares rewarding independent suppliers of land, labour, and capital.

James Mill had recognized this difficulty as a practical matter,

---

[10] Jones, *A Short Tract on Political Economy, Including Some Account of the Anglo-Indian Revenue Systems* (as reprinted by Whewell in the *Literary Remains*, p. 273).
[11] Ibid., pp. 273–4.

but he had not regarded it as an insurmountable obstacle to the implementation of his programme. The net rent could be approximated, he maintained, by direct inspection of individual plots of land. Accordingly, revenue officers in the field were instructed to conduct cadastral surveys to insure that the tax demand was adjusted to the fertility of the soil. Though Mill well understood that the translation of the Ricardian message in India involved administrative strains, he denied that any question of principle arose. If reality diverged from the requirements of the model, reality—not the model—should be adjusted to produce a closer fit.

As Jones saw the issue, Mill's proposed solution was beside the point. To map, measure, and appraise 'the land in its numerous allotments' was 'a gigantic task, that never could be efficiently done!'[12] But the main difficulty was not an administrative but a conceptual one. The *ryotwari* plan of 'settlement' in Madras had, in fact, turned Ricardian doctrine upside down. The theory held that rent was what remained after the costs of agricultural production had been met. The strategies pursued in India, however, treated rent, as approximated in the tax demand, as the first claim on the output of the peasantry. Wages and profits, rather than rent, had thus become residual shares. The consequences, in Jones's judgement, had been disastrous. Even so, he asked his readers 'to keep in mind' that the policies of British administrators had 'originated in the most equitable intentions, and an earnest desire to improve the condition of the natives. The dispatches of the home authorities, and the reports of their servants in India, attest these right and honourable dispositions . . .'[13]

III. JONES AND THE UNOFFICIAL RICARDIAN MODEL

Though Jones's central preoccupation was with the distribution of income in agrarian economies, his scepticism toward deductive reasoning as a support to policy guidelines also touched the orthodox optimism on the uplifting effects of free markets. He did not spell out his position on this question systematically. It was clear, none the less, that he again parted company with his more prominent contemporaries.

Part of the difficulty could be traced to 'an abuse of language'

[12] Ibid., p. 288.   [13] Ibid., p. 289.

by the main body of political economists. Erroneously, they had regarded wealth as 'consisting of all commodities of an exchangeable value . . .' From this proposition, it had been 'deduced that exchanges were the main subject of Political Economy'.[14] This view of the subject systematically excluded a substantial part of economic reality. There was no place in market-oriented models for economic activities conducted within the framework of self-sufficient households. In its total impact, this exclusion was not insignificant. Much of the energy of the world's peasantry was, after all, directed to production for subsistence purposes.

The failure of standard economics to look beneath the veil of the money economy was, in turn, responsible for serious misperceptions about economic policy in agrarian societies. In India, for example, British administrators had demanded payment of the land tax in cash. From the orthodox perspective, the wisdom of this procedure had seemed to be self-evident. No revenue collector wished to accept the inconvenience of dealing with a miscellaneous assortment of goods which would then have to be graded, stored, and ultimately marketed.[15] There was thus an administrative imperative to the insistence on the use of money in the settlement of tax claims. Moreover, it seemed natural to those schooled in the orthodox way of thinking to regard an enlargement of market participation as necessarily healthy.

Jones challenged the presuppositions of these arguments. He maintained that it would be hard 'even for the most wise and honest government to impose a definite money payment that shall not be oppressive'.[16] The problem arose because a tax obligation fixed in money terms could not make satisfactory allowance for two of the basic facts of agrarian economic life: seasonal fluctuations in output and instability in market prices. A peasant family was never in a position to calculate with confidence how much of its real output it would be obliged to surrender to obtain the cash required to satisfy the revenue officer. It was indeed conceivable that situations might arise in which the marketed volume of agricultural product increased while the

---

[14] Jones, *A Short Tract on Political Economy*, p. 195.

[15] Among the earlier British economic commentators on India, only Sir James Steuart had been sympathetic to such a practice. See chap. 4.

[16] Jones, *A Short Tract on Political Economy*, p. 282.

quantity of output retained in peasant households diminished. In short, growth in market participation was not an infallible index of improvement in the welfare of the peasantry. The forced marketing implied by a monetized tax system might mean that the circumstances of peasant families had deteriorated.

Though Jones did not develop these points with notable rigour, his message was still unmistakeable. The *laissez-faire* strand of Ricardianism—no less than the scientific tax strand of the doctrine—was conceptually handicapped. Other approaches were required if the problems of India were to be dealt with in realistic terms.

IV. CONSIDERATIONS PERTINENT TO A MORE REALISTIC PERSPECTIVE ON INDIA'S ECONOMIC PROSPECTS

For Jones, there was no escape from the fact that the general condition of India was miserable and that an important job needed to be done. India's difficulties, however, would not be relieved by strategies inspired by theories alien to the Indian environment. Solid progress was still possible, but it would necessarily be slow and could only occur when linked with the local institutional base. British administration still had an important role to play in creating a climate of integrity and security. Ultimately, the 'happy day' might come when 'the condition and character of the Hindoos shall have been elevated by English energy and influence to a level with their masters'. But he added a caution: 'That day, we cannot disguise from ourselves, is still far distant.'[17]

Good government still had to be paid for and, in the light of the country's economic structure, there was no alternative to continued reliance on the taxation of land. Those who had called for a large reduction in the land tax (as, for example, had McCulloch) were 'well meaning, perhaps, but not wise'.[18] There was ample room for improvement, however, in the procedures for raising revenue from the country's agrarian base. The intellectual bankruptcy of the scientific tax formula had already been demonstrated. The permanent settlement in Bengal—as an exercise in imposing a different English model to Indian conditions—was also deficient. Whether dealing with *ryots* or with *zemindari*, British administrators had acted in 'perverse contrariety to the cherished

---

[17] Ibid., p. 286.   [18] Ibid.

feelings and the inveterate habits of the people'.[19] In Jones's judgement, it was far more promising to build a tax system on the village unit by making its members as a group responsible for obligations to the state. Some attempts to implement this recommendation had already been made and a number of them, he acknowledged, had failed 'signally' and 'completely'. These disappointments, he insisted, did not discredit the approach. They had arisen because the traditional village system had been only partially reconstructed; in its new incarnation, some of the checks and balances on the authority of the village headman had been left out. There were still grounds for hope. Jones noted particularly that 'in the Bombay Presidency, which has had the good fortune to be ruled by very wise men, the Hindoo institutions have been preserved, and gradually improved and reformed.'[20]

Though Jones held that sound policy required some accommodation with traditional institutions and attitudes, it was not his intention to glorify the *status quo*. Improvement in economic performance was much to be desired. The pace at which it could occur would, in his view, ultimately be determined by the productivity of the labour force which, in turn, could be sub-divided into three components: '1. the continuity with which it [labour] is exerted; 2. the skill with which it is directed; 3. the power by which it is aided'.[21] But the effectiveness with which labour could be utilized was also related to the structure of the economy. When economic advance reached a point at which a substantial proportion of the labour force was employed for wages, the continuity and efficiency of labour input could be expected to increase. Workers would then be 'subject to the vigilant eye of their masters' and would not be permitted 'to relax their diligence'.[22] No comparable disciplines on labour utilization would be found in family-based traditional agriculture. Peasant communities thus tended to be trapped in a vicious circle of poverty. Moreover, the difficulties of escape from the trap were compounded because in-

---

[19] Jones, *A Short Tract on Political Economy* p. 287.   [20] Ibid., p. 290.

[21] Ibid., p. 189. For a modern parallel, see the discussion of labour utilization in Gunnar Myrdal, *Asian Drama: an Inquiry into the Poverty of Nations* (New York, 1968), esp. vol. 2.

[22] Jones, *A Short Tract on Political Economy*, p. 193. In the modern development literature, Albert Hirschman, for example, has used a similar argument to support the build-up of a modern industrial sector in poor countries. See *The Strategy of Economic Development* (New Haven, Conn., 1958).

efficiency in agriculture frustrated the production of the food surpluses needed to support a growing non-agricultural population. The rate of growth in other sectors was thus constrained. This restriction slowed the pace at which jobs subject to disciplined labour efficiency could be created.

But did it then follow that peasant communities could anticipate no fundamental improvement in their lot? Jones argued that this was not the case. Economists who had absorbed the orthodox classical teaching on saving—i.e. that it could be expected only from the profit share of income—might easily be led to this conclusion. Their insights, however, were faulty and encouraged undue pessimism. After all, productive capital formation could be supported from other forms of income, as indeed had happened at earlier moments in history. The standard doctrine was too culture-bound and too ahistorical to penetrate this truth. Capital accumulation, Jones wrote, was 'in the first instance, the effect and not the cause of social improvement; afterwards they move in a circle, mutually producing and produced.'[23] Though the pace of accumulation might not be dramatic, a stable institutional environment could be expected to induce socially useful saving.

A poor country might, of course, accelerate the rate of growth in its capital stock by inviting inflows from abroad. This device might, at times, be expedient, but it offered no satisfactory solution to the long-term problem. Foreign investment could 'never augment the efficiency of labour so extensively or so permanently as capital generated and accumulated upon the soil itself'.[24] On this point, Jones's suspicions of *laissez-faire* Ricardianism again showed through.

While he questioned both the official and unofficial approaches to economic policy, Jones still accepted James Mill's basic diagnosis of the condition of India. An administration which was incorruptible and fair-minded was a prerequisite to progress. A break from the traditional pattern—in which 'to be rich would

[23] Jones, *A Short Tract on Political Economy*, p. 230.

[24] Ibid., p. 230. To reinforce this point, Jones submitted the following: 'Our Indian fellow subjects are about ninety millions in number, and may be divided into about eighteen millions of families, of which it may be estimated that nearly sixteen millions are agricultural. Could the condition of this class of laborers be so much improved that each family should be able to lay by annually £2, in the shape of profits, the amount of capital annually accumulated would be £32,000,000, and, in ten years, would be swelled to the immense sum of £320,000,000. What a length of time would it take to transfer such a mass of capital from England, and to circulate it through India.' (Ibid., p. 230.)

have been a peril and a crime'—[25] demanded governmental guarantees to the security of property. Moreover, a political and social structure which assured equality of opportunity could be expected to unleash formerly untapped sources of saving. Jones held that there could 'hardly be a stronger incentive to industry in producing, and carefulness in accumulating, capital' than 'the desire of elevation in the social scale'.[26] An enlightened government might also serve as a catalyst to economic uplift in yet another way: by encouraging the formation of sound financial institutions. In company with McCulloch, Jones was sympathetic to the creation of financial intermediaries to stimulate saving (particularly among the lower classes) and to channel it into worthwhile investment.

There was thus an important mission for administrators of British India to discharge. Mistaken though the more zealous Ricardians may have been in their prescriptions for policy, the task of uplifting its peoples ought not to be abandoned. Jones admonished government to abstain 'from an extreme abuse of its position and opportunities'. India needed outside guidance and Britons could long supply it, 'provided justice and a moderate forebearance are our guides'.[27]

V. THE CRITIQUE AND ITS 'REALISM'

Jones was a staunch advocate of painstaking study of the facts of economic life. His own command of the details of the Indian economy was far from comprehensive[28] and he had no first-hand knowledge of the sub-continent. The materials at his disposal, however, were more than sufficient to persuade him that blueprints for policy derived from formal models of the Ricardian variety were out of touch with reality. Both his criticisms of orthodox approaches and his alternative recommendations were based far more on intuitive insights into the structure of a problem than on any systematically collected body of empirical data.

Though his position lacked the thoroughness his own methodology would have required, there were indications that Jones's

[25] Jones, *A Short Tract on Political Economy* p. 231.   [26] Ibid., p. 232.

[27] *Textbook of Lectures on the Political Economy of Nations, delivered at the East India College, Haileybury* (as reprinted in *The Literary Remains*, p. 457).

[28] This point has been emphasized by William L. Miller, 'Richard Jones on the Indian Economy', *History of Political Economy*, vol. 3 (1971).

general sense of the Indian situation had some foundations. Spokesmen for the residents of Madras—where the bite of Mill's directives on land revenue had been most sharply felt—offered corroborative support in their petitions to Parliament in the 1850s. It is unlikely in the extreme that members of the Madras Native Association then had any acquaintance with Jones's writing. Yet the grievances for which they sought relief had a remarkable overlap with problems Jones had identified.

In the first instance, it was argued that Mill's specifications for the *ryotwari* settlement were administratively unworkable. The procedures in Madras, they asserted, had been 'commenced without the aid of a single surveying instrument, except a chain of 33 feet, or a glimpse of scientific knowledge beyond that of their native cutcherry gomastahs or clerks, who, as a part of their duty, were to instruct others in the art of mensuration, an art in which being completely untaught themselves, they had to acquire from no better education than the progress of their own survey'.[29]

But this was not the least of the difficulties. Even if plots had been accurately measured, the problem of classifying land by its fertility would remain. According to the account of the petitioners, the task was undertaken 'by sending two assessors to classify the space measured by ten surveyors; their business was to arrange it under the principal divisions of wet, dry, and garden land, subdividing these again into various classes according to the presumed quality by a process so perfectly arbitrary, that in some districts the wet land had 12 classes, the dry 20, and the garden land as many ... As might have been expected, these assessors, partly from ignorance, and partly from the persuasion of bribery, made a great many erroneous classifications ...'[30] Meanwhile the costs of administering the scheme continued to swell and the receipts from the land revenue to fall. These results might have been acceptable had confidence in the accuracy of assessments been justified. But, in the view of the petitioners, there was no reasonable basis for such a conclusion.

The regulations on the form in which the land tax should be paid had introduced an additional complication. By requiring tax payments in cash rather than in kind, British administrators had

---

[29] The Humble Petition of the Madras Native Association, and others, Native Inhabitants of the Presidency of Madras, *Parliamentary Papers, 1852–53*, vol. 27, p. 443.   [30] Ibid., p. 440.

unwittingly inflicted severe hardships on cultivators. When the tax obligation was fixed in money terms, the peasantry, of necessity, offered a substantial proportion of its output for sale. From the standard Ricardian perspective, this requirement was altogether salutary: market participation was itself a vehicle for mass education. It had, however, further consequences. The marketed proportion of total agricultural product tended to increase, even when the volume of aggregate output did not. As the Madras petitioners described the result: 'The immediate consequence of this commutation was a gradual and general fall in the price of all grains, which, for a long series of years past, has been so low as to reduce all but the most substantial *ryots* to a state of almost beggary . . .'[31] It is a reasonable guess that Jones's position on the peculiarities of peasant economies would have been better understood by Indian *ryots* than it was by his contemporaries in England.

VI. THE RECEPTION OF JONES'S MESSAGE

In his own times, Jones's critique of orthodoxy left little mark. The Ricardian school—confident that it was armed with accurate analytic equipment—largely ignored him. Nor did Jones's cautions about economic policies win significant attention. The views of some cadets for the Indian administration may well have been influenced by his lectures at Haileybury. Strategies for economic policy, however, were formulated at a higher level. In the middle third of the nineteenth century, they emerged as an amalgamation of official and unofficial Ricardian approaches to India. Implementation of the scientific tax—though subject to some procedural modifications—remained a central objective. Meanwhile, the free traders were gratified with measures designed to widen market space (especially for British merchants and investors).

Why should Jones's criticisms have been so little noticed? On matters of economic policy, the answer is straightforward. Jones spoke to no politically relevant constituency. The *laissez-faire* Ricardians had a natural audience in Manchester and those who heard their message carried weight in Parliament. The official Ricardian model was securely entrenched at East India House. Petitioners in Madras had no comparable claim on influential thinking.

31 *Parliamentary Papers, 1852–53*, vol. 27, p. 440.

It is more productive to speculate on the failure of Jones's conceptual criticisms to stir serious debate among economists. Part of the explanation must be found in his own shortcomings. His work left much to be desired in organizational tidiness. Moreover, his suspicions of deductive procedure were such that he did not always comprehend the intricacy of the doctrines he attacked. The manner in which he challenged Ricardian reasoning on diminishing returns revealed, for example, that his understanding of the role of assumptions in analytic argument was deficient.[32] Such blind spots made it easier for his opponents to dismiss him altogether. McCulloch, who produced one of the few reviews of the *Essay on the Distribution of Wealth*, could more plausibly assert that Jones had missed the point of Ricardian method. It had been intended as a contribution to analysis and could not, therefore, be judged by 'a merely practical standard'. It was not relevant to Ricardo's purpose to discuss rent 'in the ordinary and vulgar sense of the word'.[33] As McCulloch summarized his evaluation of Jones: 'His efforts to overthrow the theory of rent have been signally abortive: he has not weakened the authority of a single principle or doctrine involved in it . . . The fact that Mr. Jones's book should have attracted any attention, shows how very little the principles of the science are understood.'[34]

Jones did not lack opportunities to clarify and strengthen his argument. He was not, however, energetic in doing so. His plan to produce a major treatise on income distribution was not put into execution; only the first part of the promised work appeared.[35]

---

[32] With this type of lapse in mind, Schumpeter indicted Jones for 'typical errors that are again and again committed by would-be theorists who have disdained to learn the art of theorizing' (*History of Economic Analysis*, p. 676). In a more charitable vein, Schumpeter congratulated Whewell for bringing out the edition of Jones's works, noting that Whewell thereby displayed 'sense of quality' (ibid., p. 448).

[33] McCulloch, 'Jones on the Theory of Rent', *Edinburgh Review* (September 1831), p. 85.

[34] Ibid., p. 99.

[35] Even the perpetual needling of Whewell, his loyal champion, failed to stir him. In a letter of 13 November 1833, Whewell nudged him as follows: 'If I ask about your book, I suppose you will tell me about your face. I . . . wish heartily that your face may diminish, and your book increase.' (I. Todhunter, *William Whewell, D.D., Master of Trinity College, Cambridge: an Account of His Writings with Selections from His Literary and Scientific Correspondence* (London, 1876), vol. 2, p. 172.) Jones is reported to have enjoyed good living. At Haileybury, he was described (in words attributed to Sydney Smith) as a man who carried 'a vintage in his countenance' (*Memorials of Old Haileybury College*, ed. Frederick Charles Danvers (Westminster, 1894), p. 176).

On Indian affairs, much of his criticism of orthodoxy was contained in essays which appeared in print only after his death. Nor was he aggressive in enlightening those readers who misconstrued his message. His friend Malthus, for example, maintained that he had revised the second edition of his *Principles of Political Economy* to include consideration of 'all the different kinds of rent referred to by Mr. Jones, in his late and valuable account of the state of rents and the various modes of paying labour in different parts of the world'.[36] None the less, Malthus insisted— in opposition to one of Jones's crucial propositions—that 'the amount of rent which can be received from a given extent of land will rise according to all the different degrees of fertility above that which will only support the actual cultivators.'[37] Though James Mill appeared to have ignored Jones altogether, his son took note of the *Essay on the Distribution of Wealth*, referring to it as 'a copious repository of valuable facts'.[38] In this reading, Jones offered only typology, not conceptual criticism.[39] Though Jones could depend on Whewell for dedicated support, the latter's advocacy was not helpful on all points. As an enthusiast for inductive method (not only in the natural sciences and political economy, but also in moral philosophy), Whewell's primary interest was in enlisting recruits in methodological battles. He promoted Jones's work for its method, not its substance. Whewell had little taste for the subject of land rents and none for Indian problems.

But there was a more fundamental obstacle to the effective transmission of Jones's teachings. Jones was not—and could not be—a grand intellectual system-builder. Those who sought to comprehend the functioning of economic systems should, he insisted, assign priority to study of their particularities. The fascination of political economy derived far more from the differences than from the similarities in the world's economies. Moreover, the

[36] Malthus, *Principles of Political Economy* (2nd edn., 1836), p. 153.

[37] Ibid., p. 154.

[38] John Stuart Mill, *The Principles of Political Economy* (London, 1848), vol. 1, p. 295.

[39] Whewell was enraged by this condescending remark by John Stuart Mill. As he wrote to Jones on 30 April 1848: 'Now this is very disparaging praise and, whether he means it or not, is the way in which people speak of books, when they want to deny them originality and philosophical value. The criticism is extremely unreasonable with regard to your book, because its peculiar and distinctive character is its originality in the point of view with which the facts are regarded, and its philosophical classifications.' (Todhunter, op. cit., vol. 2, p. 345.)

potential of the discipline to guide improvement in the human condition depended on a correct appraisal of the significance of those differences. Recommendations offered by those who claimed a universal insight were likely to be more productive of harm than good.

In the marketplace of ideas, conceptual criticism of the type Jones practised tends to have little appeal. The analytic mind in economics abhors a conceptual vacuum. Though Jones could point to limitations in the Ricardian master model, he offered no analytically satisfying substitute. Logically coherent conceptual systems seldom yield to demonstrations of their inadequacies. They are more likely to be successfully challenged by rival conceptual systems. Though some of his attacks on Ricardianism were on target, Jones was not equipped to perform the task of analytic reconstruction.

But another property of the Ricardian faith blunted the impact of charges that it lacked realism. To the believer, the 'facts' that counted were yet to be revealed. Data on the current condition of the Indian economy were not of decisive significance. The relevant test of the model's adequacy lay ahead: i.e. at that point in time when the responses to Ricardian prescriptions could reasonably be analysed. James Mill spoke to this point in 1831 when he deflected Parliamentary critics of his scientific tax: 'It does not appear to me to have been as yet long enough in operation to have produced any conspicuous effects upon the population: the effects which it is likely to produce I think must as yet be matter of inference, and cannot be expected to be very apparent as matter of experience.'[40]

[40] James Mill, Testimony of 11 August 1831, *Parliamentary Papers, 1831*, vol. 5 p. 327.

PART IV

The Post-Mortem : 1857–1858 and Later

A chain of events which began at Meerut, a garrison town to the north east of Delhi, in May 1857 abruptly reversed the fortunes of the East India Company and its administration. The proximate cause of this disturbance was a dispute over the use of cartridges, greased with animals fats, in native units of the Indian army. Isolated incidents of unrest in military compounds had been known before and had been quickly put down. On this occasion, the challenge to authority was not localized. The revolt of the sepoy regiments at Meerut was soon followed by disturbances which touched much of northern and central India.

Whether this moment in Indian history is labelled as the 'Indian Mutiny' or as 'the First War of Indian Independence' is of little consequence for the present discussion. What matters for our purposes is the impact on the structure of the system created by the East India Company. The costs in life and property were horrifying enough, but the psychological damage was perhaps more shattering. There was no precedent for an uprising of such scale by native peoples within the British colonial empire.

How was this phenomenon to be understood? To judge from the types of evidence most readily accessible to Englismen, the record of the East Indian administration during the preceding half-century had, on the whole, been one of high achievement. The privateering activities of Company officials which had so offended the national conscience in the later decades of the eighteenth century had been eliminated. Moreover, standards in the performance of official duties had steadily been raised. Though the level of general competence found among Haileybury graduates had its critics, the new generation of administrators was seldom faulted for lapses in integrity. Steps had already been taken to broaden the recruitment base to the Indian service. With the reforms of 1854, appointments were tied to the results of competitive examinations. There was thus considerable justice in the claim that the civil administration of India was among the best in the world. Certainly it was not rivalled by the home civil service in Britain.

These steps toward the provision of good government seemed also to have been reflected in the behaviour of the measured indices of economic performance. In the preceding decades the volume of trade had grown enormously. By the mid-1850s, export earnings were nearly three times as great as they had been when the Company's charter was renewed in 1833 and exceeded £23 million in the financial year 1855/56. Meanwhile, imports had grown at an even faster rate.[1] Another fact was also impressive: India had become one of Britain's most important customers, accounting for about one-eighth of her foreign sales and for nearly one-sixth of the exports of her major product line.[2]

Change in the volume of trade had also been accompanied by a transformation in its commodity composition. By the mid-1850s, India's merchandise imports were composed almost entirely of industrial products and her exports of primary commodities. Her own textile exports had all but vanished from the trade lists; by 1855 they accounted for only about five per cent of the total. Instead the returns had been moved by expanded shipments in agricultural products, and most particularly by opium which then contributed more than 30 per cent of the total value of exports.[3] Opinions might differ on the longer-term merits of such specialization in primary production. There could be no question, however, that it had been associated with growth in foreign exchange earnings. That incomes of producers had also improved seemed to be amply documented by the rising demand for imports. Altogether, the economy appeared to display a healthy flexibility by adjusting to new opportunities.

Enlargement in the government's revenues seemed to testify further to the basic soundness of the economy. In the financial year 1855/56, revenue receipts had set a new record, approaching an aggregate figure of £29 million. The taxation of land continued

[1] 'Memorandum of the Improvements in the Administration of India during the Last Thirty Years', *Parliamentary Papers, 1857–58*, vol. 43, p. 11.

[2] Albert Imlah has calculated that cotton textile products represented about 40 per cent of United Kingdom exports in 1850. Of total exports of manufactured cotton goods (including twists and yarns) of about £28 million, India was the buyer of quantities valued at more than £4·5 million. (*Economic Elements in the Pax Brittanica* (Cambridge, Mass., 1958), esp. pp. 104 and 209.)

[3] Romesh Dutt, *The Economic History of India in the Victorian Age* (7th edn., London, 1950), p. 162.

by far to be the most important single source. With broadening
in the monetary base, however, other internal revenue sources
had become more productive. But the most notable change had
occurred in the opium monopoly which supplied nearly £5 million
to the exchequer.[4] All of this receipt was accounted for shipments
to China.

Blessed with rising revenues, government expenditures had
also swollen. Outlays for civil administration and for defence
continued to make the major claims on public funds. The day had
not yet arrived when resources would be made available in substantial quantity for programmes of social improvement and for
capital investments in infrastructure. In the 1850s, however,
provision for these latter categories of expenditure had become
more generous and the outlook seemed to be bright.

This was not, of course, the whole story. Aggregative data do
not speak directly to the distribution of income nor to the economic welfare of the bulk of population. Governments, then as
now, tend to rely heavily on statistics which can be gathered in
the organized sectors of the economy. Less formal economic
activity—especially the production of peasant households—is not
easy to trap within the statistician's net. The agrarian population
contributes, of course, to movement in the aggregates by paying
taxes, by supplying export crops, and by purchasing imports.
Whether or not the course of these activities, as measured in
aggregated form, provides an accurate gauge to trends in agrarian welfare is less certain. While Jones, for example, had offered
grounds for scepticism on this score, most economic commentators—then as now—are readily disposed to form judgements on
the basis of the visible variables to the neglect of those which are
less readily quantifiable.

Another aspect of the structure of the Indian economy might
also have merited more attention than it received. There was a
substantial gap between the country's export income and the
capacity of its peoples to purchase in world markets. Transfers
to satisfy the 'home charges' had long been a part of the financial
apparatus linking India and England. By the 1850s, the magnitudes had swollen to some £3 million per year on official account
and perhaps another £1 million was required to facilitate private
remittances. Meanwhile, the financing network had become more

[4] McCulloch, *Dictionary of Commerce* (1859), p. 566.

complex. Increasingly, the opium trade with China had taken on a strategic significance in the transfer system. With the boom in imports of British textiles, India had tended to be in a deficit position in its merchandise trade with Britain. These deficits were cleared—with enough to spare to cover the 'home charges'—by export surpluses with China. The link provided by the opium traffic was thus crucial to the operation of the larger international clearing system.[5] This was not quite the pattern anticipated by the plan drafted in 1793, though it did reproduce one of its characteristics: India was committed to a persistent net transfer of resources to Britain. From the official perspective, these transfers were not a 'drain', but a payment for invisible imports—particularly of administrative services. The implications of the magnitudes and the modes of transfer for the longer-term development of the economy were seldom seriously investigated.

By mid-century, the over-all record of the East India Company's administration could plausibly be regarded as commendable. It had tackled difficult problems and could demonstrate reasonable progress in solving them. When the charter was renewed in 1853, Parliament broke sharply with precedent: no date for renegotiation and review was stipulated. Instead, the Company—under the supervision of the Parliamentary Board of Control—was confirmed in its administrative responsibility for an 'indefinite' term. This ambiguity was then understood as reflecting a sense of confidence in the Company's stewardship.

In this mood of high Victorian optimism, India did indeed seem to be 'brightest jewel in the Crown of Empire'. Yet something had gone wrong. The mutineers in Meerut had touched unexpectedly sensitive nerves.

5 For an excellent analysis of this network, see Michael Greenberg, *British Trade and the Opening of China, 1800–42* (Cambridge, 1951).

CHAPTER 13

The Assessments of 1857–1858

THE events of the Mutiny suggested that a fresh evaluation of the British connection with India was called for. There was no lack of candidates to perform this function. A battery of instant experts offered interpretations of the problem, though few of them would win high marks for the thoroughness of their penetration.[1] From the economists, a more substantial analysis could reasonably be expected. Each of the main nineteenth-century strands of analytic interpretation contributed to the discussion of Indian questions at this time. Not surprisingly, each read the situation differently. They shared, however, one conviction: that the times were indeed extraordinary.

I. A RESTATEMENT OF THE OFFICIAL MODEL: JOHN STUART MILL AT EAST INDIA HOUSE

John Stuart Mill (1806–73) recognized that 'a calamity unexampled in the history of British India' had occurred.[2] Certainly nothing comparable had happened during his years as an East India administrator. He had entered the employ of the Company at the age of seventeen as an apprentice in the office of the Examiner of the India Correspondence and had followed his father's footsteps by rising to the position of Chief Examiner in 1856. Unlike his father, he made little attempt to bring radical innovation to India. Throughout most of his career at the Company's head-

---

[1] One strand of British opinion, for example, traced the source of the uprising to the permissiveness of the government. As 'An Old Indian' put it in a tract published in 1857 under the title *Why Is the Native Army Disaffected?*: 'In our dealings with native soldiers, . . . we commenced by paying more respect to their prejudices than their own rulers paid them. We were all for caste . . . We honoured and pampered our native soldiers to the extremest bound' (p. 3). Some Indian opinion, on the other hand, maintained that the revolt had been touched off by English 'missionary colonels' who seemed bent on converting reluctant sepoys to Christianity. This view was advanced by 'A Hindu of Bengal' in a pamphlet entitled *Causes of the Indian Revolt*, ed. Malcolm Lewin, (London, 1857).

[2] 'Memorandum of the Improvements in the Administration of India during the Last Thirty Years', *Parliamentary Papers, 1857–58*, vol. 43, p. 1. This document was the Company's official brief and it was drafted by Mill.

quarters in Leadenhall Street, John Stuart Mill specialized in the
dealings between the government of British India and the nomin-
ally independent Princely States. His memoranda on these matters
fill volumes in the India Office archives but they are concerned
mainly with routine administrative details.[3]

Before 1857 John Stuart Mill had been content to practice
'normal science' in his approach to Indian affairs. The intellectual
framework he had inherited seemed to be eminently satisfactory.
The Mutiny might thus have been regarded, not just as a 'calamity', but as an intellectual challenge. The younger Mill did not so
construe it. He made no systematic attempt to explain its origins.
Instead he reaffirmed the correctness of the official strategy and
took it as his duty to remedy 'the deficiency of correct information on the subject'.[4]

John Stuart Mill's defence of the East India Company's
administration was informed by one fundamental presupposition:
that the programme for uplift devised by James Mill was now at
the point of paying handsome dividends. In the revenue administration, for example, erroneous assessments—which, though unfortunate, had been unavoidable in the initial stages—had now
been corrected. The 'beneficial results' could be seen in the 'improved condition of the population' and in the 'ease and punctu-
ality' with which a revenue could be collected.[5] These achievements
were a tribute to the foresight of his father. In phrases reminiscent
of those James Mill had used a quarter-century earlier, he wrote
of the land tax as follows: 'The public necessities of the country
may be said to be provided for, at no expense to the people at
large. Where the original right of the State to the land of the
country has been reserved, and its natural, but no more than its
natural, rents made available to meet the public expenditure,
the people may be said to be so far untaxed.'[6] So long as the
government's claim did not exceed 'the amount which the land

---

[3] Though John Stuart Mill was conscientious in discharging his official duties, they
seldom gripped his enthusiasm. He conveyed his attitude toward his work at East
India House as follows: 'I do not know any one of the occupations by which a subsistence can now be gained, more suitable than such as this to anyone who, not being
in independent circumstances, desires to devote a part of the twenty-four hours to
private intellectual pursuits.' (*Autobiography of John Stuart Mill* (New York, 1944),
p. 58). Indeed the reader of Mill's own account of his career would scarcely be aware that
for three and a half decades his livelihood had been drawn from the pay-roll of the East
India Company.   [4] 'Memorandum of the Improvements . . .', p. 1.
[5] Ibid., p. 5.   [6] Ibid., pp. 7–8.

could pay as rent if let to a solvent tenant (that is, the price of its
peculiar advantages of fertility or situation),' the scientific tax
brought gains to all. By reserving to itself only the 'profit of a
kind of natural monopoly', government intervention along such
lines perfected the market. The cultivator could count on 'the same
reward of his labour and capital which is obtained by the remainder of the industrious population'.[7]

Nor was it difficult to identify the intellectual ancestry of
John Stuart Mill's views on other sources of Indian revenue. The
sums procured through the opium monopoly, for example, were
no hardship to the people of India because the impost was 'paid
wholly by foreigners'.[8] Moreover, controls exercised through a
state monopoly sheltered India—'which has hitherto been comparatively free from this kind of hurtful indulgence'—from a
flooding of 'the article at a low price'.[9]

Altogether, the wisdom of government, Mill maintained, had
given rise to 'a great and rapid growth of general prosperity'.
Population had increased, cultivation had been extended, and
foreign trade had grown enormously. Meanwhile, wage rates had
risen 'to an unexampled height' and, over large districts, ordinary
cultivators were, 'for the first time in memory, out of debt to
money lenders and to their landlords'.[10]

These healthy developments had been accompanied by growth
in the revenues of government. In turn, the government's ability
to finance programmes to improve the life of the people had been
enormously enhanced. Mill observed that the government had
'frequently been charged with niggardliness' in its allocation of
expenditures for public works and that 'there was some, at least
apparent, ground for the charge, in former generations'.[11] Now
the government was in a position to act more imaginatively. In
the recent past, large scale irrigation projects had been launched
and major improvements in transport and communications undertaken. The government's role in stimulating railway construction
was also noteworthy. Though capital for the massive rail network
now under way was to be supplied by private investors, the government had agreed to underwrite interest payments to holders of
India railway bonds.

But the record of improvement included still more. State

[7] Ibid., p. 8.   [8] Ibid.   [9] Ibid.
[10] Ibid., p. 11.   [11] Ibid., p. 19.

BETI—H

support for educational expenditures had been substantially increased and ambitious plans for further extensions in the educational system had been drafted. Nor had the state been idle in the research and development field. Experiments, at governmental expense, had been undertaken to improve the cultivation of cotton. Similarly, the state had developed experimental stations for tea and was prepared to offer free seeds and plants to those who proposed to take up its cultivation.

Over-all, it could thus plausibly be maintained that James Mill's expectations for British India were now in the process of fulfilment. His son concluded that 'few governments, even under far more favourable circumstances, have attempted so much for the good of their subjects, or carried so many of their attempts to a successful and beneficial issue.' He was well aware that a credibility gap existed. To those who might be swayed by the passions of the moment, he offered the following counsel: 'A Government of foreigners over a people most difficult to be understood, and still more difficult to be improved,—a Government which has had all its knowledge to acquire by a slow process of study and experience, and often by a succession of failures (generally, however, leading to ultimate success), has a right to take pride to itself for having accomplished so much; and most certainly cannot be justly reproached by any existing Government or people with not having effected more.'[12]

Arguments that the East India Company had made the best of an extremely difficult situation were not, however, sufficient to quiet the clamour in England in 1858. Parliamentary pressures for a fundamental change in the structure of governance were daily growing more insistent. In a series of pamphlets published anonymously, Mill again sought to enlighten the public on the type of government India required.[13] The brief he presented echoed doctrines which had been articulated long before.

In his judgement, the central problem was still the one James Mill had identified more than four decades earlier: to find an

12 'Memorandum of the Improvements . . .', p. 35.
13 These pamphlets carried the following titles: *A President in Council the Best Government for India; Practical Observations on the First Two of the Proposed Resolutions on the Government of India; Observations on the Proposed Council of India; The Moral of the India Debate; A Constitutional View of the India Question;* and *A Report to the General Court of the East India Company from the Court of Directors upon the Two Bills Now Before Parliament Relating to the Government of India.*

appropriate mode of governance for '150 millions of Asiatics, who cannot be trusted to govern themselves'.[14] It remained the case that India had not yet 'attained such a degree of civilization and improvement as to be ripe for anything like a representative system'.[15] It was therefore incumbent on Britain to serve the country with the best talents it could offer. The qualifications of those who staffed its administration should be highly professional and, as he had urged when testifying before a Parliamentary Committee in 1852, 'the study of India must be as much a profession in itself as law or medicine.'[16] Admittedly, the system of recruitment and training associated with Haileybury had not been ideal, but steps to raise standards were now being taken.[17] The danger to be avoided was the politicization of the system. The substitution of direct Parliamentary control for Company government invited a situation in which the country would be run by a minister 'ignorant of India, appointed because a Cabinet office must be found for him, and because public opinion will not allow him to be placed in any other than that of Indian Minister'.[18] India deserved a better fate—and so also did Britain. Should the Indian patronage fall into the hands of politicians, it would be 'dangerous to the liberty and the safety of the nation'.[19] Through Mill's pen, a theme prominent in the debates of the 1780s was revived in 1858.

Under a regime of experts, however, what assurance could be offered that the Indian people would be advanced and protected? Mill maintained that 'the great security for the good government of any country is an enlightened public opinion.'[20] Within India, however, the minimum conditions for enlightenment had not yet been achieved. In the circumstances, the best approach available was the one which had been adopted by the East India Company. The major strength of its arrangements rested on the fact that

[14] A President in Council the Best Government for India (London, 1858), p. 3.
[15] John Stuart Mill, Testimony of 22 June 1852, Parliamentary Papers, 1852–53, vol. 30, p. 314.   [16] Ibid., p. 313.
[17] With the Charter renewal legislation of 1853, passage through Haileybury ceased to be a condition for entry into the Indian Civil Service. Applications were invited from graduates of the leading universities and appointments were based on the results of competitive examinations. Shortly thereafter, Haileybury ceased to function as the East-India College.
[18] The Moral of the India Debate (London, 1858), p. 4.
[19] A Constitutional View of the India Question (London, 1858), p. 5.
[20] Mill, Testimony of 21 June 1852, Parliamentary Papers, 1852–53, vol. 30, p. 301.

'the whole Government of India is carried on in writing. All the orders given, and all the acts of the executive officers, are reported in writing, and the whole of the original correspondence is sent to the Home Government; so that there is no single act done in India, the whole of the reasons for which are not placed on record.'[21]

India, in this view of matters, could thus be soundly governed by Englishmen of competence, integrity, and independent judgement. It was quite legitimate for Parliament to have powers of review, similar to those it already possessed through the Board of Control. Continuity and stability in the operational direction of Indian affairs was, however, essential. In 1852 Mill maintained that the case for the retention of the East India Company's sovereign position ultimately rested on the 'difficulty, if not impossibility, of forming a system of government which would be likely to work better'.[22] By 1858, Mill still regarded the *status quo* as superior to any of the suggested alternatives. The Board of Control mechanism, he insisted, afforded the Crown ample scope for general superintendence; moreover, the delegation of administrative authority to the East India Company was not, in principle, unlike the pattern which had been developed for the Bank of England. An arrangement whereby a President in Council—resident in India, but free of all political ties at home—held the supreme authority was, however, acceptable should change be unavoidable.[23] In all significant particulars, this was the same scheme James Mill had recommended in 1810.

John Stuart Mill's general approach to India lacked originality. He had inherited a set of premises about the state of Indian society, about the types of government appropriate to its condition, and about the strategies for economic improvement to be pursued. The younger Mill updated the facts, but he made no substantial modifications to his father's position. That he did not take a more independent view of this range of issues is itself noteworthy. His theoretical contributions to political economy and social philosophy had not been restrained by filial piety. In his *Principles of Political Economy*, for example, he broke with the standard Ricardian doctrine by arguing that the laws of distri-

---

[21] *Parliamentary Papers*, vol. 30, *1852–53*, p. 301.   [22] Ibid., p. 305.
[23] See his discussion of this point in *A President in Council the Best Government for India*.

bution were not immutable, but subject to human control.
Similarly, he discarded the orthodox Benthamite position when,
in his writings on utilitarianism, he insisted on the priority of
qualitative over quantitative satisfactions.

Though revisionism was part of his temperament, it did not
extend to his thought about India. Even the Mutiny failed to
stimulate a fundamental rethinking of his position. On the contrary, it appeared to strengthen his original convictions. After all,
what evidence could be more persuasive that Indians could not
safely govern themselves? And what could testify more tellingly
to the continued need for the civilizing influence of high-minded
British administrators?

II. INTERPRETATIONS FROM THE PERSPECTIVE OF UNOFFICIAL ORTHODOXY

The Mutiny came late in McCulloch's lengthy career as a
leading spokesman for an unofficial orthodoxy on Indian affairs.
He had long been on record as a severe critic of the East India
Company and its works. Even though the passage of time had
eroded much of the Company's economic power, its influence on
the natural course of markets had been stifling. Free markets,
McCulloch consistently maintained, had the capacity to uplift
even the most depressed peoples. But the Indian administration
had arrested their healthy growth by taxing the cultivating
population oppressively, by frustrating capital inflows, and by
misallocating public resources. While public works which might
have opened new market space had been neglected, outlays for a
top-heavy administration (both civilian and military) had swollen.

These conditions could explain shortfalls from levels of performance which were well within the reach of the Indian economy.
They were insufficient, however, to account for a violent uprising. McCulloch took the view that the insurrection could best
be understood as a 'moral panic or epidemic'.[24] That the sepoys
should have behaved outrageously reflected the influence of irrational religious prejudice. Once they had departed from rational
norms of conduct, their example had been widely imitated.
Though there was no doubt that maladministration of the economy had generated an ample store of grievances, the events

[24] McCulloch, notes to his edition of Smith, *The Wealth of Nations* (1863), p. 574.

of 1857–8 should be regarded as a form of psychological contamination.

By implication, McCulloch suggested that this distressing episode could have been averted if government in the preceding half-century had properly perceived the educative power of participation in free markets. Maximum exposure to the range of consumption and production possibilities opened by international contacts might have worked wonders as a solvent to backward traditional attitudes. But this had not been allowed to happen. The central significance of the Mutiny was that it exposed unmistakably the intellectual bankruptcy of the official position. It was a severe indictment of the East Indian administration, he observed in 1859, that the uprising had 'failed to bring forward a single native chief of talent. In every contest the inferiority of even the best drilled sepoys, when brought face to face with Europeans, has been most striking . . . They continue to be precisely what they were at Plassey . . .'[25]

Past misjudgements—well-intentioned though they may have been—had now created a situation in which Britain faced an awkward choice. Earlier opportunities to induce modernization in Indian attitudes, and in days when it might have been done by indirect means, had been allowed to pass. Direct intervention would now be required if traditional behaviour patterns were to be changed for the better. Conceivably, a government could enforce certain norms and proscribe others if it chose to pay the price. At the minimum, it would require the maintenance of major force levels 'to suppress any disturbance' and it was highly doubtful that such a commitment of resources could be justified.[26] The alternative was to accommodate to traditional practices. This course was unattractive, though it had two recommendations: economy and expediency. Short of the total evacuation of a British presence in the sub-continent, McCulloch saw no other options. In retrospect, he questioned whether a territorial involvement in India should have been undertaken. British trade (apart from the demand for British goods generated by the Indian army) was probably no greater than it would have been had the government remained in native hands. In the light of the unfortunate policies pursued by British administrators, the condition of the Indian people had not improved as much as the British public had a

[25] McCulloch, *Dictionary of Commerce* (1859), p. 565.   [26] Ibid.

right to expect. But the mistakes of the past were bygones. Having assumed a demanding responsibility, it was incumbent on Britain to see the job through. It was undoubtedly sound, however, to relieve the East India Company of this task.[27]

In 1858 McCulloch did not produce a direct rejoinder to John Stuart Mill's apologia for the Company. He had already attacked most ingredients of the official case at great length on earlier occasions. A point-by-point refutation of its latest statement could be left to others. McCulloch would have found little to quarrel with in the pamphlet prepared in 1858 by one John Freeman who identified himself as '25 years a resident in Bengal, a landed proprietor and extensive indigo planter'. Mill's rhetoric, he argued was mere sham. Two 'dreadful words, *monopoly* and *tax*, seem to produce', he wrote, 'a sort of *spasm* in Leadenhall Street if alluded to in England, though in poor India, they are "household words".'[28] No one should be misled by claims that ingenious strategies emanating from East India House had left the bulk of the population untaxed. Nor should the East India Company's government be allowed to take credit for the few improvements in the economy which had occurred. The beneficial outcomes were the product of free trade and private initiative. The happy part of the record would have been brighter still had not the Company's government deterred capital inflows by giving native judges jurisdiction over Europeans in civil cases.

Faith in an orthodoxy had again survived dismaying events. A tragedy had indeed occurred though, in this reading, it might have been avoided. Had sounder policies been adopted earlier, a more satisfactory reality would have been observable in 1858.

III. THE HETERODOX PERSPECTIVE OF MARX ON INDIA OF THE 1850s

By the time of the Mutiny, Richard Jones—the most noteworthy critic of orthodoxies within the British community of economic thinkers—was dead. Part of the critical space he had

[27] McCulloch summarized his position on this matter as follows: 'It would not be difficult to show that it would have been far more for the advantage of England had she never become an Indian power. But the die having been cast, it is our duty to make the most of the situation in which we are placed, and especially to provide, as far as may be in our power, for the well-being of the vast population we have subjected to our dominion.' (Notes to his edition of Smith, *The Wealth of Nations* (1863), p. 574.)

[28] John Freeman, *A Reply to the Memorandum of the East-India Company or an Insight into British India* (London, 1858), p. 14. Emphases in the original.

occupied was filled by a far more formidable figure whose views on the mainsprings of social change differentiated him sharply from the British intellectual tradition.

Karl Marx (1818–83) brought his analytic perspective to bear on the events of 1857–8 in a series of articles composed in English for the *New York Daily Tribune*. By that point, he was no stranger to published materials on East India affairs, though (like the major economic thinkers of native British stock) he had no first-hand acquaintance with the sub-continent. In connection with journalistic assignments in 1853 (when renewal of the Company's charter was under debate), he had done extensive homework on the background to these problems.

With only modest semantic adjustments, Marx absorbed much of the official doctrine on the condition of India. Whereas James Mill had put Hindu society at the bottom of 'the scale of civilization', Marx substituted the expression 'Oriental despotism' and did not conceal his contempt for it. In writing of traditional social structures, he urged his readers not to forget that 'they restrained the human mind within the smallest possible compass, making it the unresisting tool of superstition', that they generated 'wild, aimless, unbounded forces of destruction, and rendered murder itself a religious rite', and that they 'were contaminated by distinctions of caste and of slavery'.[29] Like James Mill, he had no patience for the view that India had once enjoyed a 'golden age' from which it had lapsed only after European intervention. The 'commencement of Indian misery' went deep into antiquity.[30] Britain indeed had a 'mission' to perform.

In the analysis of the nature of that mission, however, Marx's position could not have been further removed from the official one. To the Mills, enlightened plans, when carried into effect by a patient and dedicated administration, promised over the longer run to produce constructive improvement. To Marx, on the other hand, the British mission was twofold: 'The annihilation of old Asiatic society, and the laying of the material foundations of Western society in Asia'.[31] Englishmen were the unwitting instruments of history. Though change would certainly come, it could neither be manipulated nor restrained by the policy

---

[29] Karl Marx, *New York Daily Tribune*, 25 June 1853, as published in *K. Marx and F. Engels on Colonialism* (Moscow, n.d.), p. 38.   [30] Ibid., p. 33.
[31] *New York Daily Tribune*, 8 August 1853, in loc cit., p. 84.

planners. The directives of officials in East India House had no
bearing on reality. They had merely 'succeeded in transforming
the Indian government into one immense writing machine'
presided over by 'old obstinate clerks, and the like odd fellows'.[32]

The forces propelling change in India, though they originated
in Britain, had a totally different character. They sprang from
the drive of the 'moneyocracy' and the 'millocracy' which had
succeeded first in excluding India's finished textiles from British
markets and, later, in flooding India with products of Britain's
power looms. Throughout this process, the craftsmen of the sub-
continent had been defenceless. 'British steam and science',
Marx wrote, 'uprooted, over the whole surface of Hindustan, the
union between agriculture and manufacturing industry.'[33] The
social fabric of the traditional village had thus been destroyed,
but the clock could not be turned back. Marx would have dismissed Gandhi's appeal to twentieth-century Indians 'to rebuild
our villages' as sentimental nonsense.

This reading of matters also stood in sharp contrast to the unofficial strand of orthodoxy. Free trade clearly had consequences
—but it did not bring benefits to all. The consumers of imported
textiles may have gained from the availability of lower-priced
products of a superior technology. But an entire system—that of
family communities 'based on domestic industry, in that peculiar
combination of hand-weaving, hand-spinning and hand-tilling
agriculture which gave them self-supporting power'—had been
crushed.[34] As a result, the 'only *social* revolution ever heard of in
Asia' had transpired.[35]

Laissez-faire had sent shock waves throughout the country-
side and had left misery behind. In such an environment, it would
not be surprising should accumulated grievances erupt in violence.
But what forms might it take? Those who were most distressed
were too poor, too weak, and too ill-organized to fight. On the
other hand, even petty grievances among the better-organized
could spark trouble. It was in these terms that Marx understood
the immediate circumstances of the Mutiny. 'The Indian revolt',
he wrote in 1857, 'does not commence with the *ryots*, tortured, dis-
honoured and stripped naked by the British, but with the sepoys,

---

[32] *New York Daily Tribune*, 20 July 1853, in loc, cit., p. 69.
[33] *New York Daily Tribune*, 25 June 1853, in loc. cit., p. 36.
[34] Ibid., p. 37.   [35] Ibid., p. 38. Emphasis in the original.

clad, fed, petted, fatted, and pampered by them.'[36] But even this
group would be unable to mount a sustained or successful rebellion. Writing a month after the capture of Delhi by the sepoys,
Marx asserted that it was 'preposterous' to expect them to hold
the city for long: '. . . a motley crew of mutineering soldiers who
have murdered their own officers, torn asunder the ties of discipline, and not succeeded in discovering a man upon whom to
bestow the supreme command, are certainly the body least likely
to organize a serious and protracted resistance.'[37]

During the next year, Marx's appraisals altered slightly in tone.
Delhi indeed fell to government forces, though its recapture was
delayed for four months. Marx did not revise upward his low
opinion of Indian military competence. He suggested, however,
that the intensity and duration of fighting had itself added a
dimension to the scene. As a result of the behaviour of the sepoys,
British supremacy had ceased to seem unchallengeable—even to
normally docile groups within the population. By May 1858,
Marx expected subversive action to continue for some time. The
prospect before the British, he wrote, was 'a long and harrassing
guerrilla warfare . . .—not an eviable thing for Europeans under
an Indian sun'.[38] At the same time, the prospect before Indian
insurrectionists was hardly promising. Their efforts at this stage
in history would finally be frustrated by superior organization and
by superior military technology.

Ultimately, British intervention in the economy would sow the
seeds of its own destruction. The more fully India's economy became integrated through the expansion of markets and through
modernization of its transport and communications systems, the
more cohesive would Indian interests become. This process could
not be expected to mature quickly. Nevertheless, its end was

---

[36] *New York Daily Tribune*, 16 September 1857 in loc. cit., pp. 146–7. A similar
interpretation was later offered by H. Montgomery Martin, a long-standing radical
critic of Britain's involvement in India: 'Under a despotic government, with an
enormous army of native mercenaries, the outbreak of rebellion would naturally
occur among the soldiery. While they were contented, the people would almost
necessarily remain in complete subjection; but if the soldiery had grievances, however
slight compared with those of the people, the two classes would coalesce; the separate
discontent of each part reacting upon the other, the army would initiate rebellion, and
the people would maintain it.' (H. Montgomery Martin, *The Indian Empire* (London,
1860), vol. 2, p. 122.

[37] *New York Daily Tribune*, 4 August 1857, in loc. cit., p. 135.

[38] *New York Daily Tribune*, 25 May 1858, in loc. cit., p. 173.

clear. The transformation in India's economic structure set in
motion by contact with Western capitalism would some day produce a genuinely revolutionary situation. Ameliorative policies
could not divert the flow of historical forces.

This line of interpretation grew out of a broader model which
sought to lay bare the 'laws of motion' of modern society. Marx's
view of what should go into a 'scientific' analysis of social processes separated his approach and most of his conclusions from
those of his contemporaries. Yet his treatment of some points of
detail was still within the classical framework. On the long-vexed
question of tribute, for example, he echoed views similar to those
James Mill had advanced nearly a half-century earlier. India was
a net drain on the resources of the British public. As he put it:
'Directly, that is in the shape of tribute, of surplus of Indian receipts over Indian expenditures, nothing whatever reaches the
British Treasury. On the contrary, the annual outgo is very large.'[39]
Private individuals, to be sure, had gained handsomely from the
British connections with India—not least the civil servants whose
pay scales were grossly inflated. On balance, it was not clear that
private gains would always be sufficient to offset the costs borne
by the British tax-payer. Though Marx took note of the transfers
required to settle the 'home charges' and described them as an
'annual drain' on India, his treatment of this issue had more in
common with that of his orthodox British contemporaries than
with the interpretations later offered by a school of Indian nation-
alists. In the view of the latter, the unilateral transfers India was
compelled to make to Britain systematically stripped the country
of resources and thus perpetuated poverty. This doctrine was effectively enunciated in the 1870s by Dadabhai Naoroji.[40] It was to
play a central part in the ideology of the nationalist movement.[41]
Marx did not pursue this theme: he was at greater pains to argue,

[39] *New York Daily Tribune*, 21 September 1857, in loc. cit., p. 157.

[40] Its classic statement is to be found in Naoroji's *Poverty and Un-British Rule*,
published in London in 1901. For a further discussion, see Joseph J. Spengler, *Indian
Economic Thought* (Durham, N.C., 1972), esp. pp. 146–8.

[41] A modern version of this interpretation of India's stagnation goes as follows:

This drain consisted of various payments to the United Kingdom, for which
India did not get any returns. These payments represented savings of the country;
and India got not only no returns on the savings but, worse still, they were completely lost to her . . . This drain constituted, on a very conservative estimate, about
2–3 per cent of India's national income during 1757 to 1939. If this amount had
been invested in India for her development, she would have been able to attain a

as had the British classical economists, that the Indian domain was of doubtful national economic advantage to Britain. Moreover, his sights were trained on flows in the other direction—i.e. British investments in India, particularly for railway construction—and their impact on the Indian economic structure.

On one other matter, Marx shared more the perspective of orthodoxy than that of its critics. While he respected Jones for his insistence on structural distinctions between agrarian systems and capitalistic ones, he had no taste for Jones's plea for careful study of individual peasant economies. The Indian peasantry—no less than the peasantry of Europe—could be regarded as a 'bag of potatoes'. Production for subsistence purposes simply did not count in his scheme of economically interesting activities. What mattered was 'commodity production', defined as the production of values which had a social nexus through exchange. It was thus beside the point to engage with the intricacies of agrarian problems on their own terms. As market participation widened, these traditional structures would necessarily be phased out.

IV. DEATH AND TRANSFIGURATION

Spokesman for each of major analytic traditions concurred in the judgement that the Mutiny was an event of unusual significance. Conceivably, its unprecedented character might have inspired fresh leaps in the analytic imagination. In fact, it did not. Though neglected dimensions of reality had been brought into sharper focus, each tradition had the capacity to supply an interpretation of an extra-ordinary set of events without amendment in its central premises or categories.

From the perspective of the official model, the Mutiny seemed to confirm the importance of continued efforts to uplift India through rational planning—in isolation, it was hoped, from the distractions of partisan pressures in Britain. To the *laissez-faire* Ricardians, the tragedy seemed to support earlier indictments of the gross errors committed by too interventionist an administration. To the new strand of heterodoxy as represented by Marx, the

---

growth rate, only a little lower than that attained by the United States and the United Kingdom during the nineteenth century. (V. V. Bhatt, *Aspects of Economic Change and Policy in India, 1800–1960* (Bombay, 1963), p. 51.)

uprising was a natural by-product of structural changes generated by sustained contact between societies at contrasting stages in economic evolution. Neither the moment of violent confrontation nor its form could be predicted with precision. But Marx could claim that those who correctly understood his analysis should not have been surprised by the outbreak of rebellion nor by its suppression.

If the Mutiny did not spur adjustments in the categories of analytic understanding, it did produce remarkably swift change in the structure of government for British India. The new parliamentary disposition was codified in the royal proclamation of 2 August 1858 which terminated the official life of the East India Company and transferred governing responsibility to the British state. Under this dispensation, general authority for the government of India was vested in a fifteen-member council presided over by a Secretary of State. Two provisions for the composition of the council were especially noteworthy: it was stipulated that a majority of its members should have served or resided in India for ten years and that the tenure of their appointments should be analogous to that of the judiciary. At least part of John Stuart Mill's hope for a governing structure which would bring expertise and continuity to Indian affairs—and in an atmosphere of independence from British party politics—seemed to have been fulfilled.

The East India Company died in character. Even as it expired, it sustained the tradition of organizational innovation which had been associated with it for more than two and a half centuries. In the seventeenth century, it had pioneered methods of corporate and financial organization and its behaviour then would entitle it to be regarded as one of the world's first multi-national firms. By the late eighteenth century, it was again in the vanguard of innovation when it became the first publicly regulated private enterprise. With the surrender of the Company's governing authority to the British state, a fresh phase was entered: the government of India, in effect, became Britain's first nationalized industry. The administrative model designed for this purpose in 1858 is strikingly similar to the one which guided the structuring of British public corporations after the Second World War.

As was to be expected, spokesmen for each of the main analytic traditions reacted differently to this resolution of the problem of governance. John Stuart Mill expressed his view as follows in July 1858:

The East India Company has fought its last battle, and I have been in the thick of the fight. The Company is to be abolished, but we have succeeded in getting nearly all the principles that we contended for adopted in constituting the new government, and our original assailants feel themselves much more beaten than we do. The change—though not so bad as first seemed probable—is still, in my opinion, much for the worse. The difficulty of governing India in any tolerable manner, already so much increased by the Mutiny and its consequences, will become an impossibility if a body so ignorant and incompetent on Indian (to say nothing of other) subjects as Parliament, comes to make a practice of interfering.[42]

Mill was offered an appointment to the newly constituted council, but declined.

McCulloch understood the displacement of the Company by Imperial administration differently. The 'disasters in India' had strengthened 'the incipient prejudice against the Company', though he added 'without much reason'.[43] Presumably there was ample reason for dissatisfaction with its conduct of affairs quite apart from the events of Mutiny. Marx was still more succinct. He likened the 'exit of the East India Company . . . to the compromise effected by a bankrupt with his creditors'.[44] The eligibility of insolvent industries for nationalization has not diminished since 1858.

[42] John Stuart Mill to Judge Chapman, 8 July 1858, as reproduced in the *Letters of John Stuart Mill*, ed. Hugh S. R. Elliot (London, 1910), vol. 1, p. 211.

[43] McCulloch, *Dictionary of Commerce* (1859), p. 552.

[44] *New York Daily Tribune*, 24 July 1858, loc. cit., p. 203.

Epilogue: The Economic Mind and India

MUCH—though certainly not all—of the realignment in international economic relationships over the long sweeps of history can usefully be analysed through inspection of the basic destabilizers of economic activity: i.e. changes in technology, tastes, and population. But a less tangible element in significant change is no less real—the force of ideas and the approaches to economic policy which they sustain or inspire. The most influential economic thinker of the twentieth century drew attention to this point when he wrote: '... the ideas of economists and political philosophers, both when they are right and when they are wrong, are more powerful than is commonly understood. Indeed the world is ruled by little else. Practical men, who believe themselves to be quite exempt from intellectual influences, are usually the slaves of some defunct economist ... I am sure that the power of vested interests is vastly exaggerated compared with the gradual encroachment of ideas.'[1]

During the lifespan of the English East India Company, ideas did indeed contribute to the reshaping of economic reality. But the British connection with India also helped to give shape to economic ideas. There was always an intellectual dimension to its practical problems. Men in each age asked whether or not established modes of thought were well suited to the case of India and whether or not fresh conceptual formulations should be constructed for its circumstances.

These central questions were persistent but they received no final answers. The mere search for answers, however, speeded the germination of important conceptualizations of the economic process—and ones which were to have an impact extending well beyond the immediate context of Indian controversies. The success of seventeenth-century pamphleteers in arguing the uniqueness of the Indian commerce, for example, redirected thought on the

[1] John Maynard Keynes, *The General Theory of Employment, Interest and Money* (London, 1949), p. 383. In this context, it deserves to be noted that the young Keynes took his first employment as a civil servant in the India Office in 1905 and that his earliest publications on economic questions dealt with monetary problems in British India.

role of foreign trade in the promotion of economic expansion and gave thereby a special twist to English theoretical development during the era of 'mercantilism'. The unprecedented situation in which the East India Company found itself a century later spurred more systematic inquiry into the economic implications of monopoly. Similarly, the Indian puzzles of the early nineteenth century—which called, on the one hand, for an explanation of backwardness in the traditional economy and, on the other, for a blue-print for economic improvement—added richness to the major analytic innovation of that time. Though the doctrine of differential rent would have emerged had there been no British involvement in India, the apparent fit of the doctrine to Indian conditions added credibility to its claims.

While the Indian connection helped to mould the major orthodoxies in each of these periods, it also offered far more material for analytic innovation than in fact found its way into the dominant master models. In each phase in the evolution of this relationship, at least one analyst of stature diagnosed the central issue of the day in ways which could not be accommodated within the conventionally accepted framework. Contributions such as those of Sir James Steuart in the 1770s, of Lauderdale in 1809, or of Richard Jones in the 1830s and 1840s were little noted and not long remembered.

Each generation employs techniques for the sorting of economic ideas. Some ideas are welcomed into the main currents of thought while others are diverted into a backwater. The way in which the selection process works is not susceptible to simple generalization. It would appear, however, that candidacy for the mainstream is enhanced when novel ideas can be presented as part of—or at least can readily be assimilated into—a broader conceptual framework. Most of the heterodox commentaries were too piecemeal in their presentation to pass this test. But analytic coherence is not itself sufficient to win influence for a new view of the world. The author of *Considerations Upon the East-India Trade* stirred no waves in 1701, even though his work would have been regarded as an analytic achievement a century later. At the time he wrote, there was no audience for his message and he had no allies to assist him in capturing one.

The success stories were another matter. The ideas that did move the world in which British and Indian interests intersected appear to have shared two properties. In the first instance, they spoke a language which seemed to convey a plausible account of an aspect of observable reality which was a matter of current concern. In addition, they offered a vision of an alternative —and supposedly superior—state of affairs. This was the case in the seventeenth century when Mun, as an official spokesman for the East India Company, charted a course which opened a fresh path toward economic expansion. By the late eighteenth century, outsiders set the pace of analytic innovation; the new breed of classical economists identified an unsatisfactory present state of affairs with the monopoly form of organization, and sketched the outlines of a happier future in which the commerce would be open to all and the governance of India removed from private hands. In the first half of the nineteenth century, the East India Company recaptured part of the analytic initiative. To the extent that it succeeded, it did so by appropriating a model which seemed to offer to India the blessings of the most advanced economic teaching. The new official model was not, of course, unchallenged. But the challenge of most significant practical consequence—that offered by the *laissez-faire* strand of Ricardian theorizing—drew its strength from the same source. It also seemed able to diagnose the ills of the present and, simultaneously, to prescribe logically consistent remedies.

The success of analytic systems in economics in influencing the course of events derives largely from their dual character: i.e. their capacity, on the one hand, to be relevantly factual (though necessarily selectively so); and their capacity, on the other, to be persuasively counter-factual in their visions of alternate future states. They thus exist in two time-dimensions concurrently. This ambivalence is at once a source of weakness and of strength. Without such dualism, organized systems of ideas would be less well equipped to gain control of men's minds and, in turn, to influence the course of events. But the same dualism also arrests further analytical innovations—including ones which might be appropriate to a new reality which ideas have themselves helped to produce.

Well-constructed analytic systems thus may be the victims of their own success. To the extent that they guide events along a fresh course, the factual element of their initial base tends to be eroded. Nevertheless, perception of this phenomenon is typically delayed. Potentially awkward facts seldom come within the range of vision and are thus systematically neglected. From some perspectives, for example, it might have seemed pertinent for economists of the nineteenth century to inspect more closely the character of India's agrarian structure or to analyse in detail the implications of the transfer mechanisms for India's developmental prospects. The self-confident orthodoxies, however, looked elsewhere for evidence relevant to judgements about the country's economic condition and performance.

But even when awkward facts are too visible to be ignored, there can be no guarantee that they will themselves prompt a fundamental rethinking of conceptual systems. The counter-factual ingredient of well-constructed models assures a degree of detachment from the observed world. The response of the various analytic traditions to the events of the Mutiny is a case in point. Though the shock effect of the uprising was not uniformly distributed, none was well prepared for the actual sequence of events. Yet the interpretations offered by spokemen for each of these traditions did not stimulate revisions in conceptual systems. On the contrary, extraordinary events tended to reinforce confidence in the correctness of the original positions. The conceptual adequacy of the master models was secure in a world of 'could be's' or 'might have been's'.

The experience of British economic thinkers who concerned themselves with Indian matters during the days of the East India Company is now remote in time. Nevertheless, there is an intellectual kinship between development economists then and now. The vast enrichment in the technical resources of the discipline in recent decades should not obscure this continuity. Modern students of the economics of the Third World cannot escape a fundamental question: what types of conceptual apparatus are appropriate to understanding and improving the economic condition of the poorer countries? If the theorists who dealt with India in an earlier era could now be restored to life, they would find the contours of the modern intellectual landscape familiar.

Select Bibliography

SOURCES used in this book have been noted in the footnotes accompanying the text. The abbreviated listing below of the more significant materials may be useful to those interested in further study of these issues.

. PERTINENT WORKS BY PRINCIPAL ECONOMIC
  COMMENTATORS

JONES, Richard, *An Essay on the Distribution of Wealth and on the Sources of Taxation*, Cambridge, 1831
——*Literary Remains, Consisting of Lectures and Tracts on Political Economy of the Late Rev. Richard Jones*, ed. William Whewell, London, 1859
LAUDERDALE, see Maitland
McCULLOCH, J. R., 'Ricardo's Political Economy', *Edinburgh Review*, June 1818
——'East and West India Sugar', *Edinburgh Review*, February 1823
——'East India Company's Monopoly—Price of Tea', *Edinburgh Review*, January 1824
——'Value of Colonial Possessions', *Edinburgh Review*, August 1825
——'Progress and Present State of the Silk Manufacture', *Edinburgh Review*, November 1825
——'Revenue and Commerce of India', *Edinburgh Review*, March 1827
——'Rise, Progress, Present State and Prospects of the British Cotton Manufacture', *Edinburgh Review*, June 1827
——'Institution of Castes—Indian Society', *Edinburgh Review*, September 1828
——'Sugar Trade—Duties on Sugar', *Edinburgh Review*, January 1830
——'Rise, Progress and Decline of Commerce in Holland', *Edinburgh Review*, July 1830
——'East India Company—China Question', *Edinburgh Review*, January 1831

McCulloch, J. R. 'Jones on the Theory of Rent', *Edinburgh Review*, September 1831

—— 'Supply and Consumption of the Precious Metals', *Edinburgh Review*, April 1832

—— 'Recent Commercial Policy of Great Britain', *Edinburgh Review*, July 1832

—— *A Dictionary, Practical, Theoretical, and Historical, of Commerce and Commercial Navigation* (The *Dictionary of Commerce*), London, 1832, 1834, 1840, 1844, 1846, 1847, 1852, 1854, 1856, 1859

—— *Reasons for the Establishment of a New Bank in India with Answers to Objections Against It*, London, 1836

—— *A Statistical Account of the British Empire, exhibiting its extent, physical capacities, population, industry, and civil and religious institutions*, London, 1837, 1839, 1847, 1854

—— (ed.), Adam Smith, *Inquiry into the Nature and Causes of the Wealth of Nations*, London, 1838, 1849, 1863

—— *A Dictionary, Geographical, Statistical, and Historical, of the Various Countries, Places, and Principal Natural Objects in the World* (The *Geographical Dictionary*), London, 1841–2, 1845–6, 1849, 1852, 1854

—— (ed.), *A Select Collection of Early English Tracts on Commerce*, London, 1856, reprinted by Cambridge University Press, Cambridge 1970

Maitland, James [Lord Lauderdale], *An Inquiry into the Practical Merits of the System for the Government of India under the Superintendence of the Board of Controul*, Edinburgh, 1809

Malthus, T. R., *A Letter to the Rt. Hon. Lord Grenville Occasioned by some Observations of His Lordship on the East India Company's Establishment for the Education of Their Civil Servants*, London, 1813

—— *An Inquiry into the Nature and Progress of Rent*, London, 1815

—— *An Essay on the Principle of Population*, fifth edition, London, 1817

—— *Statements Respecting the East-India College with an Appeal to Facts in Refutation of the Charges Lately Brought Against It in the Court of Proprietors*, London, 1817

—— *Principles of Political Economy, Considered with a View to*

Their Practical Application, London, 1820, second edition, London, 1836

MARX, Karl, *K. Marx and F. Engels on Colonialism*, Moscow, n.d.

—— *Capital*, Chicago, 1912

MILL, James, 'Affairs of India', *Edinburgh*, April 1810

—— 'East India Monopoly', *Edinburgh Review*, November 1811

—— 'Malcolm on India', *Edinburgh Review*, July 1812

—— 'East Indian Monopoly', *Edinburgh Review*, November 1812

—— 'Bruce's Report on the East-India Negotiation', *Monthly Review*, 1813

—— *History of British India*, London, 1817

—— *Elements of Political Economy*, London, 1821

—— 'Colony', *Encyclopaedia Britannica*, 1826

—— Minutes of Evidence before the Select Committee on the Affairs of the East India Company, *Parliamentary Papers*, *1831*, vol. 5, *1831–2*, vol. 9, *1831–2*, vol. 14

—— Observations on the Land Revenue of India, *Parliamentary Papers*, *1831–2*, vol. 11, Appendix 7

—— *Selected Economic Writings*, ed. Donald Winch, London, 1966

MILL, John Stuart, 'Foreign Dependencies: Trade with India', *Parliamentary History and Review*, 1826–7

—— *Principles of Political Economy*, London, 1848

—— Minutes of Evidence before the Select Committee on the Affairs of the East India Company, *Parliamentary Papers*, *1852–3*, vol. 30

—— Memorandum of the Improvement in the Administration of India during the Last Thirty Years, *Parliamentary Papers*, *1857–8*, vol. 43

—— *A President in Council the Best Government for India* London, 1858

—— *Practical Observations on the First Two of the Proposed Resolutions on the Government of India*, London, 1858

—— *Observations on the Proposed Council of India*, London, 1858

—— *The Moral of the India Debate*, London, 1858

—— *A Constitutional View of the India Question*, London, 1858

—— *A Report to the General Court of the East India Company from the Court of Directors upon the Two Bills Before Parliament Relating to the Government of India*, London, 1858

MILL, John Stuart, *Letters of John Stuart Mill*, ed. H. S. R. Elliot, London, 1910

MUN, Thomas, *A Discourse of Trade from England unto the East-Indies*, London, 1621

—— *The Petition and Remonstrance of the Governor and Company of Merchants of London, Trading to the East Indies*, London, 1628

—— *England's Treasure by Forraign Trade*, London, 1664

RICARDO, David, *The Works and Correspondence of David Ricardo*, ed. P. Sraffa, Cambridge, 1952–5

SMITH, Adam, *An Inquiry into the Nature and Causes of the Wealth of Nations*, ed. Edwin Cannan, London, 1904

STEUART, James, *The Principles of Money Applied to the Present State of the Coin of Bengal*, London, 1772

—— *The Works of Sir James Steuart*, London, 1805

II. SIGNIFICANT SECONDARY WORKS

BEARCE, George D., *British Attitudes Towards India, 1784–1858*, London, 1961

BHATT, V. V., *Aspects of Economic Change and Policy in India, 1800–1960*, Bombay, 1963

BUCHANAN, Daniel H., *The Beginnings of Capitalistic Enterprise in India*, New York, 1934

CHAUDHURI, K. N., *The English East India Company: a Study of an Early Joint Stock Company*, London, 1965

—— (ed.), *The Economic Development of India under the East India Company, 1814–1858*, London, 1971

CLARK, G. N., *Guide to English Commercial Statistics, 1696–1782*, London, 1938

DUTT, Romesh, *The Economic History of India*, seventh edition, London, 1950

FOSTER, William, *John Company*, London 1926

—— *The East India House: Its History and Associations*, London, 1924

FURBER, Holden, *John Company at Work*, Cambridge, Mass., 1948

GREENBERG, Michael, *British Trade and the Opening of China, 1800–42*, Cambridge, 1951

KHAN, Shafaat Ahmad, *The East India Trade in the XVIIth Century*, London, 1923

KRISHNA, Bal, *Commercial Relations Between India and England, 1601–1757*, London, 1924

LETWIN, William, *The Origins of Scientific Economics: English Economic Thought, 1600–1776*, London, 1963

MARSHALL, P. J. *Problems of Empire: Britain and India, 1757–1813*, London, 1968

MUKHERJEE, S. W., *Sir William Jones: A Study in Eighteenth-Century British Attitudes to India*, Cambridge, 1968

MYRDAL, Gunnar, *Asian Drama: an Inquiry into the Poverty of Nations*, New York, 1968

O'BRIEN, D. P., *J. R. McCulloch: A Study in Classical Economics*, London, 1970

PARSHAD, I. Darga, *Some Aspects of Indian Foreign Trade, 1757–1893*, London, 1932

PHILIPS, C. H., *The East India Company, 1784–1834*, Bombay, 1961

RAMSEY, G. D., *English Overseas Trade During the Centuries of Emergence*, London, 1957

SAUL, S. B., *Studies in British Overseas Trade, 1870–1914*, Liverpool, 1960

SCHUMPETER, J. A., *History of Economic Analysis*, London, 1954

SINHA, J. C., *Economic Annals of Bengal*, London, 1927

SPENGLER, Joseph J., *Indian Economic Thought*, Durham, N.C., 1972

STOKES, Eric, *The English Utilitarians and India*, Oxford, 1959

SUPPLE, Barry E., *Commercial Crisis and Change in England, 1600–1642*, Cambridge, 1959

SUTHERLAND, Lucy S., *The East India Company in Eighteenth Century Politics*, Oxford, 1952

THOMAS, P. J., *Mercantilism and the East India Trade*, London, 1926

VINER, Jacob, *Studies in the Theory of International Trade*, New York, 1937

WRIGHT, H. R. C., *East-Indian Economic Problems in the Age of Cornwallis and Raffles*, London, 1961

Index

242 INDEX

Malthus, T. R.—*contd.*
College, 146–147; formulation of the rent doctrine, 147–152; re-interpretation of the traditional tax system, 152–155
Martin, H. Montgomery, 226n.
Martin, Henry, 57n.
Marx, Karl, 197, 223–228, 230; on the condition of India, 224–225; appraisal of the Indian Mutiny, 225–226; on tribute, 227
Mercantilism, interpretations of: 25–27, 232
Mill, James; 126ff., 156ff., 177, 187–188, 198–199, 209, 216, 224, 227; on monetary problems of Bengal, 83–84; initial interest in Indian affairs, 126–128; the interpretation of Indian society and its apparent backwardness, 128–134; critique of East India monopoly, 134–136; on impossibility of tribute from India, 135–138, 172; on the structure of government for India, 138–140; as an East India executive, 156–158; on application of Ricardian rent theory to the Indian tax system, 158–163; on strategy for public expenditure, 163–166; on opium and salt monopolies, 173–174; continuity through work of John Stuart Mill, 216ff.
Mill, John Stuart, 109n., 208, 215–221, 223, 230; on East India Company's procurement practices, 109n.; on Richard Jones, 208; career with East India Company, 215–216; assessment of the Company's performance, 216–218; recommendations on the governance of India, 218–221
Mir Kasim, 96n.
Misselden, Edward, 9
Money: role of in Mun's analysis, 16–19; Steuart's views on, 80–85; James Mill on, 83–84; McCulloch on, 188–190
Monopoly: attacks on in seventeenth century: 31, 38ff., 44–45; defenses in seventeenth century, 21–22, 42–43, 48–54; analysis of in *Considerations Upon the East India Trade*, 58ff.; Smith on, 95ff.; official defense of 1793, 101ff.; James Mill on, 133–135; McCulloch on, 178ff., 223
Mun, Thomas: 10ff., 31, 109, 113, 233; role in East India Company, 10; on

shortcomings of bullionist doctrine, 10–12; on significance of re-exports, 12–19; on policy for economic expansion, 19ff.; impact of his argument, 31ff.
Munro, Sir Thomas, 149, 161
Myrdal, Gunnar, 202n.

Naoroji, Dadabhai, 227
North, Sir Dudley, 40n., 57n., 63

Orientalist school, 130

Papillon, Thomas, 31n., 43
Peacock, Thomas Love, 158n., 177n., 192n.
Permanent Settlement (see Taxation, Cornwallis, and Rent, doctrine of)
Place, Francis, 127, 157n.
Pollexfen, Chief Justice, 31
Pulteney, William, 89

'Regulated company': seventeenth-century usage, 40–42, 48; eighteenth-century usage, 102–105
Rent, doctrine of: formulation of, 147ff.; application to India, 147–152; 158–163; criticisms of, 196ff.
Revenue (see Taxation)
Ricardo, David: as a member of the East India Court of Proprietors, 147, 157–158; on the rent doctrine, 133, 150, 155; on free trade, 182–183; and relationship of Mill and McCulloch, 177
Roy, Ram Mohun, 174
Ryotwari settlement (see Rent, doctrine of, and Taxation)

Say, Jean-Baptiste, 173n.
Schumpeter, J. A., 26n., 63, 207n.
Smith, Adam, 83, 86ff., 106–108, 125, 146: and relationship with the East India Company, 88–89; on economic stagnation of Hindustan, 89ff.; critique of East India monopoly, 94–100; on disposition of surplus revenues, 99; on Indian tax system, 132–133, 148–149
Smith, Sydney, 147, 207n.
Steuart, Sir James: 73ff. 88, 99, 114, 125, 190, 200n., 232; on the economic distress of Bengal, 74–76; on the measures to uplift the economy, 76–79; on proposals for a note issuing bank, 80–83; on quantity theory of money, 84–85

Stigler, George, 197n.

Taxation: Smith on, 90, 132–133, 148–
149; Malthus on, 152–155; James Mill
on, 158–163; McCulloch on, 184–185,
192–193

Trade, patterns of: in the early seventeenth century, 12–15, 20; in the late
seventeenth century, 29–34, 49–50; in
the eighteenth century, 67–71; the
projections of 1793, 109–113; in the
early nineteenth century, 115ff., 141;
in the 1820s and 1830's, 178–184, 187–
188; in the 1840's and 1850's, 212–214

Treasure (see Money)

Tribute: James Mill on, 135–138, 172–
173; Lauderdale on, 117ff.; Marx on,
227; Say on, 173n.

Tucker, Henry St. George, 173

Turkey Company, 39–42

Viner, Jacob, 17, 63

Voltaire, 131

Wellesley, Lord, 116, 145–146

West, Edward, 150

Whewell, William, 207n., 208

Zemindari settlement (see Rent, doctrine
of, Taxation, and Cornwallis)